Benched Justice

Benched Justice

How Judges Decide Asylum Claims and Asylum Rights of Unaccompanied Minors

Claire Nolasco Braaten and Daniel Braaten

LEXINGTON BOOKS

Lanham • Boulder • New York • London

Published by Lexington Books
An imprint of The Rowman & Littlefield Publishing Group, Inc.
4501 Forbes Boulevard, Suite 200, Lanham, Maryland 20706
www.rowman.com

86-90 Paul Street, London EC2A 4NE

British Library Cataloguing in Publication Information Available

Library of Congress Cataloging-in-Publication Data

Names: Braaten, Claire Nolasco, 1973- author. | Braaten, Daniel, 1980-
    author.
  Title: Benched justice : how judges decide asylum claims and asylum rights
    of unaccompanied minors / Claire Nolasco Braaten and Daniel Braaten.
  Description: Lanham : Lexington, 2023. | Includes bibliographical
    references and index. | Summary: "This book presents a gripping analysis
    of the hidden factors that affect the asylum claims and rights of
    unaccompanied minors in the US. This book reveals how politics,
    economics, and social pressures shape the decisions of immigration
    judges and how federal courts respond to policies impacting these
    vulnerable minors"-- Provided by publisher.
  Identifiers: LCCN 2023029948 (print) | LCCN 2023029949 (ebook) | ISBN
    9781666934465 (cloth) | ISBN 9781666934472 (ebook)
  Subjects: LCSH: Unaccompanied refugee children--Legal status, laws,
    etc.--United States. | Asylum, Right of--United States. | Children's
    rights--United States.
  Classification: LCC KF4836 B73 2023 (print) | LCC KF4836 (ebook) | DDC
    342.7308/3--dc23/eng/20230802
  LC record available at https://lccn.loc.gov/2023029948
  LC ebook record available at https://lccn.loc.gov/2023029949

♾️™ The paper used in this publication meets the minimum requirements of American National Standard for Information Sciences—Permanence of Paper for Printed Library Materials, ANSI/NISO Z39.48-1992.

To Olivia, with hope for a better world. May your journey be filled with purpose, and may your efforts light the path for others to follow.

Contents

List of Abbreviations

ABA	American Bar Association
ACLU	American Civil Liberties Union
AOR	Area of Responsibility
AORW	Age Out Review Worksheet
APA	Administrative Procedures Act
ATD	Alternatives to Detention
AWO	Affirmation Without Opinion
BIA	Board of Immigration Review
CAM	Central American Minors
CBP	Customs and Border Patrol
CDC	Center for Disease Control
CHSI	Comprehensive Health Services Incorporated
CNCS	Corporation for National and Community Service
DHS	Department of Homeland Security
DOJ	Department of Justice
ECCF	Essex County Correctional Facility
EO	Executive Order
EOIR	Executive Office of Immigration Review
FEMA	Federal Emergency Management Agency
FOIA	Freedom of Information Act
FOJC	Field Officer Juvenile Coordinator
FRA	Federal Records Act
FRC	Family Residential Centers
FTCA	Federal Tort Claims Act
GAO	Government Accountability Office
HHS	Department of Health and Human Services
HSA	Homeland Security Act
ICE	U.S. Immigration and Customs Enforcement
IHSC	ICE Health Services Corp

IIRIRA	Illegal Immigrant Reform and Immigrant Responsibility Act
IJ	Immigration Judge
IJP	Immigration Justice Project
IMF	International Monetary Fund
INA	Immigration and Nationality Act
INS	Immigration and Naturalization Services
JLP	Jose L.P.
KIND	Kids in Need of Defense
LPR	Lawful Permanent Resident
MPP	Migrant Protection Protocols
MS-13	Mara Salvatrucha
NARA	National Archives & Records Administration
NGO	Non Governmental Organization
NOH	Notice of Hearing
NPR	National Public Radio
NTA	Notice to Appear
OCIJ	Office of Chief Immigration Judge
OIJ	Office of Inspector General
OPPM	Operating Policies and Procedures Memorandum
ORR	Office of Refugee Resettlement
POE	Port of Entry
PSG	Particular Social Group
PTS	Political Terror Scale
ProBAR	The Texas Pro Bono Asylum Representation Project
SIJ	Special Immigrant Juvenile
SVJC	Shenandoah Valley Juvenile Center
TRO	Temporary Restraining Order
TVPRA	Trafficking Victims Protection Reauthorization Act
UAC	Unaccompanied Alien Children
UDHR	Universal Declaration of Human Rights
UNCRC	United Nations Convention on the Rights of the Child
UNHCR	United Nations High Commissioner for Refugees
US VISIT	U.S. Visit and Immigrant Status Indicator Technology
USBP	United States Border Patrol
USCBP	United States Custom and Border Protection
USCIS	United States Citizenship and Immigration Services
VAWA	Violence Against Women Act
V-DEM	Varieties of Democracy Index

Introduction

In the summer of 2019 the director of the Executive Office for Immigration Review ("EOIR"), James McHenry, issued a series of memos to the Attorney General Jeff Sessions recommending the hiring of six new judges to the Board of Immigration Appeals ("BIA") (Misra 2019). This seemingly routine bureaucratic procedure hid what many considered to be a very political act. In a footnote McHenry stated that the judges, who were all immigration judges ("IJ"), would be hired for the BIA without the traditional two-year probationary period and would be automatically hired permanently. Since this was during the Trump administration it should be no surprise to know that these specific judges were also among some of the most restrictive immigration judges in the country who denied asylum claims at rates well above most other judges (Misra 2019). Furthermore, significant complaints had been leveled against three of the judges with the most notorious being against Judge V. Stuart Couch who yelled at a two-year-old Guatemalan boy in his courtroom stating he was going to sic a dog on him if he wouldn't be quiet (Lanard 2019).

The same year marked policy moves under former President Trump's administration that aimed to dilute the protections given to unaccompanied alien children ("UAC") under current U.S. laws. One example was the United States Citizenship and Immigration Services ("USCIS") policy memo dated May 31, 2019 that became effective on June 30, 2019. The 2019 memo revised the rules in a prior USCIS policy issued in 2013 for determining whether a child is an unaccompanied minor and eligible for protections under existing laws. The 2019 memo required asylum officers to make independent factual inquiries to determine whether the child was an unaccompanied minor on the date they filed the asylum application. This was in contrast to the 2013 memo that required asylum officers to accept the findings of other immigration agencies regarding the child's unaccompanied minor status without needing to redetermine their eligibility.

In another move during the Trump administration, the Department of Homeland Security ("DHS") and the Department of Health and Human Services ("HHS") attempted to terminate the 1997 *Flores* Settlement by jointly publishing final regulations implementing it in August 2019. The 1997 *Flores* Settlement resulting from litigation in *Flores v. Reno* (1997) provides specific protections for unaccompanied alien children, including their custody, transfer, release, and detention. These regulations by the DHS and by HHS consisted of two sets of rules governing the apprehension and processing of both unaccompanied and accompanied minors and the care and custody of accompanied minors. These two policies became the subject of multiple litigation in federal courts.

The start of the Trump administration also marked the beginning of his policy of separating families at the United States–Mexico border through a pilot program that started in July 2017. Pursuant to this policy, government officials targeted families for prosecution, separated children from parents, classified the children as unaccompanied minors, and sent the children across the country without documenting the familial relationship.

Concomitant with these policies marked the first recorded instance of person-to-person spread of the 2019 novel Coronavirus in the U.S. on January 30, 2020. The COVID-19 pandemic gave the Trump administration reason to suspend the introduction of persons into the U.S. with the aim of stopping the spread of the disease. On March 24, 2020, the Centers for Disease Control ("CDC") issued a new regulation that established a procedure for suspending the introduction of persons from designated countries. DHS agents were instructed to transport covered aliens to the nearest U.S. port of entry and immediately return them to their point of transit, whether Mexico or Canada. The CDC orders did not exempt unaccompanied alien children from forcible expulsion.

How did these policy and personnel moves affect the plight of unaccompanied minors in the U.S.? At the first instance, asylum outcomes are determined by immigration judges who are political appointees. At the second instance, the political and legal context within which asylum decisions are made in the U.S. presumably affect the ability of unaccompanied minors to participate in asylum proceedings. With these points in mind, the main questions this book addresses are: 1) to what extent do immigration judges decide unaccompanied minor asylum cases based on the law but also based on politics, economic, and social factors, and 2) how have federal courts responded to executive policies and programs that significantly affect the rights of unaccompanied minors? We answer these questions using two different methodologies appropriate to each question. For the first question we analyze over 12,000 immigration court decisions from 1997 to 2021 regarding asylum claims by unaccompanied minors. Here we utilize a variety of statistical procedures to determine the relative influence of political, social, and economic factors that influence judicial decision making. For the second question we turn to doctrinal analysis and analyze over 200 federal court cases involving unaccompanied minors to determine how federal courts have defined their procedural and substantive rights.

Analysis of the above issues are even more critical considering the persistent arrival of unaccompanied alien children into the United States. In FY2021, there were 146,925 encounters with unaccompanied alien children, representing 9 percent of the 1,734,686 US Border Patrol ("USBP") encounters at the Southwest border (U.S. Customs and Border Protection "U.S. CBP" 2021a). This number exceeded levels for all previous fiscal years. For example, in 2020, encounters with unaccompanied minors (33,329) was 7 percet of total encounters (total encounters consist of accompanied minors, adult, family units, single adult) while in 2019, encounters with these minors (80,634) was 8 percent of total encounters (977,509). The majority of apprehensions in the first 10 months of FY2021 occurred within the Rio Grande (TX), El Paso (TX), and Tucson (AZ) border sectors (51%, 17%, and 13%, respectively) (U.S. CBP 2021b). DHS expects these apprehensions to continue at their current elevated levels (Caldwell & Hackman 2021). For example in FY2022, there were 152,057 encounters of unaccompanied minors at the U.S. border.

The recent growth of unaccompanied alien children coming to the United States over the last few years has raised complex legal issues regarding how and when they should be detained upon apprehension in the United States, who they should be released to, and what rights they should be accorded in immigration enforcement proceedings (Amuedo-Dorantes and Puttitanun 2018; Nolasco 2018; Nolasco and Braaten 2019; Shea 2014). These legal issues exist in the context of broader political debates ongoing in the U.S. over levels of immigration and possible large-scale reforms to U.S. immigration policy (Corona 2017; Gil 2017; Nolasco and Braaten 2019). In addition to the legal questions that surround their presence in the U.S. immigration system, they present significant ethical questions as well (Chavez and Menjívar 2010; King 2013).

Under Section 279(g)(2) of the Homeland Security Act of 2002 ("HSA"), an unaccompanied alien child is defined as an individual who: (1) has no lawful immigration status in the United States; (2) is under the age of eighteen; and (3) must have either (a) "no parent or legal guardian in the United States"; or (b) "no parent or legal guardian in the United States" available to provide "care and physical custody" (*DB v. Cardall* 2016, 732–733). These minors are particularly vulnerable since by definition they are children, traveling alone and undocumented, into a country not their own (Smith 2017). Many of these children are fleeing violence and extreme poverty in their home countries

(Amuedo-Dorantes and Puttitanun 2016; Keles et al. 2018; Boursier 2019). Three primary source countries of unaccompanied minors to the U.S.—El Salvador, Guatemala, and Honduras—have high levels of extreme poverty and violence (Marzouk 2016; Sawyer and Márquez 2017), and have a proliferation of transnational gangs that target and victimize many UAC (Kandel et al. 2014). Additionally, many of these children come to the U.S. seeking reunification with family members, mostly parents, who have emigrated earlier (Sotomayor-Peterson and Montiel-Carbajal 2014). The factors motivating these minors to leave their home country and enter the U.S. underlie the legal questions regarding how justice is given to them when they enter the U.S. immigration system (Nolasco and Braaten 2019). The complexities of immigration proceedings, especially for a class of noncitizens who are vulnerable to the inherent coercive nature of the proceedings, necessitate an analysis of the legal and political issues surrounding their processing within the U.S. (Nolasco and Braaten 2019; Villarreal 2004).

Kandel et al. (2014, 1) identified push and pull factors associated with the recent growth in UAC. Push factors are causes in the migrant origin countries that encourage outmigration of UAC. Several major *push* factors contributing to out-migration of UAC from their home countries include rising crime, economic conditions, poverty, and violent transnational gangs (Kandel et al. 2014; Finklea 2018; Vaughan 2018). In 2012, the homicide rate per 100,000 inhabitants was 90.4 in Honduras (the highest in the world), 41.2 in El Salvador, and 39.9 in Guatemala (Kandel et al. 2014). By 2019 the homicide rates for Honduras and Guatemala had declined but were still high respectively to much of the rest of the world, while the rate in El Salvador had increased significantly. In 2019 the homicide rate in Honduras was 66.9 per 100,000 people and in Guatemala it was 25.09 per 100,000 people, but in El Salvador the homicide rate increased to 85 per 100,000 people (World Health Organization 2021). Economic growth rates in these countries in 2013 ranged from 1.6 percent to 3.5 percent, compared with other Central American countries—45 percent of Salvadorans, 55 percent of Guatemalans, and 67 percent of Hondurans live in poverty. By 2020 the average gross national product (GNP) in the Northern Triangle countries was $3,603 which still ranks them toward the bottom of all countries in Latin America (Savoy and Sady-Kennedy 2021).

The Texas Pro Bono Asylum Representation Project ("ProBAR"), a pro bono project on the Texas/Mexico border, also explains that UAC flee their countries of origin due to violence and threats from criminal gangs and drug cartels (ABA Commission on Immigration 2015). Criminal groups either forced them to join or coerced them to pay large sums of money, threatening harm or death to themselves or their family members. Other unaccompanied minors represented by ProBAR describe being victims of domestic violence, trafficking, exploitation, and neglect. Other causes of Central American migration to the U.S. include lack of employment opportunities (Catholic Relief Services 2020), socio-economic and security conditions (Meyer 2021), corruption and weak governance (Call 2021), climate change, natural disasters, and food insecurity (Kitroeff and Volpe 2021; Masters 2019; Rodriguez 2021; Sieff 2021; Soboroff and Ainsley 2019; World Bank Group 2018).

In 2013, the UN High Commissioner for Refugees ("UNHCR") conducted interviews with a representative group of about 400 UAC from El Salvador, Guatemala, Honduras, and Mexico who arrived in the United States in FY2012 (UNCHR 2014). Their study showed that almost half of all unaccompanied children experienced serious harm or threats by organized criminal groups or state actors, and one-fifth experienced domestic abuse. The UNHCR found that 58 percent of the children interviewed in a 2013 study raised actual or potential legal protection concerns (UNHCR 2014). More than half of these minors personally experienced danger, abuse or neglect, making them eligible to apply for asylum or other forms of relief such as the Special Immigrant Juvenile visa. However, many of the gang-violence cases for asylum are denied by immigration judges and federal courts because they do not meet the legal standard for asylum. Applicants for asylum must show that he or she suffered past persecution or has a well-founded fear of future persecution based on race, religion, nationality, political opinion or social group (8 U.S.C. § 1158(b)(1)). Asylum applications invoking credible fear of gang violence not based on any one of the five protected grounds are denied, even if credible. Immigration judges and federal courts sometimes find credible allegations of fear based on gang violence but ultimately deny these applications because their fear is not based on one of the five protected grounds (ABA Commission on Immigration 2015).

Violence from criminal groups, state actors, and family members also played a large role in their decisions to emigrate. Surveys showed that 48 percent of unaccompanied minors experienced serious harm or were threatened by organized criminal groups or state actors and more than 20 percent experienced domestic abuse (UNCHR 2014). Poverty also caused them to emigrate—16 percent of those interviewed mentioned economic deprivation as a motive. Salvadorans were more likely to cite societal violence and Guatemalans were more likely to cite economic deprivation as motives for emigration (Kandel et al. 2014; UNCHR 2014).

Crime and violence are long standing problems in El Salvador, Guatemala, and Honduras (Kandel et al. 2014; Meyer and Seelke 2015). Gangs such as Mara Salvatrucha (MS-13) and the 18th Street gang also are significantly present in these countries (Seelke 2016). In the Rampart area of Los Angeles in the 1960s, Mexican youth who were not accepted into existing Hispanic gangs formed the 18th Street gang. In the 1980s, Salvadorans in Los Angeles who fled El Salvador's civil conflict formed the MS-13 (Diaz 2011). Both gangs expanded their operations to Central America when the U.S. began deporting illegal immigrants, many with criminal convictions, back to the northern triangle region (El Salvador, Guatemala, and Honduras) after the passage of the Illegal Immigrant Reform and Immigrant Responsibility Act ("IIRIRA") of 1996.

The MS-13 and 18th Street gangs engage in various activities, such as kidnapping, extortion, and forced recruitment. The UNHCR (2014) survey found that 27 percent of unaccompanied alien children reported harm from and threats by these gangs, including nearly 62 percent of the Salvadorans. On October 11, 2012, the U.S. Department of Treasury (2012) designated the MS-13 as a transnational criminal organization whose assets are subject to economic sanctions pursuant to Executive Order 13581. State Department officials estimate that 85,000 members of MS-13 and 18th Street gang reside in these northern triangle countries, with the highest per capita concentration in El Salvador (Brownfield 2012).

As U.S. border security tightened, more unauthorized Central American migrants used smugglers who pay money to transnational criminal organizations such as Los Zetas (Siskin and Rosen 2014). These smugglers lead the migrants through Mexico across the U.S.-Mexico border (Dickson 2014; Office of the Vice President 2014). An estimated 75–80 percent of unaccompanied minors traveled with smugglers in 2014 and these numbers have maintained in the years since. Some smugglers reportedly trafficked these migrants, selling them into forced labor or prostitution to recover their costs (Martinez 2014). Other smugglers' failure to pay Los Zetas resulted in massacres of groups of migrants (Martinez 2014). Mass grave sites of executed migrants have been discovered in recent years (Kandel et al. 2014).

In contrast to *push* factors that drive these minors to flee their countries, multiple *pull* factors attract these children to migrate specifically to the United States such as increased economic and educational opportunities, family reunification, and more favorable treatment of non-Mexican and non-Canadian migrant children by U.S. immigration law (Kandel 2014, 2021; U.S. DHS 2018). Many unaccompanied alien children also seek to reunite with family or pursue perceived opportunities in the United States. The UNHCR's (2014) survey showed that 21 percent of unaccompanied minors wanted to join a family member, 51 percent pointed to economic opportunities, and 19 percent mentioned education. These perceptions of economic opportunities, however, are in conflict with current realities in the U.S. (Kandel et al. 2014).

Current employment levels in the U.S. for minority youth are low compared to all other labor market groups (Fernandes-Alcantara 2018). The potential for unaccompanied minors to participate in the U.S. labor market is limited by their lack of English language skills, limited educational attainment, and the extent to which U.S. laws permit minorities to participate in the labor force (Kandel et al. 2014; Wassem 2007). These limitations would likely restrict them to low-skilled, low-wage sectors of the U.S. economy. Additionally, many UACs have been hired to work long hours in dangerous jobs in contravention of child labor laws in the U.S. (Dreier 2023).

Unaccompanied children also cite educational opportunities in the U.S. as a primary reason for their arrival. The U.S. Supreme Court's decision in *Plyler v. Doe* (1982) allows them access to free public education through high school. The Supreme Court considered whether a 1974 Texas education law that allowed Texas to withhold state funds from local school districts for educating children of illegal aliens violated the Equal Protection Clause of the Fourteenth Amendment (*Plyler v. Doe* 1982). The Court declared that states cannot restrict access of children to public elementary and secondary education based on immigration status. The Court's ruling, however, did not include access of unauthorized migrants (including unaccompanied minors) to postsecondary education. Both the federal government and some states have adopted measures that limit unauthorized migrants' eligibility for admission to public institutions of higher education, in-state tuition, or financial aid (Bruno 2015; Smole 2013).

Family reunification is further cited as a primary reason for their migration to the United States (UNHCR 2014). The UNHCR's (2014) survey found that one of the main reasons these children want to migrate to the U.S. was their desire to reunite with family who were separated from them. Family separation occurs when one or both parents migrate to a destination country for more lucrative employment (Chishti and Hipsman 2014). Prior to the mid-1990s, migrants from Mexico and Central America who worked temporarily in the United States often returned regularly to their families in their origin countries (Moran-Taylor 2008). Increased border enforcement in the mid-1990s made unauthorized entry into the United States more difficult and expensive (Argueta 2016). This encouraged unauthorized aliens to settle permanently in the United States rather than working temporarily and regularly returning home (Argueta 2016; Rosenblum and Brick 2011).

The Office of Refugee Resettlement ("ORR") reports that from October 2020 through September 2021, the top six states for reunification include Texas, Florida, California, New York, New Jersey, and Maryland (Office of Refugee Resettlement 2021a). The top six cities for reunification include Baltimore, Dallas, Houston, Miami, Los Angeles and New York (Office of Refugee Resettlement 2021b). As of February 2015, New York City has the immigration court with the largest number of pending unaccompanied alien children cases, followed by Baltimore, Arlington, Miami, Houston and Los Angeles (ABA Commission on Immigration 2015).

The length of time before removal hearings occur may also play a role for incentivizing these minors' migration to the United States (Kandel et al. 2014). As of March 2014, the average wait time nationwide for all immigration proceedings was 29 months (TRAC 2021). By 2022 the average wait time was 4.3 years (TRAC 2022). The length of time until a final judgment varies further depending on appeals and individual circumstances (Kandel et al. 2014). The long backlog in cases and the potential for family reunification reportedly have reached emigrant-sending communities in Central America (Nakamura 214; Preston 2014).

Against the socio-economic context within which unaccompanied minors migrate to the U.S. to seek asylum, this book discusses the political realities of their introduction into the U.S. immigration system, the laws governing their processing, and federal court cases that have decided on their substantive and procedural rights and due process. The unique circumstances of vulnerable minors and the distinct procedures and legal principles applicable to this population also require a more focused study on how judges decide their asylum claims and asylum rights.

This book is divided into two parts. We analyze outcomes of asylum claims of unaccompanied alien children in immigration courts and the Board of Immigration Appeals in part I and their asylum rights as decided by federal courts in part II. Analysis of each of these related issues is equally important to fully understand the conditions and challenges these minors face while they await their asylum cases in the U.S. In the first part of our book, we discuss the legal, political, social, and economic context of judicial decision making in asylum proceedings involving these minors. We utilize multiple statistical methods to argue that judges are affected by a variety of factors beyond the laws on asylum. We provide empirical evidence that various political and social factors affect decisions of immigration judges and the BIA when deciding asylum claims of unaccompanied alien children. In the second part of our book, we discuss federal court cases involving these minors, narrate the factual basis of their claims, and discuss how the courts resolved their procedural and substantive rights. We examine broad themes relating to procedural and substantive rights of unaccompanied alien children that have been decided in these federal courts.

Chapter One discusses the legal and political context of asylum proceedings involving unaccompanied minors in the U.S. The chapter discusses the 1997 *Flores* Settlement Agreement that settled all claims regarding the detention conditions of unaccompanied minors. The chapter also explains U.S. laws affecting unaccompanied alien children, the processing of unaccompanied alien children from initial contact with Customs and Border Protection agents at or between U.S. ports of entry to appellate judges in federal district and circuit courts, and the various administrative actions under the Obama,

Trump, and Biden presidency. The chapter analyzes how each of these administrations strengthened or diluted the principle of "best interests of the child" in the treatment of unaccompanied minors' asylum claims through policies and executive orders issued by their implementing authorities. The chapter then ties the legal and political backdrop to judicial decision making that takes place within this evolving milieu. We argue that immigration judges, who are political appointees, are not immune from the social and political pressures of the time. In contrast, the decisions of tenured federal court judges who may be more isolated from political pressures may be predisposed to decide based on legal precedents and judicial doctrine.

Part I, consisting of chapters 2 and 3, examines judicial decision making in asylum proceedings involving unaccompanied minors in the U.S. at the level of immigration courts and BIA proceedings. We empirically analyze asylum outcomes in cases involving unaccompanied minors by applying theories of judicial decision making and parsing out the factors that affect whether immigration judges grant or deny asylum to unaccompanied minors.

Chapter 2 discusses the three models of judicial decision making and current scholarly literature testing these models. Using three models of judicial decision making—the attitudinal-cognitive model, principal-agent models, and local context factors, which includes cultural threat theory and contact theory, this chapter conducts a macro-level analysis of immigration judges' decisions on asylum claims of unaccompanied minors in the U.S. from 1997 to 2020. Statistical analyses of individual asylum cases were conducted to determine the influence of individual factors of the asylum applicant such as presence of legal representation, country level variables such as U.S. political and economic interests in the applicant's home country, judge level variables such as judicial ideology and judicial partisanship affect the likelihood of granting asylum. We also include multiple county and state level variables in our model measuring social, economic, and political factors at those levels to account for the milieu in which immigration judges make decisions. The results of this multivariate and multi-level analysis of 12,826 cases indicate that several factors affected asylum outcomes. We find that the level of democracy of the home country the child is fleeing, whether the child is coming from a country where Spanish is the primary language, along with the child having an attorney representing them at their asylum hearing have a large effect on whether they receive asylum or not. Additionally, the partisanship and ideology of the immigration judge also play a significant role in asylum decisions, and finally, the county level of support for the Democratic candidate for President also significantly influences asylum decisions for unaccompanied minors.

Chapter 3 employs a macro-level analysis of BIA decisions on asylum claims by unaccompanied minors in the U.S. from 1997 to 2020. BIA decisions are the result of an unaccompanied minor appealing their initial ruling from an immigration judge. In this chapter we examine the results of "negative" decisions toward UACs that are appealed to the BIA both descriptively and with multivariate analyses. We utilize a similar model as was used in the previous chapter but without the added county and state level variables since BIA decisions are made by a panel of judges in Falls Church, VA and have a national jurisdiction. Additionally, we employ a selection model to account for the fact that not all cases before an immigration judge get appealed to the BIA. In this analysis we test if the BIA supports the primary missions of an appellate court—error correction and policy-making. In terms of policy-making we examine whether the BIA is more likely to affirm decisions from "generous" judges or "harsh" judges. We find some evidence that for UAC cases, the BIA is more likely to affirm decisions from more generous judges than from harsher judges. With regards to the policy-making functions of the BIA, we measure this indirectly by focusing on how political factors influence the decisions of the BIA with regards to UAC appeals. We find that when the composition of the BIA is filled with more judges who were appointed by Democratic Attorney Generals than the BIA is more likely to affirm the negative decisions made by immigration judges regarding UAC asylum cases Moreover, we find that one of the biggest drivers in how the BIA makes decisions on appeals from UACs is their workload.

Part II examines cases brought in federal district and circuit courts involving challenges to laws, policies, orders, and programs that affect the rights of unaccompanied minors at various stages of the asylum proceedings—from the moment of their apprehension, release, transfer to custodial settings, and conditions of detention—and more importantly in cases involving direct appeals from asylum decisions of the Board of Immigration Appeals. Part II provides a more detailed picture of how courts have construed, expanded, or restricted the legal protections and privileges of unaccompanied minors while in custodial settings with the Office of Refugee Resettlement, of the United States Department of Health and Human Services, or the U.S. Immigration and Customs Enforcement ("ICE") of the U.S. Department of Homeland Security. We also wanted to determine in what ways federal courts have acted as a counterbalance or a check on the exercise of executive powers (through orders and issuances) when administrative agencies enforced policies that undermined the rights of unaccompanied minors delineated in the 1997 *Flores* Settlement Agreement. Part II consists of chapters 4 and 5.

Moving from a macro-level quantitative analysis of immigration judges' decisions, Chapter 4 of the book employs a micro-level inductive/qualitative analysis of 293 federal district and court cases involving procedural due process and procedural rights raised by unaccompanied alien children concomitant with or subsequent to their claims for asylum. This chapter organizes these cases into broad themes as they relate to executive policies and procedures that were challenged in federal courts as well as procedural due process issues raised by unaccompanied alien children on appeal. In terms of policies and procedural due process, federal courts granted relief to unaccompanied minors who challenged executive policies and guidelines that negatively affected their procedural due process and substantive rights. Examples of challenged policies include those that retroactively transferred initial jurisdiction over their asylum applications from asylum officers to immigration judges, affected their ability to file applications beyond the one-year deadline for filing, and affected conditions of their custody, release to sponsors, and their detention during the COVID-19 pandemic. At the same time, federal courts hesitated to allow federal damages claims against government officials who implemented Trump's family separation policy in 2018.

Chapter 5 similarly employs a micro-level inductive/qualitative analysis of 293 federal district and court cases to determine issues on substantive due process and substantive rights that have reached Article III courts. This chapter analyzes themes in court cases relating to executive actions that allegedly transgressed the substantive rights and substantive due process of unaccompanied alien children on appeal. Substantive issues that have been litigated in federal courts include the rights of former unaccompanied minors who aged out of HHS custody after reaching 18 years old, legal standards for abuses experienced while in detention (including sexual abuse), standard of medical care while detained in ORR facilities, basis for the grant of asylum, and the right to abortion while in federal custody. Doctrinal analysis of jurisprudence indicates that federal judges arrived at similar outcomes on some of these substantive issues but arrived at disparate outcomes at other times, depending on the forum of the asylum application. Applying the law to the facts of the case has led some federal courts to arrive at divergent outcomes on the same litigated issue.

For purposes of this book, the terms unaccompanied alien child, unaccompanied minor, and unaccompanied child (both in the singular and plural form) are used interchangeably Unaccompanied alien child is the legal definition used by the U.S. government but for readability we vary the terminology. The dataset for part I, chapters 2 and 3, were constructed from data obtained through a Freedom of Information request from the U.S. Justice Department Executive Office of Immigration Review. Specifically, we requested information on decisions of immigration judges and Board of Immigration Appeals relating to asylum claims of unaccompanied minors. Overall, the data we received contained 13,772 cases decided from November 18, 1997 to June 4, 2021.

The dataset for part II, chapters 4 and 5, were gathered through the WESTLAW database which contains electronic copies of all published and unpublished court decisions. A keyword search was used to gather cases on unaccompanied minors decided by all federal courts in the U.S. The advanced search parameters required that the term "unaccompanied alien child" appeared in the main body of the case as of 2022 (N = 293). The authors then read each case individually and determined that not all cases were relevant to the article, either because the case did not involve UAC or did not contain sufficient facts to enable full analysis. Also, some cases were repeated because of the appeal process through the federal courts. Instead of an empirical, quantitative approach, we used inductive doctrinal analysis of federal cases to determine how federal judges are constrained by legal precedent, the plain meaning of statutes, and the intent of the framers of statutes. We organized these decisions around major issues and themes that unaccompanied minors raised at the federal courts. Scrutinizing these decisions are necessary since judicial decisions have the force and effect of law and affect the rights of these unaccompanied minors as they go through the U.S. asylum system. The issues raised in federal courts do not necessarily involve the grant or denial of asylum but the procedural and substantive rights of unaccompanied minors under current U.S. laws and policies as they navigate the asylum process. Some of these cases were filed by unaccompanied minors pending their asylum claims or subsequent to the resolution of their asylum claims. The constitutionality or legality of laws, executive orders, and regulations are often raised through the federal court process. These decisions are important for unaccompanied minors seeking asylum in the U.S. because they serve as precedents, binding on the immigration judges, Board of Immigration Appeals, and other government agencies involved in the process.

Chapter 1

Legal Background of U.S. Asylum Proceedings Involving Unaccompanied Alien Children

Examining the current legal landscape in the United States seemingly reveals that protections are in place for unaccompanied alien children entering the country. As early as the *Flores* Settlement of 1997 (*Flores v. Reno* 1997), the courts have recognized the vulnerability of these minors and have mandated preferential treatment for this specific class of foreigners. Subsequent laws such as the Homeland Security Act of 2002 and the Trafficking Victims Protection Reauthorization Act of 2008 ("TVPRA") further supplement the legal protections accorded to these minors. In practice, however, incumbent officials in the Executive Branch, especially during the Trump administration, have either attempted to circumvent or dilute these legal protections by enacting policies, programs, or executive issuances aimed at bypassing the rights and privileges accorded to these minors.

After a pilot program in the El Paso area, for example, the Trump Administration in the spring of 2018 started separating children from their parents upon crossing the U.S.-Mexico border and detaining them separately. Over 2,300 children were separated from their parents between May 5 and June 9 (Lind 2018a). Minors separated from their parents were then legally treated as unaccompanied alien children. The Trump administration bowing to political pressure stopped the separation policy in favor of a family detention policy (Lind 2018b). This policy of unrestricted detention of children contravenes the *Flores* Settlement but the Trump Administration forged ahead claiming it had no other choice. President Trump's Executive Order ("EO") 13841 on June 20, 2018 (*Affording Congress an Opportunity to Address Family Separation*) stopping family separation ordered the Attorney General to request a modification to the *Flores* Settlement to allow the government to detain immigrant families together for the entirety of the process. President

Biden revoked Trump's order on February 2, 2021 through EO 14011 which also sought to reunify separated children from their families.

Personnel changes in the immigration courts and Board of Immigration Appeals have exacerbated the plight of unaccompanied minors whose asylum proceedings are entrusted to immigration judges, who have even less independence than federal judges appointed under Article III of the constitution, or administrative law judges who adjudicate for different agencies such as the Social Security Administration. Article III judges are appointed with life-tenure and are confirmed by the U.S. Senate while administrative law judges derive their power through the U.S. Congress' legislation, namely, the Administrative Procedures Act of 1946 ("APA"). In contrast to administrative law judges who may only be fired for good cause after an independent hearing process, immigration judges under current U.S. Department of Justice ("DOJ") rules are "attorneys whom the Attorney General appoints as administrative judges" and are appointed to act "as the Attorney General's delegates in the cases that come before them" (TRAC 2021). These rules reinforce the notion of immigration judges as political subordinates, acting under the direction of the Attorney General.

Appellate court rulings have also questioned the legal ability or temperament of some immigration court judges and called for increased scrutiny and supervision of immigration judges. Seventh Circuit Court of Appeals Judge Richard Posner noted in one case that "the adjudication of [immigration] cases at the administrative level has fallen below the minimum standards of legal justice" (TRAC 2008). Third Circuit Appellate Judge Julio Fuentes similarly wrote in September 2005 that "time and time again, we have cautioned immigration judges against making intemperate or humiliating remarks during immigration proceedings" (TRAC 2008).

These developments call into question the validity of decisions made by immigration judges in asylum proceedings involving unaccompanied alien children. Equally important is the degree to which current U.S. legal protections for unaccompanied minors have been enforced in immigration courts. While federal courts are not vested with primary jurisdiction over asylum proceedings of unaccompanied minors, their power to interpret the laws and determine the legality of executive acts and programs enable them to plausibly act as vanguards in enforcing the rights and privileges of unaccompanied minors. While we tackle these two related issues in subsequent chapters, we discuss in this chapter the legal landscape within which unaccompanied minors are processed—from their entry into the U.S., while they await their asylum proceedings, and if placed in removal proceedings.

Several legal sources provide the basis for protections accorded to unaccompanied minors. Chief and foremost is the case of *Reno* v. *Flores* (1993) which ultimately resulted in a court settlement that serves as the basis for release and custodial conditions of these minors. Prior to 2003, the Immigration and Naturalization Service ("INS") was responsible for the care and custody of unaccompanied alien children arrested in the U.S., suspected of being eligible for deportation, and who had no responsible parent or legal guardian (*DB v. Cardall* 2016). The INS was also tasked with prosecuting removal proceedings against them in immigration courts (*DB v. Cardall* 2016). During the late 1980s and into the 1990s, an increasing number of unaccompanied alien children began migrating to the U.S. from Central America seeking reunification with separated relatives who entered ahead of them to flee the violence in their home countries and to pursue better economic opportunities (Lopez 2012; Navarro 1998). In response to their increased flow into California, the INS Western Regional Office adopted a policy in 1984 of limiting the release of detained minors to a parent or lawful guardian, except in "unusual and extraordinary cases" allowing release to a responsible individual who agrees to provide for the care, welfare, and wellbeing of the child (*DB v. Cardall* 2016, 732; *Flores v. Meese* 1990, 994).

The following year, Jenny Flores, a 15-year-old child from El Salvador entered the United States without inspection to be reunited with her aunt in the United States (Lopez 2012). She was arrested at the border, handcuffed, strip searched, and placed in a juvenile detention center where she spent the next two months waiting for her deportation hearing (Lopez 2012). The INS did not release Jenny to her aunt because at that time the INS regulations prohibited release of unaccompanied minors to third-party adults (Lopez 2012). On July 11, 1985, the American Civil Liberties Union ("ACLU") and four minors, including Jenny, filed a class action lawsuit in *Flores v. Meese* with the District Court for the Central District of California on behalf of all aliens under the age of 18 detained by the INS Western Region because a parent or legal guardian failed to personally appear to take custody of them (*Flores v. Meese* 1988).

Pending litigation in 1988, INS adopted a modified rule codified as 8 CFR §242.24_allowing alien juveniles to be released to a: (1) parent; (2) legal guardian; or (3) adult relative (e.g., brother, sister, aunt, uncle, grandparent), except in "unusual and compelling circumstances" and unless the INS decided that detention was necessary to ensure the unaccompanied alien child's safety or appearance in deportation proceedings (*Reno* v. *Flores* 1993, 296). The District Court granted the INS partial summary judgment and in late 1987 approved a consent decree that settled all claims regarding the detention conditions (*Reno* v. *Flores* 1993, 296). A divided panel of the Ninth Circuit Court of Appeals reversed but an *en banc* Ninth Circuit vacated the panel opinion and affirmed the District Court (*Reno* v. *Flores* 1993, 299). On certiorari, the Supreme Court in *Reno v. Flores* reversed the *en banc* decision of the Court of Appeals and remanded the case for further proceedings (*Reno* v. *Flores* 1993, 315).

On remand, the district court approved in 1997 an agreement that settled all claims regarding the detention conditions of unaccompanied alien children ("*Flores* Settlement" or "*Flores* Agreement") (*Flores v. Sessions* 2017). The *Flores* Settlement established a nationwide policy for their detention, release, and treatment (*DB v. Cardall* 2016; *Flores v. Sessions* 2017; Lincoln 2017). Among other things, it: (1) defined a minor as any person under the age of eighteen (18) years detained in the legal custody of the INS; (2) supported family reunification; (3) listed the preferred order of individuals to whom detained minors may be released; and (4) provided for the custody and right to a bond hearing of minors who cannot be immediately released *(Flores v. Sessions* 2017).

The *Flores* Settlement is binding on all successor agencies of the now defunct INS, including the Office of Refugee Resettlement, and the Department of Health and Human Services (Nolasco and Braaten 2019). It creates procedures for the processing of UAC after their arrest, including: (1) providing them with a notice of rights and segregating them from unrelated adults; (2) establishing a general policy favoring their release without unnecessary delay to their parents, legal guardians, adult relatives, certain other adults or entities designated by their parent or guardian, or licensed programs willing to accept legal custody, in that order of preference, unless their continued detention was necessary to secure their timely appearance before immigration authorities or immigration court, or to ensure their or other persons' safety (*Flores v. Reno* 1997). Juveniles who are not released must, within 72 hours of arrest, be placed in juvenile care facilities that meet or exceed state licensing requirements (*Reno* v. *Flores* 1993). Studies indicate that the mental health of UAC depend on the degree of trauma and acculturation upon migration into the country of refuge (Bean et al. 2007; Bronstein and Montgomery 2011; Jensen et al. 2014; Keles et al. 2018; Unterhitzenberger et al. 2015). Hence, the necessity of release and placement is essential to the wellbeing of the UAC.

The *Flores* Settlement requires alien minors in federal custody to be treated with dignity, respect and special concern due to their vulnerability as minors (Manuel and Garcia 2014; *Flores v. Reno* 1997). It also required immigration officials detaining these minors to provide (1) food and drinking water, (2) medical assistance, (3) toilets and sinks, (4) adequate temperature control and ventilation, (5) adequate supervision to protect minors from others, and (6) separation from unrelated adults whenever possible (Kandel 2021). Under the *Flores* Settlement, the government must hold minors in safe and sanitary facilities that are the least restrictive setting based on the minor's age and special needs (*Flores v. Rosen* 2020).

Before September 11, 2001, families apprehended while entering the United States illegally were often released because of a limited amount of family bed space in detention facilities (*Flores v. Lynch* 2016). After 2001, the government imposed a more restrictive immigration policy marked by tougher enforcement and extensive expedited removal of inadmissible aliens (*Flores v. Rosen* 2020, 729). Prior to 2014, ICE generally released parents who were not flight or safety risks. In 2014, however, ICE changed its practice by detaining families fleeing from Central America in its newly opened family detention centers in Texas that operated under internal standards that did not comply with the *Flores* Settlement. In *Flores v. Lynch* (2016), plaintiffs argued that ICE violated the terms of the *Flores* Settlement by holding minors in secure, unlicensed facilities and by failing to release a minor's accompanying parent who was not a flight or safety risk. The government countered that the *Flores* Settlement did not apply to accompanied minors.

The Ninth Circuit held that the *Flores* Settlement covered accompanied minors but did not require the government to release or separate the detained parents from their children (*Flores v. Lynch* 2016). If the government did not release the parents, the parents had the choice to exercise their children's right to be released to a suitable sponsor or waive their children's rights and keep their children with them. A year later in *Flores v. Session* (2017a), the Ninth Circuit held that the Homeland Security Act or the TVPRA did not relieve the government from providing detained, unaccompanied minors with bond hearings as required by the *Flores* Settlement. The Ninth Circuit noted that the bond hearing is a "fundamental protection" guaranteed to unaccompanied minors under the *Flores* Settlement, providing them with "meaningful rights and practical benefits" (*Flores v. Session* 2017, 867).

The *Reno v. Flores* (1993) case and the resulting *Flores* Settlement have been important in protecting the rights of children in different contexts. Although the *Flores* Settlement was developed in response to a case involving unaccompanied minors in INS custody, the detention standards set forth in the *Flores* Settlement apply to all children in the custody of the now defunct INS and its successor agency the DHS (Lopez 2012). For instance, in the 2007 case of *In Re Hutto Family Detention Center* (2007), the *Flores* Settlement was invoked as justification for the District Court of the Western District of Texas to approve a settlement agreement improving the detention conditions of ten plaintiffs who were accompanied minors detained with their parents in the Hutto family detention center.

The 1997 *Flores* agreement was originally set to terminate (except for the requirement that minors generally be housed in licensed facilities) at the earlier of (1) five years after its final approval by the court, or (2) three years after the court determines that federal officials are in substantial compliance with the agreement (*Flores v. Reno* 1997, par. 40; Manuel and Garcia 2014). A 2001 stipulation and order extended it 45 days after the federal government promulgated final regulations implementing the *Flores* Agreement (*Flores v. Reno* 2001). However, implementing regulations have not yet been promulgated (Manuel and Garcia 2014).

U.S. LAWS AFFECTING UNACCOMPANIED ALIEN CHILDREN

Prior to 1996, foreign nationals arriving at a U.S. port of entry without proper immigration documents could attend a removal hearing before an immigration judge to determine whether they were admissible and to request asylum if eligible under the current laws (Braaten and Braaten 2021). The Illegal Immigrant Reform and Immigrant Responsibility Act of 1996 ("IIRIRA") amended this procedure by authorizing the exclusion of arriving foreign nationals without placing them in removal proceedings. The Department of Homeland Security through its Customs and Border Protection immigration officers were authorized to conduct expedited removal by summarily excluding foreign nationals arriving without proper documentation unless they expressed a fear of persecution if repatriated (Braaten and Braaten 2021). The 1997 *Flores* settlement in the case of *Reno v Flores* (1993), however, established a nationwide policy for the detention, treatment, and release of unaccompanied alien children (Nolasco and Braaten 2019; *Flores v. Sessions* 2017). Based on the *Flores Settlement*, the INS issued a policy guidance that unaccompanied alien children would not generally be subject to the expedited removal procedures of the IIRIRA and instead could seek asylum during removal proceedings before an immigration judge (Virtue 1997; Wasem 2014).

Since the *Flores* Settlement, Congress enacted the 2002 Homeland Security Act and the 2008 Trafficking Victims Protection Reauthorization Act both of which affirmed the authority of the Office of Refugee Resettlement over the care and placement of unaccompanied alien children (*Tabbaa v. Chertoff* 2007).

Homeland Security Act of 2002

The Homeland Security Act of 2002 divided responsibilities for the processing and treatment of unaccompanied alien children between the newly created Department of Homeland Security, the Department of Health and Human

Services, and the Office of Refugee Resettlement (Wasem 2014). Section 462 of the Homeland Security Act of 2002 transferred responsibility for the care of unaccompanied alien children (but not accompanied alien children) from DHS to ORR (6 U.S.C. §279). Once DHS or any other federal agency classifies a minor as an unaccompanied alien child, they must transfer the child to the custody of ORR within 72 hours (8 U.S.C. §1232(b)(3). Upon transfer, ORR coordinates and implements their care and placement (6 U.S.C. §279(b)(1)(A) by placing them in state-licensed care facilities and foster care (Office of Refugee Resettlement 2021). However, their transfer from DHS to ORR custody does not preclude any removal proceedings against them (8 U.S.C. §1232(a)(5)(D)). If an unaccompanied minor in ORR custody is ordered removed by an immigration judge, DHS may take physical custody of the child to enforce his or her removal.

Under the HSA, DHS handles the arrest, transfer, and return of unaccompanied alien children to their countries of origin. ORR handles their care and placement in appropriate custody, reunites them with their parents, maintains and publishes a list of legal services available to them, and collects statistical information on them. The HSA required the ORR to ensure that "the best interests of the child" are considered in decisions and actions concerning their care and custody (*Flores v. Sessions* 2017, 870). The HSA has a "savings clause" that recognizes as effective and valid all administrative actions (e.g., orders, agreements, grants, contracts, certificates, licenses, registrations, and privileges) entered into by the INS until "amended, modified, superseded, terminated, set aside, or revoked" in accordance with law (*Flores v. Sessions* 2017, 870).

The law provides for different processing of unaccompanied alien children from contiguous countries (Canada or Mexico) caught at a land border or a U.S. port of entry and who are deemed inadmissible under federal immigration laws. The child can request that they be voluntarily returned to their contiguous home country instead of being placed in immigration removal proceedings—this is known as "voluntary return" which is a process distinct from "voluntary departure" (Manuel and Garcia 2014, 7). Once apprehended, DHS has 48 hours to decide whether the child is eligible for voluntary return because they are citizens of Canada or Mexico. If DHS cannot decide within this period, or the child does not meet the criteria for repatriation, DHS must immediately transfer the child to ORR custody.

Trafficking Victims Protection Reauthorization Act

The Immigration and Nationality Act ("INA"), amended by the Illegal Immigrant Reform and Immigrant Responsibility Act of 1996, deals with the treatment of adults and families with children who illegally arrive in the U.S. In 2008, Congress adopted the William Wilberforce Trafficking Victims Protection Reauthorization Act which contained provisions relating to unaccompanied alien children. Under the TVPRA, the HHS Secretary is responsible for their care, custody, and detention. Other federal agencies were required to transfer custody to the ORR within 72 hours after determining that a minor in their custody is an unaccompanied alien child. The TVPRA requires ORR to promptly place the child in the "least restrictive setting that is in the best interest of the child." The TVPRA, like the *Flores* Settlement, provides that if release is not possible, the unaccompanied alien child may be placed in a specialized juvenile program or facility if the ORR determines that he or she poses a danger to self or others or committed a criminal offense. The ORR was also required under the law to conduct monthly reviews of any placement of an unaccompanied alien child in a secure facility.

Another significant change is incorporated in Section 235(a) to 235 (d) of the TVPRA which vests the DHS's U.S. Citizenship and Immigration Services asylum officers with initial jurisdiction over any asylum application filed by an unaccompanied alien child (Langlois 2009). Under the current law, an unaccompanied alien child can initially apply for asylum with the USCIS, even if he or she has already been issued Notice to Appear before an immigration judge (Langlois 2009, 2). The initial jurisdiction provision was effective on March 23, 2009 and applied to all unaccompanied alien children who filed for asylum on or after March 23, 2009, including those with pending removal proceedings in immigration court, cases on appeal to the Board of Immigration Appeals or on petition for review in federal court (*Flores v. Lynch* 2016; Langlois 2009). The provision grants an additional layer of protection because these minors now have the right to have their asylum cases decided in the first instance in a non-adversarial proceeding before the USCIS Asylum Office, even if they are in removal proceedings before the immigration courts (Braaten and Braaten 2019, 63).

Under current ORR guidelines (2015), field specialists initially determine whether to detain or release unaccompanied minors ("ORR Policies"). Before placing the child with a potential custodian, the ORR must: (1) ascertain whether the proposed custodian can provide for the minor's physical and mental well-being; and (2) determine the necessity of a home study. A home study is mandatory when the proposed custodian "clearly presents a risk of abuse, maltreatment, exploitation, or trafficking to the child" (*DB v. Cardall* 2016, 734). The parent or legal guardian (but not any other sponsor) has 30 days to appeal the adverse decision to the Assistant Secretary for Children and Families. Under ORR Policies, the parent or guardian does not have the right to be represented by counsel at the placement hearing (*Flores v. Sessions* 2017). The child can appeal a detention decision only if the sole reason for denial of release is that he poses a danger to himself or to others (ORR Policies 2015).

The TVPRA directed the Secretary of DHS to develop policies and procedures to ensure that unaccompanied alien children in the United States who are removed are safely returned to their countries of nationality or last habitual residence. The TVPRA requires differential treatment of unaccompanied alien children from Mexico and Canada who can be voluntarily returned to their countries compared to those from all other countries who are sheltered in the United States and placed in formal removal proceedings in immigration courts (Kandel 2021). The TVPRA revised the procedures and policies for unaccompanied alien children who file for asylum, requiring that those from contiguous countries (i.e., Canada and Mexico) be screened for possible trafficking risks and asylum claims within 48 hours of arrest (U.S. Government Accountability Office ["U.S. GAO"] 2015). The government later opted to screen all unaccompanied alien children for possible asylum claims. It also required the return of unaccompanied alien children to Mexico or Canada without additional penalties if they were found not to be human trafficking victims or were not fearful of being returned. The Secretary of State was tasked with negotiating agreements with Mexico and Canada to manage the minors' repatriation. Unaccompanied alien children from non-contiguous countries, those from Mexico and Canada arrested at the border and determined to be human trafficking victims or are fearful of returning, or those arrested away from the border are transferred to ORR care and custody and placed in removal proceedings before immigration judges.

Processing of Unaccompanied Alien Children

Different federal agencies are involved in the processing of unaccompanied alien children (Braaten and Braaten 2021; Kandel 2021a; Seghetti 2014) (see figure 1.1). A discussion of the roles of these agencies and their obligations under current laws is necessary because much of the litigation described in chapter 4 on the procedural due process rights of unaccompanied minors that reached federal courts involve the conditions under which immigration agencies detained and/or released these minors. Specifically, these minors challenged the conditions under which they were detained by DHS and ORR, alleging that these were unsafe and unsanitary, that they were deprived of appropriate medical care, that there were delays in their release and in efforts toward family reunification, and that they were placed in unlicensed facilities such as hotels prior to their expulsion under Title 42.

Customs and Border Protection apprehends, processes, and detains the majority of unaccompanied alien children arrested along U.S. borders. DHS's

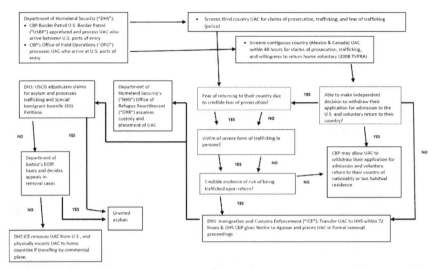

Figure 1.1.   Processing of Unaccompanied Alien Children by U.S. Federal Government Agencies. Source: Created by the authors.

Immigration and Customs Enforcement ("ICE") physically transfers them to ORR custody, apprehends them in the interior of the country, and represents the government in removal proceedings. If the unaccompanied alien children are ordered removed or voluntarily depart from the United States, ICE returns them to their home country. ORR provides temporary shelter and custody for those arriving from non-contiguous countries and contiguous countries (Canada and Mexico) who may be victims of trafficking, have an asylum claim, or do not desire to return to their country voluntarily, while their immigration hearings are ongoing. The USCIS initially decides asylum applications filed by them even after they are placed in removal proceedings. EOIR's immigration judges conduct immigration removal proceedings to determine whether they can remain in the U.S. or must be removed to their home countries. ICE repatriates unaccompanied alien children who are ordered removed from the U.S. Figure 1.1 shows the processing of unaccompanied alien children by U.S. federal government agencies.

Upon apprehension by Border Patrol agents, juveniles are transported to a CBP processing station where they are held in cells during processing. Under the Trafficking Victims Protection Reauthorization Act, CBP must determine whether they are unaccompanied alien children within 48 hours of arrest and transfer them to ORR custody within 72 hours. In practice, the children are held much longer for 15 days or more in multiple holding facilities (American Bar Association ["ABA"] Commission on Immigration 2015). After transfer to ORR shelters, these minors are able to "shower, rest, eat hot food, make phone calls and receive medical care, counseling, education and legal services" (ABA Commission on Immigration 2015, 3). Legal service providers give "Know Your Rights" presentations and perform individual screenings within days of their arrival to the shelter. The individual screenings enable their referral to *pro bono* attorneys.

The TVPRA requires that unaccompanied alien children from non-contiguous countries be placed in removal proceedings before an immigration judge and grants them the right to apply for legal relief and receive counsel "to the greatest extent practicable" (ABA Commission on Immigration 2015, 3). Unaccompanied minors from contiguous countries (Mexico and Canada) can be immediately returned to their countries after a cursory screening by a Border Patrol agent. A confidential report from the United Nations High Commissioner for Refugees (UNHCR) found these Border Patrol screenings to be inadequate and that they failed to protect Mexican children (Lind 2014). The UNHCR concluded that Border Patrol agents should not be responsible for screening children for risks of trafficking, persecution or voluntariness of return because these agents lack training to determine if or respond when an unaccompanied alien child is victimized (Lind 2014).

Customs and Border Protection

The TVPRA requires CBP to screen unaccompanied alien children who are nationals or habitual residents of a contiguous country (Mexico and Canada). However, DHS issued a policy in March 2009 that required screening for all unaccompanied alien children (Ryan 2011). Within 48 hours of apprehension, CBP personnel must screen all unaccompanied alien children to determine if: (1) he or she is not a victim of a severe form of trafficking in persons and there is no credible evidence that the minor is at risk of being trafficked upon return to his/her country of nationality or last habitual residence; (2) he or she does not have a fear of returning to his/her country of nationality or last habitual residence owing to a credible fear of persecution; and (3) he or she is able to decide independently to return voluntarily to his/her country of nationality or last habitual residence (Amnesty International 2021; Cavendish and Cortazar 2011; U.S. GAO 2015). If screening shows that all three of the above statements are true and they are inadmissible under the INA, the child must return to his/her home country. CBP can allow the child to withdraw his/her application for admission, allowing him/her to return voluntarily to their country of nationality or last habitual residence.

"Voluntary return" is a different relief from "voluntary departure" under Section 240B of the INA. Unaccompanied alien children who are citizens or residents of Canada and Mexico may be voluntarily returned to their home countries instead of being placed in removal proceedings if they withdraw their application for admission. Eligibility for voluntary return depends upon immigration authorities determining that the child (1) was not a victim of or at risk of a "severe form of trafficking" if repatriated; (2) does not fear repatriation because of a "credible fear" of persecution; and (3) can independently decide to agree to repatriation instead of being placed in removal proceedings (Smith 2020, 3–4). Unaccompanied alien children from Canada and Mexico who do not satisfy these criteria, or who do not agree to withdraw their application for admission, may be treated similarly to other children, including being placed in formal removal proceedings before an immigration judge (Manuel and Garcia 2014). Under Section 240 of the INA, unaccompanied alien children from noncontiguous countries not covered by TVPRA's special repatriation procedures for Mexican or Canadian UAC (e.g., withdrawal of application for admission) are also placed in removal proceedings. Section 240B of the INA allows them to apply for voluntary departure during these removal proceedings at no cost to them.

Immigration and Customs Enforcement

ICE agents physically transport unaccompanied alien children from CBP to ORR custody, apprehend UAC in the U.S. during immigration enforcement actions, represent the government in EOIR removal proceedings, and physically remove those who have final orders of removal or who chose to depart voluntarily from the U.S. while in removal proceedings (Siskin 2015). To enforce a removal order for UAC, the U.S. government must obtain travel documents from their country. Upon issuance by the foreign country of travel documents, ICE arranges the child's transport and escorts him/her to their home country if traveling by commercial plane. Mexican unaccompanied alien children are repatriated according to nine local repatriation agreements requiring ICE to notify the Mexican Consulate for each child repatriated (U.S. Department of Homeland Security 2019).

Office of Refugee Resettlement

ORR provides for care and custody of unaccompanied alien children apprehended and referred by CBP, ICE, or other federal agencies. Upon transfer to ORR custody, the ORR ensures: (1) that the children are placed in the least restrictive setting in their best interests; (2) timely appoint legal counsel for them; (3) that their interests are considered in decisions and actions relating to their care and custody; and (4) the viability of the infrastructure and personnel of residential facilities (Kandel 2021a). ORR also facilitates their release to family members or other sponsors who are able to care for them (Office of Refugee Resettlement 2015, 2021). The *Flores* Settlement preferentially ranks the order of sponsors for release as follows: (1) parent; (2) legal guardian; (3) adult relative; (4) adult individual or entity designated by the parent or legal guardian; (5) licensed program willing to accept legal custody; or (6) an adult or entity approved by ORR (*Flores v. Reno* 1997).

When sponsors cannot be located, these minors are placed in a long-term care setting, such as community-based foster care or extended care group home (Office of Refugee Resettlement 2015, 2021c). After placement, ORR requires its shelter care providers to conduct a *Safety and Well Being Follow-Up Call* with the child and their sponsor 30 days after his/her release to confirm the child's safety, living arrangements, school enrollment, and awareness of upcoming court dates (Office of Refugee Resettlement 2015, 2021c). Removal proceedings initiated by CBP continue while the child is placed with a sponsor. When the child in ORR custody reaches the age of 18 thereby aging out of status, ORR's legal authority to retain custody ends. ORR then transfers custody over these children to ICE custody where they are detained in adult detention facilities (Kandel 2021a).

U.S. Citizenship and Immigration Services

Section 235(d)(7)(B) of the TVPRA places initial jurisdiction of asylum applications filed by unaccompanied minors with USCIS, even for those already in removal proceedings (Bruno 2019; Kandel 2021; Seghetti 2014). USCIS also has initial jurisdiction over asylum applications filed by those who have: (1) been reunited with a parent or legal guardian, (2) pending claims in immigration court (National Immigrant Justice Center 2019), (3) cases on appeal before the Board of Immigration Appeals, or (4) petitions under review with federal courts. They must appear at any hearings scheduled in immigration court, even after petitioning for asylum with USCIS (Wasem 2014). If the asylum officer decides that the child in removal proceedings is not eligible for a grant of asylum, the child may request asylum during removal proceedings in the Department of Justice's Executive Office for Immigration Review (Langlois 2007, 2009; Wasem 2014).

USCIS Memorandum (2013) applies to any USCIS decision issued on or after June 10, 2013. The memorandum, applicable to asylum applications filed by unaccompanied alien children issued on or after June 10, 2013, requires USCIS to determine whether applicants in removal proceedings are unaccompanied alien children. In cases where either CBP or ICE already determined that the applicant in removal proceedings is an unaccompanied alien child and that status was still valid on the date the asylum application was filed, USCIS Asylum Offices should adopt that determination without another factual inquiry (Kim 2013). The USCIS has initial jurisdiction over the asylum application even if the applicant already reached 18 years of age or was reunited with a parent or legal guardian since the CBP or ICE determination (Kim 2013).

If the CBP or ICE have not yet determined whether minor applicants who are not in removal proceedings are unaccompanied alien children, the USCIS Asylum Offices will determine their status if they apply for asylum with the USCIS for the sole purpose of deciding whether they are subject to the one-year filing deadline and whether they must notify ORR that they discovered the unaccompanied alien child ("affirmative asylum process") (Kim 2013). For applicants already in removal proceedings where CBP or ICE has not determined that the applicants are unaccompanied alien children ("defensive asylum process"), Asylum Offices will determine their status for the purpose of deciding whether USCIS has jurisdiction over the case (Kim 2013). If they remain unaccompanied alien children at the time of the asylum interview, the Asylum Office must notify HHS that it has discovered the child.

Executive Office for Immigration Review

The Executive Office for Immigration Review conducts removal proceedings and decides immigration cases (EOIR 2017). During immigration removal proceedings, an immigration judge reviews evidence and testimonies presented before them to determine whether the unaccompanied alien children are removable or qualify for relief from removal (e.g., permission to temporarily or permanently remain in the United States). The TVPRA authorizes the HHS to ensure that the child has access to legal counsel and to appoint independent child advocates for child trafficking victims and other vulnerable unaccompanied children.

Section 235(b) of the TVPRA: (1) requires that HHS ensure, "to the greatest extent practicable," that they have access to legal counsel; and (2) authorizes the HHS to appoint independent child advocates for other vulnerable unaccompanied alien children (Kandel 2019, 14). Under EOIR guidelines, immigration judges should: (1) establish special dockets solely for unaccompanied alien children, (2) allow child-friendly courtroom modifications (e.g., judges not wearing robes, allowing the child to have a toy, permitting the child to testify from a seat rather than the witness stand, allowing more breaks during the proceedings), (3) provide courtroom orientations to familiarize the child with the court, (4) employ child-sensitive questioning, and (5) encourage the use of pro bono legal counsel if the child is not represented (Keller 2017). In response to the 2014 surge, EOIR issued new guidelines on July 9, 2014 that prioritized cases involving unaccompanied alien children and non-detained families above other cases in the immigration courts (Kandel

2019; Osuna 2014). EOIR's most recent guidance, issued January 17, 2018, does not prioritize these cases (Kandel 2019; McHenry III 2018).

Release from DHS or HHS Custody

DHS and HHS maintain custody over UAC for different purposes—DHS ensures their presence at removal proceedings and executes a final order of removal while HHS/ORR provides unaccompanied minors with temporary shelter care and protects them from trafficking and exploitation (Manuel and Garcia 2014). The *Flores* Settlement and DHS regulations specify when juveniles in removal proceedings may be released from custody. Although the *Flores* Settlement has a general policy favoring the release of children from detention, unaccompanied minors cannot be released when DHS determines that their continued detention is needed to ensure their safety or the safety of others, or is required to secure their presence at immigration removal proceedings (*Flores v. Reno* 1997).

DHS regulations also provide that a juvenile may be released, in order of preference, to (1) a parent, legal guardian, or other adult relative (brother, sister, aunt, uncle, or grandparent) not presently detained by DHS; (2) another adult individual or entity who is designated by a parent or guardian in DHS custody and who agrees to care for the juvenile and ensure his/her presence at removal proceedings; or (3) another adult individual or entity designated by DHS who agrees to care for the child and ensure his/her presence at removal proceedings (8 C.F.R. §236.3(b)). When the juvenile is detained by DHS along with a parent, legal guardian, or adult family member, DHS may on a case-by-case basis opt to release the juvenile and accompanying adult from detention simultaneously (Manuel and Garcia 2014).

After transfer to the HHS's ORR, the unaccompanied minor is released to the physical custody of an ORR-contracted care facility. The type of facility (e.g., shelter care, secure care, or foster care) depends upon the age of the minor, whether they pose a flight risk or a danger to themselves or others, and on their particular needs (Byrne and Miller 2012; Seghetti et al. 2014). These minors remain in the federal government's legal custody although they are temporarily in the physical custody of a licensed care provider. They remain in these facilities while there are removal proceedings against them, until they turn 18 (after which they are turned over to DHS if DHS has initiated removal proceedings against them), or until ORR finds a parent, legal guardian, or other entity who may take custody of the UAC according to the *Flores* Settlement (*Flores v. Reno* 1997).

Best Interests of the Child Principle in Treatment of
UAC Asylum Claims

Various international instruments provide guidance on the treatment of asylum claims of children. Article 3(1) of the United Nations' Convention on the Rights of the Child ("UNCRC") provides that the "best interests of the child" should be the "primary consideration" in all actions involving children (UNCRC 1989). The "best interests of the child" principle holds the State "ultimately responsible" in meeting and protecting the "basic needs" and "fundamental rights" of children (USCIS Asylum Division 2009, 8). Article 25(2) of the Universal Declaration of Human Rights ("UDHR") requires special care and assistance for children (Weiss 1998). The United Nations High Commissioner for Refugees Executive Committee Conclusion No. 47 requires that government actions involving refugee children be guided by the "best interests of the child" principle (UNHCR 1987). The UNHCR also promulgated guidelines on dealing with unaccompanied children seeking asylum (UNHCR 1997). Recognizing these international legal mandates, the USCIS (formerly the Immigration and Naturalization Service or "INS") issued on Human Rights Day 1998 guidelines addressing "child-sensitive interview procedures and legal analysis of the issues" arising in UAC asylum claims (USCIS 2009, 7). The guidelines provide that the "best interests of the child" principle of international law is a "useful measure" to determine "appropriate interview procedures for child asylum seekers" but "does not play a role in determining substantive eligibility under the U.S. refugee definition" (Weiss 1998, 2).

Although the child asylum applicant has the burden of proof in asylum proceedings, asylum officers conducting the non-adversarial interview must consider the effect of the child's age, stage of language development, background, and level of sophistication when creating a "child-friendly" asylum interview environment that allows the child to discuss freely the factual elements of the claim (Weiss 1998, 5). The guidelines encourage asylum officers to engage in child-sensitive questioning, active listening techniques, and take an active role in gathering objective evidence to evaluate the claims. Asylum officers are admonished, however, that "regardless of how sympathetic" they may be to the child's asylum claims, the "best interests of the child" principle—although useful during the interview process—does not replace or change the U.S. law's refugee definition in determining substantive eligibility (Weiss 1998, 18).

Noting the absence of guidelines for children's asylum claims in adversarial immigration proceedings, the Office of the Chief Immigration Judge ("OCIJ") issued on May 22, 2007 an Operating Policies and Procedures Memorandum ("OPPM") 07–01 providing guidance and suggestions for adjudicating cases involving unaccompanied minors (Neal 2007). Under OPPM 07–01, the best interest of the child principle is not a legal basis for the detention or removal of unaccompanied alien children (*Matter of A–E–M–* 1998). The Memorandum explicitly states that issues of law (e.g., questions of admissibility, eligibility for relief) are governed by the Immigration and Nationality Act and its regulations. Hence, the best interest of the child standard cannot provide a basis for relief that is not permitted by law. The standard may allow modification in the conduct of immigration removal proceedings, even though it is irrelevant in determining whether the child is removable. The ORR, by contrast, is required to consider the best interest of the child in decisions involving placement of unaccompanied alien children in care facilities (Manuel and Garcia 2014). In 2008, Congress mandated that ORR transfer physical custody of these minors "in the least restrictive setting that is in the best interest of the child" (*Flores v. Reno* 1997, par. 99).

The OPPM 07–01 guidelines contain the following basic principles: (1) immigration judges are required to employ "child sensitive procedures" (Neal 2007, 3); (2) the "best interest of the child" principle relates to the immigration judges' discretion to ensure a "child appropriate" hearing environment where the child can freely discuss the elements of the asylum claim but does not "negate the statute" and "cannot provide a basis" for relief that is not sanctioned by law (Neal 2007, 4); (3) the immigration judge should encourage the use of appropriate pro bono resources and provide a list of pro bono services to the child respondent who is not represented; (4) all immigration judges are trained to handle asylum cases involving unaccompanied alien children; and (5) topics to consider when a child is a respondent or witness include: "effect of age and development on the child's ability to participate in the proceedings; gender; mental health (including possible post-traumatic stress syndrome); general cultural sensitivity issues; and appropriate questioning and listening techniques for child witnesses" (Neal 2007, 4).

The OPPM 07–01 also provides guidance on permissible courtroom modifications to ensuring an appropriate courtroom setting including, courtroom orientation to allow minors familiarity with the courtroom; separate dockets or separate schedules from adult cases (EOIR 2008); courtroom modifications; use of video or telephone conferencing; and removal of judge's robe. To ensure appropriate courtroom procedures, the guidelines also recommend explaining the proceedings at the outset; allowing the interpreter to build rapport with the child; preparing the child to testify; making proper credibility assessments; controlling access to the courtroom; and employing child sensitive questioning and active listening techniques described in the USCIS guidelines incorporated as an attachment.

Under the Trump administration, the OCIJ issued OPPM 17–03 on December 20, 2017, rescinding and replacing OPPM 07–01. The new OPPM

17–03 streamlined provisions of OPPM 07–01, removing the requirement for immigration judges to employ child sensitive procedures and child appropriate hearing environment for cases involving juveniles but retaining provisions on modifications for courtroom setting and procedure (Keller 2017). OPPM 17–03 (2017, 3) cautions immigration judges that issues of law are governed by the INA and the regulations and not the "best interests of the child" standard—the new memorandum removes the immigration judges' discretion in ensuring a child appropriate hearing environment. OPPM 17–03 also omits specific child-friendly practices in the prior OPPM 07–01, notably: (1) allowing for telephonic conferences for master calendar hearings or status conferences when a child does not reside close to the immigration court; (2) guidance on child sensitive questioning and active listening techniques is no longer incorporated as an attachment; and (3) the section on "credibility and burden of proof assessments" emphasizes that "legal requirements, including credibility standards and burdens of proof, are not relaxed or obviated for juvenile respondents," and that "vague, speculative or generalized testimony" may be "insufficient by itself" to be found credible or meet the burden of proof (Keller 2017, 7). Thus, immigration judges are reminded to use the same standards when evaluating the testimony of children and adults without considering their biological, cognitive, and developmental differences.

Forms of Relief from Removal

Unaccompanied alien children may be eligible for the following forms of relief from removal (Manuel and Garcia 2014). Upon grant of the relief, they may be permitted to remain in the United States and adjust to lawful permanent resident ("LPR") status.

First, they may be granted asylum if they are unable or unwilling to return to their home country due to a well-founded fear of persecution because of race, religion, nationality, political opinion, or membership in a particular social group (Section 208 (b)(1)(A) of the INA). An unaccompanied minor granted asylum may be allowed to work in the U.S. and adjust to LPR status (Sections 208(c) and 209 (b) of the INA). Section 208(b)(3)(C) of the INA also mandates that asylum officers within USCIS have initial jurisdiction over any asylum claim made even if they are already in removal proceedings.

Second, they may be eligible for Special Immigrant Juvenile ("SIJ") status and apply as LPR (Section 101(a)(27)(J) of the INA). Eligibility for SIJ status is limited to noncitizens under 21 years of age who lack the care or custody of their parents or legal guardians. SIJ status is limited to juveniles who (1) have been declared as a dependent by a state juvenile court or legally placed by the court with a state or an appointed private entity; (2) cannot reunite with their parents due to abuse, abandonment, or neglect; and (3) whose best interests are not served by being returned to their native country or country of last habitual residence. The Secretary of HHS must consent to the jurisdiction of a juvenile court before the court may declare an unaccompanied alien child in ORR custody to be a dependent of the court or before the court may legally place the child in the custody of a state agency or a court-appointed person or entity (Section 101 of the INA). One difference between SIJ status is that it grants the noncitizen legal basis to remain in the United States, adjust their status to that of lawful permanent resident alien, and eventually apply for U.S. citizenship. Classification as an unaccompanied alien child, in contrast, does not provide any legal basis to remain in the United States or adjust to LPR status, they could potentially be able apply for various forms of relief (Manuel and Garcia 2014).

Third, they can apply for nonimmigrant visas that allow them to temporarily remain in the country (and adjust to LPR status) if they are the victims of trafficking or certain other crimes. They may apply for a nonimmigrant T visa if they are below 18 years old and victims of severe forms of trafficking (Section 101(a)(15)(T) of the INA). They can also apply for a nonimmigrant U visa if they (1) suffered substantial physical or mental abuse as victims of specific criminal activities (e.g., domestic violence, rape, trafficking, kidnapping, involuntary servitude, and felonious assault); (2) possess information regarding the criminal activity; and (3) have been or are likely to be helpful in a law enforcement investigation or prosecution of such activity (Section 101(a)(15)(U) of the INA). Both the T visa and U visa allow noncitizens to live in the United States for up to four years (subject to extension) and apply for adjustment to LPR status after three years (Sections 214(o) and 214(p) of the INA).

Fourth, in recent years, immigration judges and the BIA increasingly ordered administrative closure to remove a large number of cases from their dockets (Montano 2020). Administrative closure is "a docket management tool" used to "temporarily pause" removal proceedings and remove the case from the immigration judge's active calendar or from the BIA's docket (*Matter of Castro-Tum* 2018, 272). In most cases, administrative closure becomes permanent and unless a party moves to re-calendar the administratively closed case, the case remains "indefinitely suspended without a final resolution" (*Matter of Castro-Tum* 2018, 272). Within a span of six years (from October 1, 2011 through September 30, 2017), 215,285 cases were administratively closed. This represents 76 percent of the total cases that were administratively closed in the 30-year period between 1980 and 2011. Citing the growing use of administrative closure in immigration courts, Attorney General Jeff Sessions issued on May 17, 2018 an opinion in *Matter of Castro-Tum* (2018) holding that immigration judges and the BIA have no general authority to administratively close cases. The Fourth Circuit Court of

Appeals, however, in *Romero v. Barr* (2019) abrogated *Matter of Castro-Tum* (2018), concluding that the DOJ regulations governing the powers and conduct of immigration judges clearly vest in immigration judges the authority to administratively close cases.

RIGHTS, PRIVILEGES, AND BENEFITS OF UNACCOMPANIED ALIEN CHILDREN

Both the TVPRA and Homeland Security Act contain provisions relating to unaccompanied alien children's access to legal counsel (Manuel and Garcia 2014). Section 235 of the TVPRA requires the Secretary of HHS to ensure that unaccompanied alien children in HHS or DHS custody have counsel to represent them in legal proceedings or matters and protect them from mistreatment, exploitation, and trafficking. Section 462 of the HSA requires the ORR Director to develop a plan to ensure that qualified and independent legal counsel is timely appointed to represent the interests of each child. Consistent with Section 292 of the INA, both laws require that this legal counsel should not entail any expense on the part of the Government.

Several federal circuit courts have opined that the U.S. Constitution's Due Process Clause could require on a case-by-case basis the appointment of counsel for noncitizens who cannot represent themselves due to "age, ignorance, or mental capacity" (*Aguilera-Enriquez v. INS* 1975, 569; cf. *Wade v. Mayo*, 1948, 683–684; *Michelson v. INS* 1990, 468; *Ruiz v. INS* 1996, 1297; *Barthold v. INS* 1975, 690–691). Section 504 of the Rehabilitation Act has also been interpreted as allowing the appointment of counsel at the government's expense for unrepresented immigration detainees with "serious mental disorders or conditions" that make them "mentally incompetent" to "meaningfully participate" in immigration proceedings (*Franco-Gonzales v. Holder* 2010, 1045–1046; Executive Office of Immigration Review 2013, 1).

Access to Counsel and Due Process Concerns

Legal representation in removal proceedings is correlated with obtaining successful relief—73 percent of represented children were granted the right to remain in the United States compared to 15 percent of unrepresented children (Transactional Records Access Clearinghouse 2014). The EOIR began to expedite the cases of unaccompanied children who were released from detention and reunified beginning in May 2014. These "rocket dockets" require children's cases to be set for an initial master calendar hearing within 21 days of release from detention (ABA Commission on Immigration 2015, 8). These expedited rocket proceedings raise significant due process concerns due to lack of proper notice and lack of access to counsel in immigration courts (Fritze 2014). Although initial master calendar hearings are required to be expedited, the Chief Immigration Judge clarified that immigration judges can use their discretion to allow adjournments in subsequent hearings as necessary (O'Leary 2015).

Pro Bono Legal Services

There is no central agency coordinating the legal representation of unaccompanied alien children after they are reunified with sponsors. Some non-profit groups provide pro bono legal services in major cities. For example, Kids in Need of Defense ("KIND") operates in eight major cities including Baltimore, Washington DC, Boston, Houston, Seattle, Los Angeles, New York and Newark (ABA Commission on Immigration 2015). Several federal grants also support free legal services for reunified unaccompanied alien children. The ORR awarded grants of over $2 million each to two non-profit agencies—the U.S. Committee for Refugees and the U.S. Conference of Catholic Bishops—for post-release legal services serving reunified unaccompanied alien children in removal proceedings (Children and Families Administration 2014). Also, the Department of Justice and the Corporation for National and Community Service in June 2014 created the "justice AmeriCorps" a grant program intended to enroll 100 lawyers and paralegals in the U.S. to provide legal services to vulnerable children in removal proceedings who meet certain criteria (Executive Office for Immigration Review 2014).

The majority of unaccompanied alien children who arrived in the U.S. in 2014 came from three countries: El Salvador, Honduras and Guatemala, a region in Central America known as the Northern Triangle. Since 1989, the ABA has operated the Texas Pro Bono Asylum Representation Project, a *pro bono* project on the Texas/Mexico border. ProBAR provides legal services to indigent, detained adults and unaccompanied children in the Rio Grande Valley of lower South Texas. In 2014, ProBAR served 10,403 detained unaccompanied alien children and 1,981 detained adults (ABA Commission on Immigration 2015). ProBAR gives "Know Your Rights" presentations to detained children and adults, individual screenings, and *pro bono* representation and referrals to those eligible for relief. In 2008, the ABA also created the Immigrant Justice Project ("IJP"), a pro bono project located in San Diego, California. The IJP serves both detained and non-detained individuals. It recruits, trains and mentors volunteer lawyers and law students to represent individual clients. Although IJP does not focus specifically on unaccompanied alien children, it specializes in representing detainees with diminished mental capacity, asylum-seekers, and others (ABA Commission on Immigration 2015).

U.S. ASYLUM APPLICATION PROCESS

Our discussion of the legal rights and protections accorded to unaccompanied minors under U.S. laws would not be complete without a discussion of the asylum application process itself. While chapters 2 and 3 discuss asylum outcomes in immigration courts and the Board of Immigration Appeals, chapter 5 discusses several cases that were filed in federal courts through a petition for review of decisions of the BIA. Thus, these federal cases directly discuss the legal basis for asylum, the parameters of a particular social group as a basis for the grant of asylum, and the viability of asylum claims based on the proposed social group of young men opposed to gang membership and fear of persecution on account of a protected ground.

Foreign nationals apprehended along the U.S. border or port of entry who lack immigration documents or engage in fraud or misrepresentation are generally placed in expedited removal (Wassem 2014). If they express a fear of persecution, they can receive a credible fear hearing before a USCIS asylum officer. If their fears are found credible, they are referred to an immigration judge for a hearing. To receive asylum in the United States, they must demonstrate a well-founded fear that if returned home, they will be persecuted based upon one of five characteristics: race, religion, nationality, membership in a particular social group, or political opinion.

Prior to 1996, foreign nationals arriving at a U.S. port of entry without proper documents could request a removal proceeding before an EOIR immigration judge to determine if they could be admitted into the country. They could also request asylum during the hearing and seek administrative and judicial review if the immigration judge ruled against them. However, the Illegal Immigrant Reform and Immigrant Responsibility Act of 1996 (IIRIRA, P.L. 104–208) amended the law by allowing expedited removal of these foreign nationals. DHS immigration officers could summarily exclude a foreign national arriving without proper documents, unless they expressed a fear of persecution if repatriated (Wasem 2013, 2014). Without such fear, the officer can exclude them from the country without placing them in removal proceedings (Executive Office for Immigration Review 2009).

Credible Fear

DHS immigration policy and procedures require immigration officers to ask each foreign national subject to expedited removal the following questions to identify whether they have fears of being returned to their home country: (1) Why did you leave your home country or country of last residence? (2) Do you have any fear or concern about being returned to your home country or being removed from the United States? (3) Would you be harmed if you were returned to your home country or country of last residence? (4) Do you have any questions or is there anything else you would like to add? (Wasem 2014).

Under the INA, credible fear of persecution means that there is a significant possibility, based on the credibility of the alien's statements and facts known to the officer, that the alien could establish eligibility for asylum under §208. If the asylum officer finds that the foreign national has credible fear, the officer refers him or her to an EOIR immigration judge (defensive applications for asylum) (Wasem 2011). If the USCIS asylum officer decides that the alien does not have credible fear, the alien may request that the EOIR immigration judge review that finding (Executive Office for Immigration Review 2009).

Eligibility for Asylum

Foreign nationals arriving in the U.S. may apply for asylum with the USCIS or before the DOJ's EOIR during removal proceedings. To receive asylum, they must show a well-founded fear that, if returned home, they will be persecuted based upon one of five characteristics: race, religion, nationality, membership in a particular social group, or political opinion (Wassem 2011, 2014). Case law and federal regulations provide guidance on the meaning of well-founded fear (*INS v. Cardoza-Fonseca* 1987). Asylum seekers have a well-founded fear of persecution if: (1) they have a fear of persecution in their country of nationality or, if stateless, in their country of last habitual residence, due to race, religion, nationality, membership in a particular social group, or political opinion; (2) there is a reasonable possibility of suffering such persecution if they return to that country; and (3) they are unable or unwilling to return to, or avail themselves of the protection of that country because of such fear (8 C.F.R. §208.13(b)(2)).

Treatment of Asylum Claims of Unaccompanied Alien Children

As mentioned earlier, noncitizens arriving in the United States who are deemed inadmissible by an immigration officer may be immediately ordered removed through a streamlined expedited removal process that does not require removal proceedings before an immigration judge (Manuel and Garcia 2014; Section 235(b) INA). Federal law specifically exempts unaccompanied alien children from this expedited process (8 U.S.C. §1232(a)(5)(D). Under Section 240 of the INA, inadmissible unaccompanied alien children must be placed in formal removal proceedings before an immigration judge. They also have the right to counsel at no expense to the government (8 U.S.C. §1232(a)(5)(D) & (c)(5)) and can opt for voluntary departure under Section 240B of the INA at no cost to the child (8 U.S.C. §1232(a)(4)).

Upon apprehension, unaccompanied alien children are screened to see if they may have a credible fear of returning home. The TVPRA requires that children from contiguous countries (Mexico and Canada) be screened within 48 hours of apprehension to determine whether they should be returned to their country or transferred to HHS and placed in removal proceedings (Seghetti 2014). During the screening, CBP personnel must determine whether the child: (1) has been a victim or is at risk of a severe form of human trafficking; (2) has possible claims to asylum; and (3) can make an independent decision to voluntarily return to his country of nationality or of last habitual residence (U.S. GAO 2015). Although TVPRA requires initial CBP screening only for unaccompanied alien children from Mexico and Canada, DHS issued a policy in March 2009 that made the screening provisions applicable to all unaccompanied alien children (Ryan 2011). Unaccompanied children who opt not to return voluntarily and those from noncontiguous countries are transferred to the care and custody of HHS while they go through formal removal proceedings before an immigration judge (Wassem 2014).

The TVPRA grants USCIS asylum officers initial jurisdiction over asylum applications filed by unaccompanied alien children. All applications of unaccompanied alien children for asylum are heard by USCIS, even if they are already in removal proceedings (Section 208(b)(3)(C) of the INA). By contrast, affirmative applications for asylum by other noncitizens are heard by USCIS while their defensive applications in removal proceedings are heard exclusively by immigration judges (8 C.F.R. §208.2(b)). Once either the CBP or ICE determines that the child is an unaccompanied minor and transfers the minor to ORR's custody, USCIS will decide on his or her asylum application, even when the child has reunited with a parent or legal guardian, has pending claims in immigration court, has a case on appeal before the Board of Immigration Appeals (Langlois 2009). If the USCIS denies the child's application for asylum, he/she may request asylum during formal removal proceedings before the EOIR's immigration judge (Manuel and Garcia 2014). The TVPRA requires that all unaccompanied alien children, except those from contiguous countries who agree to voluntary return, are given formal removal proceedings before an immigration judge. The TVPRA also provides that unaccompanied alien children are not subject to the time limit that requires foreign nationals to seek asylum within one year of arriving in the United States—they can file an application for asylum more than one year after their arrival in the United States (*Ogayonne v. Mukasey* 2008; 8 C.F.R. §1208.4(a)(5)(ii)).

Inadmissibility of Unaccompanied Minor Without Immigration Status

Section 212(a)(7) of the INA bars the admission to the United States of "any immigrant [who] at the time of application for admission . . . is not in possession of a valid unexpired immigrant visa, reentry permit, border crossing identification card, or other valid entry document, and a valid unexpired passport, or other suitable travel document, or document of identity and nationality." The INA differentiates admission from entry—admission is the lawful entry into the United States after inspection and authorization by an immigration officer while entry is any arrival of a noncitizen into the U.S. and may be permitted in circumstances where admission is not legally permissible (*Matter of Rosas-Ramirez* 1999).

Section 235 of the TVPRA of 2008, as amended, implicitly authorized unaccompanied alien children to enter the United States. Section 235 distinguishes between unaccompanied alien children from contiguous countries (Canada and Mexico) and those from noncontiguous countries. Unaccompanied alien children from contiguous countries passing through a port of entry or land border whom immigration officials consider as inadmissible (e.g., lack of proper documentation) may withdraw their application for admission and are returned to their home country, subject to certain conditions (8 U.S.C. §1232(a)(2)(A)). Minors from other countries are required to be transferred to the custody of the Secretary of Health and Human Services within 72 hours of being classified as unaccompanied alien children (8 U.S.C. §1232(a)(3) & (b)(3)).

Asylum Based on Gang Violence in Home Countries

To be eligible for asylum, the unaccompanied alien child has the burden of proving that he/she is unable or unwilling to return to their home country because of persecution, or a well-founded fear of persecution, on account of race, religion, nationality, political opinion, or membership in a particular social group (§208(b)(1)(B)(i) of the INA). Although not defined in either the INA or its implementing regulations, persecution means "the infliction of suffering or harm upon those who differ (in race, religion or political opinion) in a way regarded as offensive" (*Ghaly v. INS* 1995, 1431; *Osaghae v. INS* 1991, 1163). Generalized violence or lawlessness and harms not arising from governmental actions or entities whom the government cannot or will not control (*Fuentes-Chavarria* 2014; *Karki v. Holder* 2013) are different from persecution and cannot serve as basis for asylum (*Escobar v. Holder* 2012; *Jutus v. Holder* 2013). Persecution must also be the result of a protected ground (i.e., race, religion, etc.)—the protected ground serves as "at least one central reason for the persecution" (*Crespin-Valladares v. Holder* 2011, 127; *Matter of J-B-N-* 2007, 214; *Quineros-Mendoza v. Holder* 1999, 164).

Non-citizens applying for asylum based on gang violence assert that they are persecuted because of membership in a particular social group or, less commonly, political opinion (an actual or imputed political opinion that they are opposed to the gangs) (*Castillo Sanchez v. U.S. Attorney General* 2013). Applicants have experienced various degrees of success in defining the social group as (1) those who concretely or actively oppose the gangs' activities (*Pirir-Boc v. Holder* 2014); (2) those who resist gang attempts to recruit them (*Flores Munoz v. Holder* 2014; *Matter of S-E-G-* 2008); (3) former gang members who renounced their membership (*Ramos v. Holder* 2009); (3) witnesses who testified against the gangs (*Henriquez-Rivas v. Holder* 2013), and (4) families that have been affected by gang violence (*Perez-Perez v. Holder* 2014). Some administrative and judicial tribunals denied asylum on these grounds, declining to recognize their proposed social group (*Olmos Borja v. Holder* 2013; *Ulloa Santos v. Attorney General* 2014).

POLITICAL RESPONSES TO UNACCOMPANIED MINORS IN THE U.S.

Obama Administration Action

The Obama Administration implemented several measures to respond to the rise in apprehensions of unaccompanied alien children in 2014. In June 2014, the government formed the Unified Coordination Group headed by Federal Emergency Management Agency's ("FEMA"), with representatives from key agencies (Obama 2014; U.S. DHS 2014). The DOJ's Legal Orientation Program was also tasked in FY2014 with providing legal orientation presentations to sponsors of these minors in EOIR removal proceedings. To provide children with legal representation in immigration removal proceedings, EOIR partnered with the Corporation for National and Community Service ("CNCS") to create "Justice AmeriCorps" which operated from January 1, 2015 to August 31, 2017 (Fountain and Overbay 2019). The grant program enrolled approximately 100 lawyers and paralegals as AmeriCorps members (EOIR 2014).

In September 2014, the Obama Administration announced the Central American Minors ("CAM") Refugee and Parole Program to provide a safe, legal, and orderly alternative for unaccompanied alien children to join relatives in the United States (Bruno 2015; Kandel 2021). The program targeted children from El Salvador, Guatemala, and Honduras and discouraged them from migrating to the U.S., by allowing some of them to be considered for refugee status while remaining in their home countries. In August 2017, the Trump Administration terminated the CAM program. The Biden Administration reactivated the program in March 2021 and expanded its eligibility criteria (U.S. Department of State 2021).

Trump Administration Action

The Trump Administration responded by providing unaccompanied alien children with temporary housing and reducing the number of family units migrating to the United States (Singer and Kandel 2019). The Trump administration increased the use of temporary influx shelters due to the increasing caseload, encouraged sponsor information sharing between ORR, CBP, and ICE, reclassified children whose parents were prosecuted for illegal entry as unaccompanied alien children and housed them in ORR shelters, and proposed new regulations to expand their allowable detention beyond the existing 20-day limit (Kandel 2021).

To respond to surges of unaccompanied alien children arriving at the Southwest border alone or as part of family units who were later separated, ORR used temporary "influx care facilities" to provide emergency shelter, supplementing its current network of state-licensed shelters (ORR 2015, 2021c). These temporary facilities are located on federally owned land or leased properties, exempting them from state or local childcare licensing standards. Between March 2018 and July 2019, ORR temporarily opened three such shelters in Tornillo, TX (Tornillo shelter), Homestead, FL (Homestead shelter), and Carrizo Springs, TX, and closed them when they were no longer needed (Kandel 2021).

At the end of December 2018, ORR housed more than 15,000 children in its shelters (including influx shelters), an increase from 9,200 children in January 2017 (Hernández 2018; Leighton 2018). In December 2018, in response to the growing number of unaccompanied alien children in ORR custody (Moore 2018), the Trump Administration relaxed the requirements of its information collection and sharing policy relating to potential sponsors. The Biden Administration has since rescinded Trump's policy on information sharing, noting its "chilling effect" on family reunification (Ordonez 2021, 1).

Concerns About ORR Temporary Shelters

The Florida Homestead Shelter ("Homestead") was the largest shelter facility operating in the U.S. and the only one operated by a for-profit corporation, Comprehensive Health Services Incorporated ("CHSI") (U.S. Office of the Inspector General 2020a). HHS began using Homestead as a temporary shelter for unaccompanied alien children in June 2016, sheltering 8,500 children over approximately 10 months until it closed temporarily in April 2017 (Office of Refugee Resettlement 2019). In March 2018, the Homestead shelter reopened. During the time Homestead operated, allegations of sexual abuse occurring at the facility were reported to the media (Madan 2020). Some minors further alleged that they were emotionally neglected and abused. The facility was also located near a toxic military Superfund site (Cardona 2021). These issues influenced the Biden Administration not to reopen Homestead in the spring of 2021 despite the urgent need for additional housing (Kight and Nichols 2021).

ORR asserts that its temporary influx shelters have similar standards, policies, and services as conventional ORR-supervised state-licensed shelters (Office of Refugee Resettlement 2021c). In November 2018, HHS's OIG issued a memorandum identifying vulnerabilities that included insufficient personnel background checks and numbers of mental health clinicians (Chiedi 2019; Levinson 2018). In February 2019, a congressional delegation visiting the Homestead site characterized its conditions as deplorable and unacceptable (Chaplin 2019; Sesin 2019). An internal ORR report indicated that the agency had received 4,556 allegations of sexual abuse or sexual harassment in detention centers between FY2015 and FY2018 (Haag 2019; Office of Refugee Resettlement 2017).

Information Sharing Between ORR, ICE, and CBP

In April 2018, ORR, ICE, and CBP entered into a memorandum of agreement ("MOA") for the sharing of information from the time that the CBP or ICE refers the child to ORR, during his/her period in ORR custody, and upon his/her release from ORR custody to a sponsor (Kandel 2021; MOA 2018). Under the MOA, ORR agreed to collect and share with ICE and CBP information about these minors in their custody, such as arrests, unauthorized absences, deaths, abuse experienced, and violent behavior, age determination findings, and gang affiliation. The ORR would also share with ICE biographic and biometric (fingerprint) information about potential sponsors and their household members. ICE would then provide ORR with summary criminal and immigration histories of potential sponsors and all adult household members so that ORR could determine the sponsors' suitability to take custody of these minors. After the policy was implemented, ICE began arresting unauthorized aliens who volunteered to sponsor these children. From July through November 2018, ICE arrested 170 potential sponsors—109 of whom had no previous criminal histories—and placed them in deportation proceedings (Kopan 2018). Critics pointed out that Trump's immigration policies deterred potential sponsors from coming forward out of fear of being arrested, resulting in longer detentions for unaccompanied alien children (Kopan 2018).

Zero Tolerance Immigration Enforcement Policy

On April 6, 2018, DOJ implemented a "zero tolerance" enforcement policy for persons who entered the United States illegally between ports of entry (Kandel 2021b 1). Under the zero tolerance policy, DOJ prosecuted all adult foreign nationals arrested while crossing the border illegally, without exempting asylum seekers or migrants with minor children (Daniels 2018). When a parent entered the U.S. illegally with a minor and was criminally detained, DHS treated the minor as an unaccompanied alien child and transferred him/her to ORR custody. When the parent's criminal prosecution for illegal entry or reentry ended, the parent was then reunited with the child.

Due to critical public reaction, President Trump issued Executive Order 13841 (2018), authorizing DHS to maintain custody of alien families during the pendency of any criminal trial or immigration proceedings. Although CBP stopped referring most illegal border crossers to the DOJ for criminal prosecution, ICE continued to detain family units for up to 20 days (Kandel 2021, 2021b). A federal judge then issued an injunction prohibiting family separation and requiring that all separated children be reunited promptly with their families (*Ms. L v. ICE* 2018).

Reuniting families was problematic for the ORR, CBP, and ICE. The Office of Inspector General ("OIG") reports that CBP omitted information about the separated children's family members after classifying them as unaccompanied alien children and transferring them to ORR custody. There were also limitations with CBP's information technology system for tracking these minors (U.S. Office of Inspector General 2018, 2019). Due to the delay in reunifying families, between 2,000 and 3,000 children spent an indeterminate amount of additional time in ORR shelters (Dickerson 2018; Lovett and Radnofsky 2018; Prasad 2018; Schallhorn 2018).

Regulations to Replace the Flores Settlement Agreement

On September 7, 2018, the DHS and HHS under the Trump Administration jointly published proposed regulations that would have replaced the *Flores* Agreement (U.S. HHS and U.S. DHS 2018). The proposed rule amended current licensing requirements for family residential centers, allowing detention of families together with minors during their entire immigration proceedings. It also allowed ICE to overcome the 20-day immigration detention restriction for families that was imposed as part of the *Flores* Agreement. The final rule was issued on August 23, 2019 (U.S. HHS and U.S. DHS 2018). After the rule was issued, federal district judge Dolly Gee, who oversees the *Flores* Agreement, permanently enjoined it (*Flores v. Barr* 2019).

Title 42 Public Health Emergency

At the start of the global COVID-19 pandemic in 2020, the Trump Administration temporarily restricted the entry of certain foreign nationals at U.S. land and coastal borders to limit the potential spread of the virus. On March 21, 2020, the Centers for Disease Control and Prevention ("CDC") of the HHS issued a Title 42 order that suspended the arrival of specific foreign nationals traveling from Mexico and Canada into the U.S. (Centers for Disease Control and Prevention 2020a, 2020b; Harrington 2021). Under Title 42, CBP quickly expelled most unaccompanied alien children to Mexico, their country of last transit, instead of processing them under Title 9 of U.S. immigration law. Title 42 along with the pandemic's constricting impact on migration led to a decrease in *encounters* (apprehensions and expulsions) with unaccompanied alien children from 76,020 in FY2019 to 30,557 in FY2020 (Kandel 2021).

The use of Title 42 sharply reduced the number of unaccompanied children apprehended by CBP and referred to ORR. Apprehensions of these minors by CBP decreased from 18,096 in the first half of FY2020 to 12,461 in the second half of FY2020 (U.S. Customs and Border Protection 2021a). CBP referrals to ORR decreased from 13,339 in the first half of FY2020 to 1,970 in the second half of FY2020 (U.S. Customs and Border Protection 2021a). Federal district court judge Sullivan blocked in November 2020 the application of CDC's Title 42 order to unaccompanied alien children because it violated the TVPRA and other laws governing their processing (Monyak 2020; *P.J.E.S. v. Chad F. Wolf* 2020). The D.C. Circuit Court of Appeals, however, stayed the November injunction on January 29, 2021 (Aquino 2021; CDC 2021a). In February 2021, the Biden Administration stopped the use of Title 42 to expel them and required that they be processed under Title 8, including placing them in formal immigration proceedings (Centers for Disease Control and Prevention 2021a). This partly contributed to the surge of unaccompanied children arriving at the Southwest border (Miroff & Sacchetti 2021; Shear et al. 2021).

Biden Administration Action

Limited ORR Shelter Capacity

The Biden Administration was faced with a surge of unaccompanied alien children in March 2021—border agents encountered more than 19,000 children, the largest number recorded in a single month. (Shear et al. 2021). CBP Southwest land border encounters with unaccompanied minors rose from 146,925 in fiscal year 2021 to 152,057 in fiscal year 2022 compared to 80,634 in fiscal year 2019 and 33,239 during the height of the COVID-19 pandemic in fiscal year 2020. One of the problems the Administration faced was limited ORR shelter capacity, leading CBP to rapidly expand its temporary housing capacity to accommodate these arriving children (Andersson and Laurant 2021; Flores et al. 2021; Kanno-Youngs & Shear 2021). In March 2021, CBP housed almost 5,800 unaccompanied alien children in its own facilities (Greenberg 2021), including more than 4,100 children at a Donna, TX facility which could house only 250 detainees (Spagat and Merchant 2021). The CBP detained approximately 2,000 children for more than 72 hours—39 were detained for more than two weeks (Coulehan 2021; Spagat and Merchant 2021; U.S. Customs and Border Protection 2021).

The reduced ORR housing capacity resulted from both the declines in unaccompanied alien children referrals to the agency during FY2020 and CDC's Title 42 public health protocols. When referrals to ORR declined in FY2020, some shelters either reduced capacity or did not renew their expired contracts. The CDC protocols on COVID-19 also required ORR shelters to reduce their intake capacity to comply with its social distancing guidelines (U.S. Office of the Inspector General 2020b). Fewer conventional state-licensed shelters were operating at reduced capacity at the start of FY2021 hindering ORR's ability to respond to the surge (Greenberg 2021b). In March 2021, CDC ordered ORR to relax its COVID-19 related restrictions and accommodate these minors in its shelters at 100 percent capacity (Kight 2021). CDC justified this as preferable to children being detained for extended periods in CBP facilities (Alvarez 2021a).

The Biden Administration also opened previously closed and new temporary influx shelter facilities (Lind 2021; Zak 2021). These influx facilities were: (1) relatively faster to set up compared to traditional ORR-supervised state-licensed shelters that require between six and nine months to open (Greenberg 2021c); (2) not subject to state licensing requirements; (3) typically operated by private companies; and (4) cost ORR about $775 daily per child compared to about $290 daily for traditional shelters (Foster-Frau 2021). At the surge's peak in March 2021, ORR required 20,000 beds to accommodate the influx of unaccompanied alien children (Kandel 2021). It used the temporary facilities for older children and the smaller, state-licensed conventional shelters for children under 13 years old (Miroff et al. 2021). From October 2020 to September 2021, unaccompanied alien children were spending 51 days in ORR custody (U.S. HHS 2021).

Complaints arose regarding the operation of Fort Bliss EIS, one of ORR's temporary influx facilities (Drake and Cruz 2021; Government Accountability Project 2021). Two federal workers assigned to Fort Bliss filed a whistleblower complaint in July 2021 to Congress and HHS alleging gross mismanagement because employees of the private contractor running the facility did not have child welfare experience, Spanish language skills, and relevant prior training (Alvarez 2021b; Seide and Gold 2021).

The Biden Administration took other steps in response to the surge, including: (1) terminating the 2018 ICE-ORR biometric/biographic information-sharing agreement that discouraged sponsorship of these minors by potential custodians (Greenberg 2021d; Kandel 2021; U.S. HHS and U.S. DHS 2021); (2) making disaster aid funding available to border communities for migrant-related assistance (FEMA 2021); (3) requiring ORR to temporarily waive background check requirements for household members living with prospective sponsors (Arthur 2021; Office of Refugee Resettlement 2021d); (4) creating more temporary shelter facilities to relieve CBP from housing thousands of these minors in its border stations; and (5) authorizing its shelter operators to pay for some children's transportation costs (Merchant 2021). The Biden Administration also reactivated and expanded in March 2021 eligibility for the CAM Program (Rush 2021a, 2021b; U.S. Department of State 2021). In June, the Biden Administration asserted that its policies reduced the number of unaccompanied alien children in CBP custody to pre-surge levels (Kandel 2021a). As of June 8, 2021, CBP held 514 unaccompanied alien children who spent an average of 21 hours in custody—none had been in CBP custody for more than 72 hours (Shahoulian 2021). Under the Biden administration, ORR released a total of 118,486 unaccompanied alien children to various sponsors across the different states in fiscal year 2022 (October 2021-August 2022). This represents a 239 percent increase from the total 34,953 released unaccompanied minors in fiscal year 2018, a 63 percent increase from the total 72,837 released in fiscal year 2019, and a 604 percent increase from the total 16,837 released in fiscal year 2020 under the Trump administration.

CONCLUSION

This chapter analyzed the legal basis for asylum claims and asylum rights of unaccompanied minors in the U.S. and their implementation under various Presidential administrations. Analysis of the current operational framework involving these minors show that multiple government agencies are involved in handling their claims from the point of entry or arrest in the country to their transfer to ORR custody, detention, release or removal from the U.S. While the current laws specifically detail the obligations of each of these agencies, there have been efforts to curtail or dilute these legal protections through executive orders and agency regulations under the Trump administration. Much of the litigation on the procedural rights of unaccompanied minors in chapter 4 were brought and decided during the Trump years. For example, the attempt of the HHS and DHS to terminate the 1997 *Flores* Settlement through the issuance of final rules under the Trump administration was challenged in federal courts. Former President Trump's family separation policy was also the subject of several litigation in federal courts. The CDC's Title 42 Order was similarly the subject of litigation in *P.J.E.S. by and through Escobar Francisco v. Wolf* (2020) discussed in chapter 4. Also, ICE and ORR Policies during the COVID-19 pandemic were challenged by unaccompanied minors in federal courts who alleged that these agencies failed to provide them with safe and sanitary conditions or appropriate medical care. Unaccompanied minors detained in ICE Family Residential Centers due to COVID-19 infections further filed suits. Recurring substantive due process issues in federal courts included access to counsel, long periods of detention, and challenges to conditions of their confinement. All of these point to the fact that despite the definite pronouncement in the 1997 *Flores* Settlement, the legal requirements imposed under existing U.S. laws governing their custody, release and detention, and the legal obligations of each of the immigration agencies involved in their care and custody, the legal protections in place for unaccompanied minors are not strictly implemented in practice.

PART I

Chapter 2

Judicial Decision Making at the Macro-Level

How Do Immigration Judges Decide?

On July 16, 2019, an immigration judge denied an unaccompanied minor's application for asylum, reasoning, among other things, that it was likely that the minor had produced a fraudulent birth certificate and had continued to misrepresent his age because, when asked his age in immigration court, the minor had "audibly said 'hmm . . . ' and paused for nearly ten seconds before responding that he was seventeen years, eleven months old," which suggested he "may have been attempting to calculate his age during the extended pause" (Imon v. Keeton 2020, 3). This anecdote highlights the seemingly spur of the moment arbitrary nature of immigration judge's decision-making process. We know that immigration judges are subject to tremendous pressure to move through cases as fast as possible considering the large backup of cases. Early in the Trump Administration the Justice Department, under the Attorney General Jeff Sessions, evaluated immigration judges based on how fast they worked through cases and on whether their decisions were sent back by higher courts (Meckler 2018).

As we have noted, immigration judges, unlike Article III judges, are not independent but members of the Executive Branch who can be fired, removed, sanctioned, or reassigned by the Attorney General. These evaluation metrics along with the overall political priorities of the Executive Branch are liable to influence how immigration judges come to their decisions. Therefore, the purpose of this chapter is to explore the role that political, along with social and economic, factors play in immigration judge's decisions regarding asylum claims for unaccompanied minors. We do this with an analysis of 12,826 cases of asylum claims from unaccompanied minors from 1997 to 2020. The rest of the chapter proceeds with a review of relevant literature on judicial decision making including previous studies on immigration judge decision making and what political, social and economic factors may influence that process. This is followed by a thorough dissection of the 12,826 cases, specifically looking at the number of cases per judge, court, county and state and the percentage of successful and unsuccessful asylum claims by unaccompanied minors per those respective jurisdictions. Finally, we utilize multilevel logistic and ordered logistic regression to analyze the role of political, economic, and social factors on the outcomes of immigration court proceedings on asylum claims of unaccompanied minors.

THEORETICAL BACKGROUND

Decision-Making Models of Judicial Behavior

Scholars of judicial behavior in general have developed three models for judicial decision making. The attitudinal model argues that judges primarily pursue their policy preferences when making decisions (Keith et al. 2013; Segal and Spaeth 2002). The strategic model explains judicial behavior as a function of the judge's policy preferences and the preferences of other judicial actors, such as other judges on the same court, the reviewing appellate court, or other relevant institutions (Epstein and Knight 1998). Finally, the legal model explains judicial decision making as judicial decisions that are constrained by legal precedent, the plain meaning of statutes, and the intent of the framers of statutes (Gillman 2001). With regards to immigration judges, the attitudinal model suggests that asylum grant rates are influenced by extralegal factors, including US foreign policy factors such as US military aid or trade relations (Rosenblum and Salehyan 2004; Rottman et al. 2009). Therefore, one can discern that the disparities in grant and denial rates among judges result from the influence of the individual judge's policy preferences or personal biases (Ramji-Nogales et al. 2007; TRAC 2006).

Drawing from the attitudinal model of judicial choice, Miller, Keith, and Holmes (2015b, 56) explicitly add a fourth model of judicial decision-making specifically for the circumstances of immigration judges—the cognitive approach. The cognitive approach theorizes that "the policy preferences of IJs influence their decisions in asylum cases" but that the legal requirements under US asylum law "also impose some constraints on the use of the policy proclivities of an IJ." The attitudinal cognitive model of asylum decision making explains that IJs, "under tremendous time pressure and unsure of the credibility of an asylum seeker," will rely on policy predispositions to help process both legally relevant and legally irrelevant facts (Keith et al. 2013, 267). Judges assess legal factors such as the level of human rights abuses in the applicant country in a more objective "bottom-up fashion," while extralegal factors such as US material and security interests are assessed more subjectively in a "top-down fashion" based on judge's policy preferences (Miller et al. 2015b, 58). The continuum of judicial choice ranges from top-down, where the subjective predispositions of the judge predominate other factors, to bottom-up, where the judge impartially scrutinizes the facts of the case and decides objectively (Bartels 2010). Empirical studies of asylum decisions have attempted to differentiate between the importance of certain "bottom-up" factors versus "top-down" factors in asylum decisions. Table 2.1 summarizes the relevant literature on the factors affecting outcomes in asylum proceedings.

Table 2.1 Summary of Factors Affecting Outcomes in Asylum Proceedings

	Factors resulting in positive outcomes	*Factors resulting in negative outcomes*	*Factors not having any statistically significant effect*
Legal Factors			
Human rights abuses	High level of human rights abuses in applicant's country of origin (measured by Political Terror Scale) (Keith et al. 2003; Rottman et al. 2009)		
Democratic government		More democratic government of country of origin (Polity IV data combined with Polity2 variable) (Keith et al. 2003; Miller et al. 2015b; Rottman et al. 2009)	
Political Factors			
Economic and military ally	Country of origin is among the more prosperous and developed economies as measured by World Bank (Keith et al. 2003; Miller et al. 2015b)	Country of origin is important to US economic (level of trade with U.S.) and security concerns (level of military aid from U.S.) (Keith et al. 2003; Miller et al. 2015b; Rottman et al. 2009)	

(continued)

	Factors resulting in positive outcomes	Factors resulting in negative outcomes	Factors not having any statistically significant effect
Top 10 source of illegal immigration to the U.S.		Country of origin is among top 10 producers of illegal immigrants in the US (Keith et al. 2003; Miller et al. 2015b; Rottman et al. 2009)	
Change in political context		Application was filed after September 11, 2001 attacks (Rottman et al. 2009)	

Asylum Applicant Factors

Legal representation and detention status	Legal representation—percentage of cases heard by judge where applicants are represented by an attorney (Chand et al., 2017); presence of legal representation (Keith et al. 2003; Ramji-Nogales et al., 2007),	Detention status of applicant (those detained are 11 percent less likely to receive asylum than those who have never been detained) (Miller et al. 2015b)	

Judicial Proclivities (ideology and career path)

Work Experience	Judge has prior work experience with a non-profit organization (Ramji-Nogales et al. 2007)	Judge has prior work experience with DHS/INS (Ramji-Nogales et al. 2007)	Judge has prior DHS/INS work experience or prior government work experience (Chand et al. 2017)
Judicial Ideology	Liberal ideological preferences of judge (based on career path and prior work experiences) (Keith et al. 2003; Miller et al. 2015b)		
Years in Bench		Judge's total number of years in the bench (Chand et al. 2017)	

	Factors resulting in positive outcomes	*Factors resulting in negative outcomes*	*Factors not having any statistically significant effect*
Appointing Authority			Appointment by Republican attorney general (Chand et al. 2017)
Local context			
Unemployment levels	High unemployment rate in Metropolitan Statistical Area ("MSA") of immigration court increases likelihood of grant by a conservative judge (Miller et al. 2015b)	High unemployment rate in MSA of immigration court decreases likelihood of grant by a liberal judge (Miller et al. 2015b); national unemployment rate (Keith et al. 2013); national change in per capita gross domestic product (Keith et al. 2013)	Standardized scores at the county and state levels for per capita income and unemployment rates (Chand et al. 2017)
Border location	Judge serves in county bordering Mexico (Chand et al. 2017)		Immigration court is located in a border state (Keith et al. 2013)
Foreign born population	Applicant is migrating to a community with a large matching diaspora community (contact theory) (Miller et al. 2015b)	Increase in proportion of foreign-born population in MSA (cultural threat theory) (Miller et al. 2015b); percentage of applicants before the judge who are from Guatemala, Honduras, and El Salvador (Chand et al. 2017)	Percentage change in Hispanic and Latinx residents in areas where the judge served (Chand et al. 2017)
Immigrant laws	Anti-immigrant laws (Chand et al. 2017)		Pro-immigrant laws (Chand et al. 2017)
	Passage of Illegal Immigration Reform and Immigrant Responsibility Act and Real ID Act increased the grant of relief to at-risk pool of applicants (Miller et al. 2015b)		

(continued)

	Factors resulting in positive outcomes	Factors resulting in negative outcomes	Factors not having any statistically significant effect
Party control	Average Democratic vote for president in locality (Miller et al. 2015b)	Percentage of county votes for Republican presidential nominees in 2008 and 2012 (Chand et al. 2017)	Number of years each states' legislative house was controlled by a Democratic majority added to the number of years it had a Democratic governor, for years 2009 through 2014 (Chand et al. 2017)
287(g) MOA		Existence of a 287(g) MOA signed by the state (Chand et al. 2017)	Existence of a 287(g) MOA signed by the county (Chand et al. 2017)
other control variables	Female judge (Keith et al. 2003; Ramji-Nogales et al. 2007)		Female judge (Chand et al., 2017)
	Applicant is an English or Arabic speaker (Keith et al. 2013)	Persons from Spanish and Arab speaking countries (Rottman et al. 2009)	Applicants from English-speaking countries (Rottman et al. 2009)

Reprinted with Permission from Braaten and Braaten 2021.

Legal determinants of asylum outcomes include fear of violence and persecution which can be assessed implicitly by the level of human rights abuses, and degree of democracy in the applicant's country of origin (Gibney et al. 1992; Gibney and Stohl 1988; Rosenblum and Salehyan 2004; Rottman et al. 2009). With respect to political factors, IJs were less likely to grant asylum to applicants from countries with which the United States has friendly relations, countries that receive little or no US military aid, countries with higher degree of trade with the United States, countries with high levels of undocumented immigration to the United States, and countries that use Spanish or Arabic as an official language (Rottman et al. 2009; Salehyan and Rosenblum 2008, 105).

The ideological predisposition of immigration judges also influences their decisions (Keith et al. 2013). Miller et al. (2015b, 73) found that the more liberal an IJ the more likely they are to grant asylum. They note, "liberal judges are 73 percent more likely to grant withholding than conservative IJs when other relief is unlikely, but are just 13 percent more likely to grant relief when asylum is otherwise likely." Keith et al. (2013) also found that a change in IJs' immigration liberalism from the least liberal judge to the most liberal increased the probability of a grant of asylum by 25 percent. Scholars determine judicial ideology and policy preferences through such measures as the party affiliation of the judge, the appointing president's party affiliation (George and Epstein 1992; Ocepek and Fetzer 2010; Tate and Handberg 1991), or measures of the appointing president's liberalism (Segal et al. 1996).

Keith et al. (2013) created a measure based on career path and background characteristics (Gould et al. 2010) to reflect the ways in which judges' socialization processes and life experiences result in specific attitudes and predispositions toward immigration (Gryski et al. 1986; Songer et al. 2003; Tate and Handberg 1991). Miller et al. (2015b, 23) and Keith et al. (2013) coded eleven prior career experiences to represent the immigration officer's career socialization as a proxy for policy views toward immigration and asylum, categorizing officers according to whether they had previously worked for the INS and/or ICE, DHS (non-USCIS/INS), the EOIR, a nongovernmental organization ("NGO"), an immigration-related NGO, the military, a law school, or in private practice, as well as whether they had prior judicial experience, had worked in corporate law, or had worked as prosecutors. Liberal individuals were more likely to have academic experience emphasizing cultural and personal differences, tolerance, and receptivity to immigrants (Espenshade and Calhoun 1993; Fetzer 2000; Hoskin 1991) and were more likely to have had prior private practice experience (Ocepek and Fetzer 2010; Ramji-Nogales et al. 2009). Conservative individuals, on the other hand, were more likely to have pursued careers as INS agents or prosecutors and were more likely to have had prior military experience.

Principal–Agent Model of Judicial Decision Making

In addition to having their own policy preferences, as members of the DOJ, IJs are also susceptible to intense political pressure and political influence. This has been especially true during the years of the Trump administration. Unlike other administrative law judges, who are substantially isolated from agency pressures, IJs show "significantly greater deference to the positions of the public, their agency, Congress, and the president, and report more favorable attitudes toward interest groups in adjudications" (Chand and Schreckhise 2020, 171). Salehyan and Rosenblum (2008) analyzed asylum approval rates between 1983 and 2001, focusing on how domestic politics moderated the influence of humanitarian norms and US interests with respect to the granting of asylum. They proposed a framework of US asylum policy-making and enforcement within the context of a principal–agent relationship, with Congress as the principal and the executive branch (e.g., the president, asylum officers, and judges) as its agent. Agents whose interests diverge from that of the principal are more likely to deviate from the directives of their principal, while agents who share common goals with the principal are more likely to follow policy guidelines (Kiewiet and McCubbins 1991; Moe 1984).

Presidents generally view immigration through a diplomatic lens, accepting applicants from countries hostile to the United States but rejecting applicants from countries with which the United States has friendly relations (Freeman 1995; Loescher and Scanlan 1986; Moe and Wilson 1994; Rosenblum and Salehyan 2004; Teitelbaum and Weiner 1995; Weingast et al. 1981). Immigration judges who belong to the executive branch are thus more likely to consider the diplomatic and national security implications of migration policy (Rosenblum 2004; Teitelbaum and Weiner 1995; Tichenor 2002). Congressional and executive officials are also likely to diverge when office holders come from opposing political parties (Hoskin 1991). In the United States, Republicans tend to oppose the granting of asylum and refugee status, family reunification, and the extension of rights to immigrants (Comelius et al. 2004; Earnest 2006; Givens 2005). On the other hand, Democrats tend to support international human rights protections, including the granting of asylum or refugee status (Anker and Posner 1981; Loescher and Scanlan 1986; Shanks 2001; Tichenor 2002).

Local Context Factors—Contact Theory and Cultural Threat Theory

Applying their cognitive model of IJ decision making, Miller et al. (2015b) found that local conditions, as a subset of extralegal factors, influence IJ decision making in a top-down, subjective manner based on IJs' own policy preferences. The principal–agent model of decision making also suggests that IJs are not isolated from the local geographic, political, and social context within which they operate (Blue et al. 2020; Chand et al. 2017; Chand and Schreckhise 2015; Chand and Schreckhise 2020; Johnson 2004). State laws, policies, and resources also affect immigrant populations (Hlass 2014, 2017; Walker and Leitner 2011). Contact theory explains that meaningful contact with immigrants promotes tolerance for foreign-born populations, while cultural threat theory posits that economic threats or threats to cultural identity affect perceptions of immigrants (Cornelius and Rosenblum 2005; Fetzer 2000). The size of the foreign-born population or the presence of immigrant communities in the judge's area of jurisdiction can lead to favorable outcomes (Miller et al. 2015). Contrary research, however, has found that states with larger Hispanic populations and greater numbers of undocumented immigrants had more deportations (Blue et al. 2020; Chand

and Schreckhise 2015). According to cultural threat theory, IJs are less likely to grant relief in localities with high levels of unemployment and worsening economic conditions (Miller et al. 2015). It should be noted that public views toward immigration and immigrants are not divorced from the broader political context. The Republican party in particular has used immigration as a wedge issue, often demonizing immigrants and immigration in the process, to try and secure electoral success. Zoltan Hajnal and Marisa Abrajano (2015; 2016) note that the Republican party has over the last few decades polarized the issue of immigration to draw more white voters into their coalition. This political context of immigration certainly has an impact on local views toward immigration and immigration.

Table 2.1 also summarizes the various local context factors that the prior literature identifies as significantly affecting asylum outcomes. Drawing from contact theory and cultural threat theory, the following local context factors have been found to be associated with positive UAC asylum outcomes: (1) migration of applicants to communities with large matching diaspora communities (i.e., foreign-born populations of the same ethnicity) (Miller et al. 2015b); (2) the judge serving in a county bordering Mexico (Chand et al. 2017); (3) the passage of anti-immigrant laws (Chand et al. 2017), including the IIRIRA and the Real ID Act (Miller et al. 2015b); and (4) a better economy (in terms of per capita income and unemployment rates) in the county and state where the IJ's court is located (Chand et al. 2017). An increased unemployment rate had varying effects depending on the IJ's ideology—it increased the likelihood of relief by 1 percent for conservative IJs but decreased the likelihood of relief by 11 percent for liberal IJs. Liberal IJs "tend to see applicants as a potential labor threat to other segments of the local population" such as the "low-skilled segments to whom liberals may be more solicitous" (Miller et al. 2015b, 101). Conservative IJs, however, view asylum applicants as more credible when they file claims in communities with high unemployment (Miller et al. 2015b). Asylum seekers are viewed as a financial burden on their destination communities by some members of those communities, and public opposition to immigration increases when the labor market deteriorates (as measured by an increase in unemployment) (Miller et al. 2015b).

Drawing from the principal–agent model of decision making, the previous literature has found that IJs accord deference to the positions of the president, Congress, the public, and interest groups where their courts are located. IJs with significantly lower grant rates worked in counties that voted Republican in the 2008 and 2012 presidential elections; IJs also had lower grant rates in states that have Section 287g agreements between law enforcement agencies and ICE, are controlled by Republican state legislatures and governors, and have more pro-immigrant laws (Chand et al. 2017). States with a moralistic political culture, better quality of life (as measured by aggregating nineteen economic indices into one ranking) and higher poverty rates (calculated as the percentage of the state's population that lives in poverty) resettle the most refugees, but more liberal states do not resettle more refugees than more conservative states (Nolasco and Braaten 2021).

As specifically applied to UAC, cultural threat theory suggests that IJs might consider the economic threat and financial burden represented by UAC asylum applicants. Child poverty is a measure of economic threat that is unique to juveniles. IJs who are under immense political pressure may consider child poverty levels when deciding UAC asylum applications, and IJs may take these factors into consideration when deciding whether to grant or deny asylum.

The attitudinal cognitive model and principal–agent theory provide a strong theoretical grounding for our analysis of immigration court decisions for unaccompanied minors. This combination shows that immigration judges use both legal and political factors when assessing asylum claims. They are also susceptible to pressure from above in the form of executive branch policies as well as from below in the form of the local contexts in which they operate.

RESEARCH DESIGN

To test the propositions regarding how IJs make asylum decisions for UACs we use data requested from the U.S. Justice Department Executive Office of Immigration Review as a result of a Freedom of Information Act ("FOIA") request. We requested data on the following categories: 1) gender, race, country of origin of the asylum applicant, 2) place of arrest or apprehension of minor, 3) name of asylum office to which the minor's case was referred, 4) name of immigration judge deciding the case, 5) name of lawyer of unaccompanied minor, 6) whether the lawyer was appointed or retained, 7) type of lawyer assigned, 8) year of decision on asylum, 9) venue and location where case was decided, 10) grounds for asylum petition by unaccompanied minor, 11) nature and kind of custody of minor, 12) place of detention, 13) grounds for decision of asylum office and/or immigration judge, and finally, 14) decision on the case. We received data on everything requested except for what EOIR stated they do not track, that included the race of the UAC, the place of arrest or apprehension of the UAC, the name of the asylum officer in which the minor's case was referred, whether the lawyer for the UAC was appointed and retained and the type of lawyer assigned, the place of detention, and finally the reason for decision of asylum officer.

Overall, the data we received contained 13,772 cases ranging from November 18, 1997 to June 4, 2021. These are the dates decisions were made on the respective UAC cases. In order to accommodate the inclusion of necessary covariates for our subsequent statistical analysis of this data we dropped all 2021 observations from the FOIA data which left us with 12,826 cases in our analysis. The following description of the data will be based on this slightly truncated data set with observations ranging from the year 1997 to 2020.

For our statistical analysis, we utilized a multilevel model to understand the influence of the various independent variables on the dependent variable. Multilevel models are called for when "characteristics or processes occurring at a higher level of analysis are influencing characteristics or processes at a lower level" (Luke 2004, 1). This is fundamentally what we are trying to examine in this chapter—how characteristics or processes at a higher level (state, county, judge) influence characteristics or processes at a lower level (decisions in immigration courts regarding unaccompanied minors). Statistically, a multilevel model is also required, as it is highly likely that immigrant court decisions are clustered at the judge, county, and state level and are thus likely to have correlated errors that a multilevel model can account for. In addition, because our first dependent variable is dichotomous, we use logistic regression, and because our second dependent variable is ordinal with three categories, we use ordered logistic regression. The two categories of the first dependent variable are grant of relief or asylum where the child is allowed to stay in the U.S. and the second category contains all the judicial decisions where the minor could be required to leave the U.S. The categories for the second dependent variable are those negative decisions made by IJs where the minors are required to leave the U.S. a middle category for the decision of "termination" which means the case is terminated but the status for the minor is ambiguous, and the final category contains those decisions where the child is granted relief to stay in the U.S.

We treat the three categories in this dependent variable as ordered since they range from negative to positive outcomes, with neutral as the middle category. Finally, we report the odds ratios instead of traditional coefficients. With odds ratios, positive effects are greater than 1 and negative effects are less than 1—for every one-unit change in the independent variable, the odds of a positive outcome in immigration court either decreases or increases, depending on whether the value is greater than or less than 1, by the amount presented. Before we get to the multivariate analysis, we present the descriptive results from our data. We present the total number of asylum cases per year, nationality, hearing location, base city, county, state, and immigration judge. We then present the total number of positive asylum cases per year and then the percentage of positive cases per hearing location, base city, county, state, and immigration judge.

DESCRIPTIVE RESULTS

Figure 2.1 shows the number of asylum applications for unaccompanied minors from 1997 to 2020. The numbers show roughly three distinct periods of asylum claims for unaccompanied minors. From 1997 to 2005 where the number of asylum claims are miniscule, an average of 13 per year in that time period. From 2006 to 2014 the numbers rose 1,707 percent greater than 1997–2005 with the average number of asylum claims during that period increasing to approximately 235 per year. From 2015 to 2020 the number of asylum claims by unaccompanied minors rose substantially again with the average number of claims in that time period reaching 1,766 an increase of 651 percent from 2006 to 2014.

Figure 2.2 presents the top 10 UAC asylum applications by nationality for the time period under investigation in this study. Overall, there were asylum applications from unaccompanied minors from 58 different countries but for many of those countries the total number of asylum seekers was only a handful with many having only one. As figure 2.2 shows the vast majority of applicants came from only 3 countries, what are known as the northern triangle countries of—El Salvador, Guatemala, and Honduras. Applications from those countries alone add up to 11,614 or 90.55 percent of the total number of applications from 1997 to 2020.

Figure 2.3 shows the number of UAC asylum applications per year from the Northern Triangle countries compared to the non-Northern Triangle

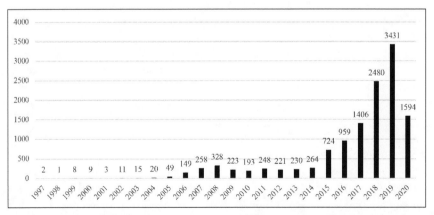

Figure 2.1.   Asylum Applications per Year, 1997–2020. Source: Created by the authors.

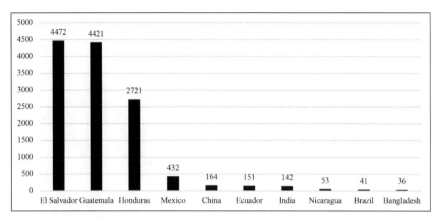

Figure 2.2. Top 10 UAC Asylum Applications by Nationality, 1997–2020. Source: Created by the authors.

countries. The first year there are any asylum applications from UACs from Northern Triangle countries is 2004 and the only year the number of applications from Northern Triangle and non-Northern Triangle countries are close is 2009 when there were 198 applications from UACs from one of the Northern Triangle countries and 177 applications from UACs from one of the non-Northern Triangle countries.

In addition to understanding where UACs are coming from it is necessary to also have a view of where the decisions are happening, i.e., the location of the immigration courts, to properly understand the outcomes in immigration court decisions for UACs. Figure 2.4 presents the top hearing locations with at least 100 hearings per the time period involved in this study. The top four locations are Los Angeles, Miami, New York City, and Houston which

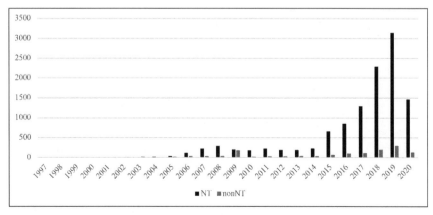

Figure 2.3. Asylum Applications from Northern Triangle Countries and Non-Northern Triangle Countries, 1997–2020. Source: Created by the authors.

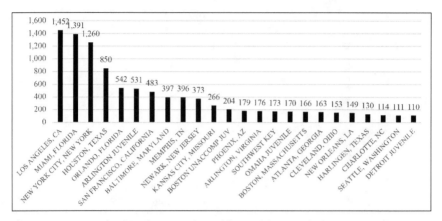

Figure 2.4. Cases by Hearing Location with a Minimum of 100 Cases, 1997–2020. Source: Created by the authors.

represent 4,953 hearings or 38.6 percent of all hearings. In total there are 174 hearing locations in 64 cities, 52 counties, and 29 states included in the dataset with some cities containing multiple hearing locations because of demand and specialization of the court.

The final chart in this section, figure 2.5, shows the number of UAC asylum cases per immigration judge (with a minimum of 100 cases). In total there are 637 immigration judges who heard at least one case involving a UAC in our dataset. What is presented in figure 2.5 is only the judges who heard a minimum of 100 cases. As can be seen four judges in particular—Ashley A. Tabaddor, John Milo Bryant, Rebecca L. Holt, and Clarease Rankin Yates—handled 1,673 cases between them which accounts for 13 percent of all cases in the dataset.

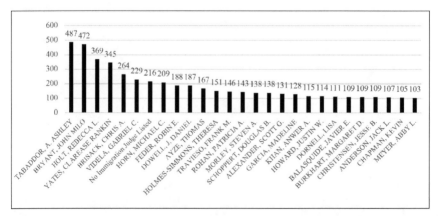

Figure 2.5. UAC Asylum Cases per Immigration Judge with a Minimum of 100 Cases, 1997–2020. Source: Created by the authors.

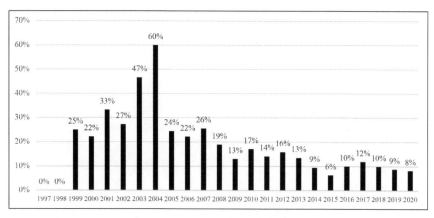

Figure 2.6.   Percent Positive Outcomes for UACs, 1997–2020. Source: Created by the authors.

The next set of figures explores the outcomes of the UAC immigration court decisions, specifically what percentage of the time UACs received a positive outcome versus a negative outcome. Figure 2.6 shows the overall percentage of positive outcomes for UACs from 1997 to 2020. One interesting trend is that the rate of positive outcomes increases from 1997 to 2004 and then steadily declines from there on out. Of course, it is important to remember that the number of cases heard from 2015 onward greatly overwhelms the number of cases that came prior.

Figure 2.7 shows the percentage of positive outcomes per hearing location with a minimum of 100 cases. Almost all of the locations have a positivity rate well below 50 percent. The exception is the court in Harlingen, TX. From 1997 to 2020 there were 130 cases involving UACs in Harlingen, TX and a

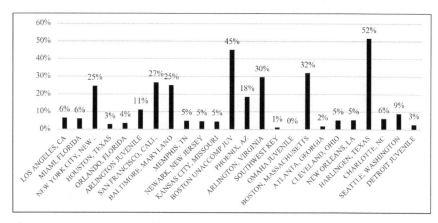

Figure 2.7.   Percent UAC Positive Decisions per Hearing Location with a Minimum of 100 Cases, 1997–2020. Source: Created by the authors.

Chapter 2

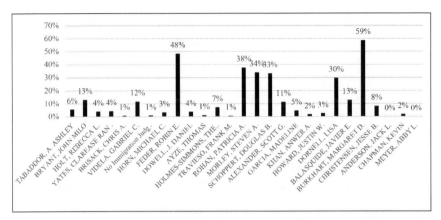

Figure 2.8. Percent Positive Decisions for UACs by Immigration Judge with a Minimum of 100 Cases. Source: Created by the authors.

52 percent positive outcome rate shows that 68 of the cases had a positive outcome for the UAC and 62 of the cases had a negative outcome.

Our final figure, figure 2.8, shows the percent positive decision for UAC by Immigration Judge with a minimum of 100 cases decided. Only one judge in the chart presented here has a positive decision rate higher than 50 percent and that is judge Margaret Burkhardt with a rate of 59 percent. Judge Robin E. Feder comes close with 48 percent. Other than those two the rates for all other judges are well below 50 percent.

Moving from descriptive statistics on the outcomes of UAC asylum cases this next section will focus on more sophisticated statistical analysis, namely logistic and ordered logistic regression. The next section will describe the dependent and independent variables used in those analyses as well as further description of the models used in the analysis. This is followed by the results of the analyses.

DEPENDENT VARIABLE

Our unit of analysis is the individual case decision and because of that we utilize two separate dependent variables in our analysis. The first dependent variable (*Decision1*) is a dichotomous measure of individual case outcomes. We code as "1" outcomes in cases in which the judge makes a grant of asylum (or relief). We code as "0" outcomes where the judge has ordered the UAC removed from the U.S. Additionally, we also include in this category outcomes where the UAC voluntarily departs the U.S., withdraws the case, or the case was terminated. We refer to these outcomes as negative because they either require the removal of the child to their home country (removal), the child decides to voluntarily leave the U.S. (voluntary departure), or their status in the U.S. is ambiguous (termination). Because termination means that the charging document against the UAC in removal proceedings was dismissed and that the UAC is not subject to removal (Kandel 2019) we also use a second dependent variable (*Decision2*). This is also a measure of individual case outcomes, but this variable is an ordinal measure with three categories. The first category, which we refer to as negative outcomes, we code as "0" outcomes in cases where there is a voluntary departure or removal. The second category, which we refer to as neutral, we code as "1" outcomes in cases where there is a termination. We treat termination this way to acknowledge some of the ambiguity of the category since the child is not subject to removal but is also not granted asylum, therefore it does not provide a final resolution, we supply it with its own category in this variable to account for that ambiguity. Finally, for the third category, referred to as positive outcomes, we code as "2" outcomes in cases where there is a grant of asylum.

INDEPENDENT VARIABLES

Human Rights Level of Home Country

We use the Political Terror Scale ("PTS"), as our measure of the level of respect for human rights in the asylum seeker's country of origin (*Human Rights*). The PTS is a five-category ordinal scale interpreted as follows: (1) "1" indicates countries under a "secure rule of law," in which people are "not imprisoned for their view," torture is "rare or exceptional," and political murders are "extremely rare"; (2) "2" indicates countries where there are "limited amounts of imprisonment for nonviolent political activity," torture and beatings are "exceptional," and political murder is rare; (3) "3" indicates countries where there is "extensive political imprisonment," or a "recent history of such imprisonment," execution or other political murders are common, and "unlimited detention, with or without a trial, for political views is accepted"; (4) "4" indicates countries where civil and political rights violations "have expanded to large numbers of the population" and "murders, disappearances, and torture are a common part of life"; and (5) "5" indicates countries where "terror has expanded to the whole population" and where leaders "do not place limits on the means or thoroughness with which they pursue personal or ideological goals" (Gibney et al. 2021).

Democracy Level of Home Country

We use the Varieties of Democracy Electoral Democracy ("V-DEM") Index (Coppedge et al. 2022), which ranges from zero to one with higher levels indicating further fulfillment of electoral democracy, as our measure of level of democracy in the UACs home country (Democracy). The index is created by country experts who rate a country's level of electoral democracy using the following criteria:

> The electoral principle of democracy seeks to embody the core value of making rulers responsive to citizens, achieved through electoral competition for the electorate's approval under circumstances when suffrage is extensive; political and civil society organizations can operate freely; elections are clean and not marred by fraud or systematic irregularities; and elections affect the composition of the chief executive of the country. In between elections, there is freedom of expression and an independent media capable of presenting alternative views on matters of political relevance.

Security and Economic Ties of Home Country

We code the U.S. military aid (*Military Aid*) measure as a dichotomous variable: "1" indicates a country that receives U.S. military aid in a given year, while "0" indicates all other countries. We code military aid this way to account for outliers in the data. We aggregate imports to the U.S. and exports from the U.S. into one measure (*Volume of Trade*) to gauge the economic impact of the country of origin on the U.S. economy and log the series to decrease the effects of outliers. The U.S. military aid data was taken from the U.S. Overseas Loans and Grants publication (otherwise known as the "greenbook") produced by the United States Agency for International Aid and Development (2020). Trade data was obtained from the International Monetary Fund's ("IMF") Direction of Trade Statistics (2020).

High Levels of Undocumented U.S. Immigration from Home Country

We code the top ten undocumented immigrant–sending countries (*High Undocumented Country*) for each year that they appear in our model as "1," and all other countries as "0." The top ten countries in order (from most to least) are: Mexico, El Salvador, Guatemala, India, Honduras, China, Dominican Republic, Brazil, Philippines, and South Korea. The list of top ten countries with the largest undocumented population in the U.S. comes from the Pew Research Center (Passel and Cohn 2019).

Primary Language in Home Country

We construct a dichotomous variable where applicants from all Spanish-speaking (*Spanish*) countries are coded as "1," applicants from all other countries are coded as "0."

Immigration Judge Ideological Preferences

Following prior research, we code prior career experiences to represent the immigration officer's career socialization as a proxy for their policy views toward immigration and asylum, coding judges according to whether they had previously worked for the USCIS/INS and/or ICE, the Department of Homeland Security (non-USCIS/INS), the EOIR, an NGO, an immigration-related NGO, the military, or a law school, as well as whether they previously worked in private practice, had prior judicial experience, had worked in corporate law, and or had worked as a prosecutor. This serves as our measure of judicial ideology (*Immigration Judge Ideology*). Based on the results of Keith, Holmes, and Miller (2013) we code as "-1" prior work experience with the USCIS/INS/ICE, the DHS (non-USCIS/INS/ICE), the U.S. federal government, EOIR, the military, corporate law, and as a prosecutor. We suggest that this type of work experience would lead one to be more conservative on immigration and asylum issues. Conversely, we code as "1" prior work experience in an immigration or non-immigration related NGO, in academia, in private practice, or in the judiciary; we suggest that this type of work experience would lead one to have a more liberal view on immigration and asylum. For each judge, we construct an ideological scale by adding their score on each of the work experience categories, with higher scores indicating greater liberalism (Miller et al. 2015; Songer et al. 2003).

Judicial Partisanship

To further account for political views that may influence an immigration judge's decision in an asylum case involving an unaccompanied minor, we also consider the party of the president (*Immigration Judge Party*) that appointed the judge ("1"=judge appointed under a Democratic administration and "0"=judge appointed under a Republican administration).

Trump Administration

To test the influence of the restrictive immigration policies of the Trump years (*Trump*) on the adjudication of UAC asylum cases, we code as "1" all cases adjudicated during the Trump years and as "0" all cases adjudicated before the Trump years. Because the Trump administration took a hardline stance against asylum claims, we test to see how those preferences filtered down to the immigration judges themselves.

The following sets of variables are what we refer to as local context variables. Local context refers to both the county and the state where the immigration court is located. We include local context variables, encompassing geographic, social, political, and economic factors for both the county and state level in the following sections.

Geography: Location Near the U.S.–Mexico Border

Following prior studies analyzing immigration decisions in border counties and states (Chand and Schreckhise 2015), we include a dichotomous variable (*County Borders Mexico)* indicating whether the county where the immigration court is located is on the U.S.–Mexico border ("1"=located in a border county, and "0"=not located in a border county). We also include a dichotomous variable (*State Borders Mexico*) for whether the state where the immigration court is located is on the U.S.–Mexico border ("1"=located in a border state, and "0"=not located in a border state).

Social Factors: Percentage of Hispanic Population

Consistent with prior literature (Chand and Schreckhise 2015; Chand et al. 2017), we include variables measuring the percentage of the population that is Hispanic in both the county (*County Hispanic Population*) and the state (*State Hispanic Population*) where the immigration court is located. Hispanic population data is taken from the U.S. Census Bureau (2020).

Political Factors: Representation and Electoral Results

We used separate variables to capture the political dimensions of local state and county contexts. We consider election of state and local officials more informative of local political context than state or county level results of the presidential election. We use a dichotomous variable (*State Democratic Governor*) of "1" if a state has a Democratic governor and "0" if a state does not have a Democratic governor. Unfortunately, we cannot use a similar measure at the county level due to variation in county elected representation, so we utilize results from the most recent Presidential elections. We include county-level vote percentage for the Democratic candidate for President as our local political context variable for the County level (*County Dem. Presidential Vote*).

Economic Factors: Unemployment Levels

Following Miller et al. (2015), we include measures of the unemployment level at both the county (*County Unemployment Level*) and state (*State Unemployment Level*) levels. County-level unemployment data comes from the U.S. Department of Agriculture Rural Atlas Data (2020) and state-level unemployment data comes from the University of Kentucky Center for Poverty Research (2020).

Economic Factors (Child Specific): Child Poverty

As specifically applied to UAC, we included child poverty as a measure of economic threat that is unique to juveniles. Because of data availability, we use two different measures for the state and county level that both capture child poverty. We include measures of child poverty because we assume that the level of child poverty in a locality would be an important contextual factor in influencing judicial decision making in cases involving UAC. At the state level, we include a measure of the percentage of the state's low-income children that lack health insurance (*State Level of Low-Income Uninsured Children*). Although this is not solely a direct measure of poverty, lack of health insurance in the United States is a function of income levels. The data is from the University of Kentucky's Center for Poverty Research (2020). Our measure at the county level is the percentage of children in the county in poverty (*County Child Poverty Rate*). Our data for this measure comes from Kids Count Data Center which compiles census data on a variety of topics related to children (2020).

CONTROL VARIABLES

We include the following as control variables, as the previous literature has established these factors as important in immigration court decisions.

Custodial Status of UAC

We construct a dummy variable measuring custody status. The variable (*Detained*), "1" indicates that the applicant was detained and never released, and "0" indicates either that the applicant was detained and released or was never detained.

Legal Representation of UAC

We also test the effect of the asylum applicant's legal representation on the likelihood of success. We create a dichotomous variable (*Attorney*) where "1" indicates that the applicant had legal counsel, while "0" indicates that they did not.

MODELS

We utilized a multilevel model to understand the influence of the various independent variables on the dependent variable. Multilevel models are called for when "characteristics or processes occurring at a higher level of analysis are influencing characteristics or processes at a lower level" (Luke 2004, 1). This is fundamentally what we are trying to examine in this book—how characteristics or processes at a higher level (state, county, judge) influence characteristics or processes at a lower level (decisions in immigration courts regarding unaccompanied minors). Statistically, a multilevel model is also required, as it is highly likely that immigrant court decisions are clustered at the judge, county, and state level and are thus likely to have correlated errors that a multilevel model can account for.

In addition, because our first dependent variable is dichotomous, we use logistic regression, and because our second dependent variable is ordinal with three categories, we use ordered logistic regression. We treat the three categories in dependent variable 2 as ordered since they range from negative to positive outcomes, with neutral as the middle category. Additionally, we report the odds ratios instead of traditional coefficients. With odds ratios, positive effects are greater than 1 and negative effects are less than 1—for every one-unit change in the independent variable, the odds of a positive outcome in immigration court either decreases or increases, depending on whether the value is greater than or less than 1, by the amount presented. Finally, we also include results with year fixed effects (in models 3 and 4). This allows for a more stringent test.

Table 2.2 presents the results of our main analysis. Model 1 uses our bivariate dependent variable (*Decision1*) and mixed effects while Model 2 uses our ordinal dependent variable (*Decision2*) also with mixed effects. Conversely, Model 3 uses the bivariate dependent variable but with year fixed effects and Model 4 uses the ordinal dependent variable also with year fixed effects. Starting with the variables in the category of characteristics of UAC applicants, the only significant variable across all four models is the level of democracy in the country the UAC is fleeing. The measure of democracy used in this study rates more democratic countries higher and since the odds

Table 2.2 Multilevel Logistic and Ordered Logistic Regression of Unaccompanied Minor Asylum Decisions, 1997–2020

Variables	Model 1 Odds Ratio	(Std Error)	Model 2 Odds Ratio	(Std Error)	Model 3 Odds Ratio	(Std Error)	Model 4 Odds Ratio	(Std Error)
Human Rights	1.24*	(.112)	.910	(.059)	1.11	(.109)	1.06	(.073)
Democracy	.152***	(.048)	.330***	(.077)	.142***	(.046)	.323***	(.076)
Military Aid	1.09	(.319)	.730	(.179)	1.20	(.370)	.774	(.194)
Volume of Trade (ln)	.986	(.036)	1.06*	(.028)	1.01	(.038)	1.02	(.028)
High Undocumented Country	.713	(.126)	.837	(.116)	.704*	(.126)	.858	(.120)
Spanish	.335***	(.054)	.308***	(.040)	.314***	(.051)	.298***	(.039)
Detained	.975	(.166)	.348***	(.032)	.916	(.161)	.358***	(.053)
Attorney	4.64	(.646)	6.01***	(.526)	4.84***	(.685)	5.82***	(.512)
Immigration Judge Ideology	1.11**	(.045)	1.09*	(.038)	1.11**	(.046)	1.10**	(.037)
Immigration Judge Party	1.47**	(.203)	1.46***	(.171)	1.50**	(.209)	1.41**	(.157)
Trump	1.35*	(.165)	.906	(.074)	.950	(.496)	1.06	(.445)
County Borders Mexico	.844	(.523)	.734	(.381)	.766	(.479)	.915	(.465)
County Child Poverty Rate	3.56	(6.84)	13.41	(18.54)	1.84	(4.13)	85.73**	(142.92)
County Dem. Pres. Vote	130.51***	(138.64)	63.03***	(52.47)	72.89***	(83.08)	23.88***	(21.99)
County Hispanic Population	2.47	(3.33)	1.12	(1.12)	4.08	(5.47)	.441	(.511)

(continued)

	Model 1		Model 2		Model 3		Model 4	
County Unemployment Level	.848**	(.054)	1.02	(.047)	.917	(.067)	.949	(.053)
State Borders Mexico	2.94	(2.14)	3.27	(2.05)	4.37	(3.77)	2.84	(2.50)
State L.I. Uninsured Child	1.10***	(.025)	1.05**	(.017)	1.07	(.037)	1.08***	(.025)
State Democratic Governor	1.06	(.137)	1.28*	(.128)	1.12	(.152)	1.22	(.128)
State Hispanic Population	.005*	(.011)	.015**	(.023)	.001*	(.003)	.043	(.131)
State Unemployment Level	1.16*	(.082)	.974	(.053)	1.10	(.111)	.907	(.069)
Observations	11,857		11,857		11,851		11,857	
LL	-3368.06833		-8084.6748		-3345.3024		-7975.5188	
N of Immigration Judges	808		808		807		808	
N of Counties	52		52		52		52	
N of States	29		29		29		29	
Residual ICC—State Level	.499		.511		.387		.773	
Residual ICC—State/County	.396		.275		.385		.287	
Residual ICC—State/County/Judge	.965		1.02		.987		.855	
Wald chi2	392.87		738.53		417.26		937.49	
LR v Log Model	677.77		1168.02		620.72		1075.3	

Created by the authors

ratios presented here are below one (and well below for that matter) this shows that UACs from countries that are more democratic are less likely to be granted asylum in the U.S. Interestingly, the results for human rights are not significant (with the exception of model 1) nor are the odds ratios greatly divergent from 1 indicating that the variable has a limited effect. What the results suggest is that UACs coming from less democratic countries are more likely to be given asylum in the U.S. but that is not necessarily the case for UACs coming from countries with worse human rights records on average. None of the other U.S. foreign policy variables (military aid and level of trade) are significant in any of the models.

Looking at the UAC specific variables (coming from a county with a high undocumented population in the U.S., coming from a country where Spanish is the primary language, being detained at some point during the process, and having an attorney or not), UACs coming from a country where Spanish is the dominant language were less likely to receive asylum (or a positive outcome) than UAC coming from countries where Spanish was not the dominant language. Coming from a country with a high undocumented population already in the U.S. was not significant in all of the models (only model 3). Custodial status (being detained at any point during the processes versus never being detained) is significant in the ordered logistic regression models indicating there is a relationship between custodial status and receiving asylum versus termination of the cases and between termination of the case and a negative outcome with having been detained leading to greater likelihood of termination versus asylum and a negative outcome more likely versus termination. Finally, with regards to UAC specific variables, whether the child had a lawyer throughout the process or not was an important factor in determining whether that child would receive a positive outcome in their case. The attorney variable is significant in all models and the odds ratio across all models are well above 1 (4.64, 6.01, 4.84, and 5.82 respectively) indicating the variable has a strong impact on whether a UAC receives a positive impact in immigration court or not.

Moving to the judge related variables, immigration judge ideology, and political party of the Attorney General appointing the judge have a statistically significant impact on the outcomes of UAC cases. For the ideological variable, UAC who come before a judge who is more liberal, they are more likely to receive asylum or a positive outcome, and for the partisan variable, UAC who come before a judge appointed by a Democratic Attorney General, they are more likely to receive asylum or a positive outcome to their case. The *Trump* variable was only significant in model 1 and not in the direction one would think in that the positive odds ratio suggests that if a judge was appointed by Trump's attorney general, they were more likely to grant asylum or a positive outcome to a UAC. However, in subsequent models 2 and

3 the sign shifts to below 1 indicating the unstable nature of the variable in the analysis meaning one cannot extrapolate much information from it. In our previous work (Braaten and Braaten 2021) we found statistically significant results for Trump appointed judges being less likely to support asylum for UACs, however that. That work however only looked at data for 9 months of the Trump administration, with this dataset we have an almost complete timeline for the Trump administration's ability to influence immigration court decisions on UACs and see that, at least of this measure, they were not able to influence outcomes as they might have liked.

Moving to the county level measures, the only variable that was significant across all four models and in the direction we would expect is the level of support for the Democratic candidate for President. The odds ratio for this variable is very large (130.51, 63.03, 72.89, and 23.88 respectively across the four models). These are large effects but it should be noted that the standard errors for each measure are also quite large so one should be cautious in overinterpreting these results. Finally, looking at the state level variables, none are statistically significant across all four models but two—state level of low-income uninsured children and state Hispanic population are significant in three out of the four. Interestingly, neither of these variables are in the direction we would expect. For example, the odds ratios for state level of low-income uninsured children, although not large, are all positive. This indicates that as the level of low-income uninsured children increases in a state the likelihood of a positive result for UACs in immigration courts in that state also increases. This would seem to contradict the notion that immigration judges in states with higher levels of low-income uninsured children (which is just our proxy measure for possible taxing of the welfare system more children might add) would be less likely to support asylum for UAC as they would have some awareness of the possible overburdens of social services available for children in the state. The sign of the state Hispanic population variable also offers a contradiction of our expectations. Our analysis indicates that as the size of the Hispanic population in a state increases, UACs in that state are less likely to receive a positive outcome in their case. This would seem to challenge our use of contact theory to suggest that in states with higher Hispanic populations, immigration judges would be more likely to support asylum for UACs.

Although statistical significance and odds ratios can tell us a lot about the relationships, we have just discussed another method that perhaps provides an even better approach. Further analysis of predicted probabilities shows more interesting results by showing us the magnitude of the effect. Table 2.3 shows the predicted probabilities of asylum for unaccompanied minors for all the variables that were statistically significant in all models. The results range from observations of two standard deviations below the mean to two standard deviations above the means (these numbers are in parentheses) except for the dichotomous variables which only have two categories.

Table 2.3 Predicted Probabilities of IJ Making a Positive Decisions on UAC Asylum Claims by Statistically Significant Results

Democracy	
1 (.335)	.141
2 (.449)	.121
3 (.563)	.104
4 (.677)	.088
5 (.791)	.074

Language	
0 (not Spanish)	.212
1 (Spanish)	.100

Attorney	
0 (No)	.036
1 (Yes)	.124

Immigration Judge Ideology	
1 (-3.824)	.078
2 (-2.154)	.090
3 (-.484)	.104
4 (1.186)	.118
5 (2.856)	.135

Immigration Judge Political Party	
0 (Republican)	.090
1 (Democratic)	.120

County Level Democratic Presidential Vote	
1 (.416)	.039
2 (.542)	.065
3 (.668)	.105
4 (.794)	.163
5 (.920)	.239

Created by the authors

Again, the UACs coming from countries with lower levels of democracy are more likely to receive asylum than those coming from more established democracies. Moving from the lowest level of democracy presented to the highest decreases the predicted mean of receiving asylum by 6.7 percent. Sticking with the UAC specific factors, those who come from countries where Spanish is the main language compared to those who are coming from countries where another language is primary see their chances of receiving a positive outcome decrease by 11 percent. Finally, UACs with attorneys see the predicted mean of receiving asylum increase by 9 percent over those who do not have an attorney represent them in immigration court.

Moving to the Immigration Judge specific variables, predicted probabilities for immigration Judge ideology and political party are also presented in Table 2.3. Here we can see the difference in how more liberal judges rule versus more conservative judges. Moving from the most conservative judicial ideology in the table to the most liberal ideology increases the probability of receiving asylum by 5.7 percent. Similarly, UACs appearing before a judge that was appointed by a Democratic administration have a higher likelihood (although it's not a big increase) of receiving asylum compared to those who appear before a judge appointed during a Republican administration. Going from a judge appointed by a Republican administration to one appointed by a Democratic one increasing the probability of asylum by 3 percent.

Looking at the county level influences; table 2.3 also shows the predicted probability for the county level Democratic presidential vote. The effect for county level Democratic Presidential votes is quite large. Moving from the lowest county vote percent for a Democratic candidate presented in the table to the largest, increases the probability of a UAC receiving asylum by 20 percent. Overall predicted probabilities provide a more nuanced view of the relationship between the variables by showing what the likelihood of a positive outcome for UACs is at every level of the independent variable.

CONCLUSION

The analysis in this chapter showed the aggregate influence of various social, political, and economic influences on judicial decisions regarding asylum claims by unaccompanied minors. Additionally, this chapter shifted the focus to immigration courts specifically as opposed to the Federal courts analyzed in subsequent chapters. What these two shifts have allowed us to do is more thoroughly examine the role of non-legal factors, such as politics, and their influence in asylum decisions for unaccompanied minors. Previous research on asylum decisions outlined in table 2.1 displayed the factors that have been shown to influence overall asylum decisions (including UACs and non-UACs). In contrast, our analysis focuses exclusively on asylum decisions for UACs. With that focus, the descriptive results presented show the number of cases overtime from 1997 to 2020 as well as a breakdown of the nationalities of UACs over the same time period. What both of those results show is that the number of UAC cases increase substantially following the first 2014 "surge" of unaccompanied minors coming to the U.S. which connects to the nationalities results as the vast majority of UAC cases involve minors from the Northern Triangle countries which is where the majority of the minors in 2014 and after were coming from.

The descriptive results also show the distribution of cases across hearing locations, base cities, counties, states, and judges, and the distribution of positive cases across those same categories. These results show that the distribution of cases and positive outcomes for UACs are not evenly dispensed across hearing locations, base cities, counties, states, or judges. Much of the distribution of cases is connected to population, as the higher population centers of the U.S. have a higher volume of cases. For example, the base cities with the most cases from 1997 to 2020 are Los Angeles, Miami, New York, and Houston each are among the largest cities in the U.S. Additionally, the distribution of positive outcomes is not evenly dispersed across any of the location categories examined. Just looking at the four base cities with the most cases one can see the variation in positive outcomes quite clearly. From 1997 to 2020 of all UAC cases decided in Los Angeles only 6 percent were positive (asylum was granted). The same percentage is seen in Miami but in New York City the positive rate was 25 percent. Finally, in Houston the positive rate over the same time period was only 3 percent.

The large variation in positive outcomes across hearing locations, base cities, counties, states, and immigration judges suggests two possibilities. The first is that the underlying composition of the cases may explain the variation across these jurisdictions. For example, perhaps the reason that 25 percent of the cases were successful asylum claims for UACs in New York but in Houston the rate was only 3 percent is that the cases in New York were more valid than the cases heard in Houston. In other words, the UACs having their cases heard in New York had more legitimate asylum claims than the ones having their cases heard in Houston. Because we do not have the specific details for all of the cases in our dataset, we cannot test this claim but regardless we are skeptical that this is the main reason for the dramatic differences in successful asylum claims across jurisdictions. Rather we favor a second explanation, that extra-legal factors influence immigration judge decision making regarding asylum claims by unaccompanied minors and the results of our multivariate statistical analysis support this explanation.

We theorize that the decision-making process of immigration judges regarding UACs is best represented by three models—the cognitive model of immigration judge decision making developed by Miller, Keith, and Holmes (2015b), principal-agent models of judicial decision making, and finally local context models particularly contact theory and cultural threat theory. These models together capture the unique nature of immigration judges making asylum decisions for UACs since they include the legal aspects of the decision-making process but also the political, economic, and social factors that also appear to influence the decision-making process. Our multivariate and multilevel model reaffirms many of the assumptions of these models but with some nuance and surprises.

Looking at the first two variables in the model, level of democracy and human rights, we see that level of democracy is significant across all models and in line with the proposition that UACs coming from more democratic countries are less likely to receive asylum. This proposition is in line with both the legal factors that influence asylum (i.e., more democratic countries are less likely to engage in repression that causes people to flee their countries) and in line with U.S. foreign policy goals of supporting more democratic countries. Interestingly, however, the human rights variable is not significant and is arguably a better measure of home country repression than level of democracy. In terms of UAC specific characteristics coming from countries in which Spanish is the main language and having an attorney both significantly impact the likelihood of receiving asylum albeit in opposite directions. Perhaps reflecting domestic policy decisions or just simply the result of personal bias of immigration judges, coming from a Spanish speaking country has a significant negative effect on a UAC receiving asylum in the U.S. Conversely, having an attorney helping you with the asylum process greatly increases the likelihood the UAC will receive asylum in the U.S.

We also find strong evidence that politics influences immigration judges' decisions as both the variables measuring judge's ideology and partisanship were significant in all models. More liberal judges, along with judges appointed by Democratic administrations, were more likely to grant asylum to UACs than more conservative judges and judges appointed during Republican administrations. The marginal effects for these two variables were not very large so one does not want to over-emphasize their impact but nevertheless the evidence is clear that they have an effect on immigration judge's decision making. Finally, with the regards to the county and state level variables in our model, most were not significant, which suggests limited impact for contextual variables in influencing immigration judges' decision making. The variable County level support for Democratic Presidential candidates was significant across all models and in line with the proposition that more "Democratic" counties would be more supportive of asylum for UACs and judges in those counties would reflect that support in their decisions. The marginal effects for this variable were the largest of any of the variables in the model as well.

The next chapter will go deeper with our analysis by looking at the results of the appeals process and BIA decision making.

Chapter 3

Judicial Decision Making at the Macro-Level

How Does the Board of Immigration Appeals Decide?

Seventeen-year-old Honduran Torres first entered the U.S. illegally in 2007 (*United States v. Torres Zuniga,* 2019). He was served a Notice to Appear ("NTA") requiring him to appear at a future removal hearing. Torres attended an immigration hearing at which he was granted voluntary departure to Honduras. He left the U.S. in October 2007 on an immigration charter flight from Houston, Texas. In 2008, Torres reentered the United States illegally and was issued a second NTA ("2008 NTA"). The 2008 NTA did not contain a date or time for Torres's immigration hearing although he was given oral notice of the time and place of his immigration hearing. He was subsequently given a Notice of Hearing containing the date of his hearing before an immigration court while detained at an Arizona unaccompanied minor shelter. Torres appeared at the immigration hearing where he was represented by pro bono counsel. The immigration court ordered his removal to Honduras. Torres was removed from the United States on an immigration flight from Houston in April 2008.

Following his removal in 2008, Torres re-entered the United States in 2012, 2013, and 2014. Pursuant to the 2008 Removal Order, he was removed from the United States. At each removal, Torres was issued (and signed) a form informing him that he was now prohibited from entering the United States for a period of 20 years because he illegally entered the United States following removal. Torres re-entered the U.S. in 2018 and was indicted for illegal reentry. Citing *Pereira v. Sessions* (2018), Torres argued that the 2008 NTA without a date or time did not vest an immigration court with jurisdiction. He filed a motion to dismiss, alleging that the 2008 removal order was void for lack of jurisdiction. The case he cited, *Pereira v. Sessions* (2018, 2110), was a Supreme Court decision where the Court dealt with a "narrow question" of whether an NTA that "fails to specify either the time or place of the removal proceedings . . . triggered the stop-time rule." The Supreme Court held that "a putative notice to appear that fails to designate the specific time or place of the noncitizen's removal proceedings is not a 'notice to appear under section 1229(a),' and so does not trigger the stop-time rule" (*Pereira v. Sessions* 2018, 2113–2114).

The case of *United States v. Torres Zuniga* (2019) illustrates the significance of BIA's decision making. After *Pereira v. Sessions* (2018), the Board of Immigration Appeals issued *Matter of Bermudez-Cota* (2018) where it held that an NTA that does not specify the time and place of an alien's initial removal hearing vests an Immigration Judge with jurisdiction over the removal proceedings so long as a notice of hearing specifying this information is later sent to the alien. Basing its decision in part on the BIA ruling in *Matter of Bermudez-Cota* (2018), the district court of the Eastern District of Virginia denied Torres's motion to dismiss, holding that removal order was not void for lack of jurisdiction even if the 2008 NTA lacked information relating to date and time of hearing (*United States v. Torres Zuniga* 2019, 661).

The Board of Immigration Appeals is the review tribunal for the U.S. immigration system. The BIA is located in Fall Church, VA and has nationwide jurisdiction to apply immigration and nationality law uniformly throughout the U.S. They do this primarily by reviewing the decisions of immigration judges. The BIA conducts what is called "paper review" of cases meaning they do not, with rare exceptions, conduct courtroom proceedings. The BIA is currently composed of 23 judges but that number has fluctuated over the previous decades. Generally, cases are reviewed by just one judge but on occasion cases can be heard by a panel of three judges and, additionally, a case can be heard *en blanc* with the full component of judges. Finally, BIA decisions can be reviewed by the Attorney General and/or appealed to U.S. Appellate Courts.

This chapter presents the results of an analysis of Board of Immigration Appeals decisions on the asylum claims of unaccompanied minors. In what follows we present a theoretical background on BIA decision making. We focus on three main drivers of BIA decision making—error correction, policy-making, and workload management. In the next section we present the research design for the chapter with first a presentation of descriptive results on cases before the BIA and how they decide. We then present the main variables used in our analysis as well as the specific models we test. This is followed by the results and the conclusion.

THEORETICAL BACKGROUND

BIA and Error Correction

In general, the goal of an appellate process is to ensure uniformity across legal jurisdictions and they achieve this through two rationales—error correction and lawmaking both of which should increase consistency in legal decisions (Hausman 2016). Steven Shavell (1995) argues that the appellate process is a superior form of error correction in a judicial system (more so than improvements at the courts of original jurisdiction) because litigants bringing appeals have knowledge about the specific errors of their cases, and if the appellate courts validate that those errors occurred, the process will develop into one where litigants only appeal cases where they are confident that appellate judges will validate their claims of errors and will not do so when they are not confident of such a ruling. This creates the overall error correcting process for appellate courts. The lawmaking process of appellate courts occurs through the issuance of precedence decisions. Lawmaking, or the issuance of precedence decisions, should increase uniformity in a judicial system by "elaborating rules that lower court judges must follow, appeals courts reduce the discretion of those judges and promote uniformity across those decisions" (Hausman 2016, 1182). These two processes—error correction and lawmaking are both responsibilities for the BIA and both, ideally, should enforce uniformity within the immigration system.

In terms of error correction, David Hausman (2016) has conducted the most thorough examination of this process for the BIA and concludes that the BIA fails in its mission in correcting errors throughout immigration courts. Hausman argues that the immigration appeals system fails "because judges not only decide whether to order immigrants deported but also influence whether immigrants choose to appeal" (2016, 1180). With the first point, Hausman examined the "correction" by the BIA of "harsh" and "generous" judges. Calculating the relief rate for each immigration judge (the rate at which immigration judges allow immigrants to remain in the U.S.) Hausman found that the BIA was more likely to reverse decisions from "generous judge" (those allowing immigrants to stay in the U.S. at much higher than average rates) but was not more likely to reverse decisions of harsh judges (those who allow immigrants to stay in the U.S. at much lower rates than average). This asymmetry in reversal rates is not consistent with the error correction possibility of an appeals process.

In terms of his second point—that immigration judges influence whether an immigrant appeals their case or not, Hausman notes that immigrants are more likely to appeal their cases if they are given time to find an attorney to file their appeal and it is the more generous judges who generally give immigrants more time to do so. Therefore, the cases that get to the BIA for review are not a random sample of cases but rather are cases appealed from more generous judges. This selection bias in the cases that get to the BIA also prohibits the error correction process from working accordingly.

BIA and Policy-Making

The twin purposes of an appeals process are error correction and law (or policy) making. In terms of the first process—error correction—the BIA is not fulfilling its task but in terms of its second task—policy-making, the picture is a bit more complicated. One way the policy-making power of the BIA is impacted is in the role of the Attorney General in selecting members for the Board as well as being able to refer cases from the BIA to themselves. The power of the Attorney General over the BIA is substantial. According to Ramji-Nogales, Schoenholtz, and Schrag (2009, 61), "the attorney general established the BIA by regulation and has the power to overrule its decisions, change its adjudicatory procedures, and appoint and remove Board members who disagree with his or her political ideology." The BIA was established in 1940 and is not a statutory body but one that was created solely by the Attorney General after the transfer of immigration policy from the Department of Labor. The authority that the Attorney General has over the BIA is important because of its policy-making role. According to Schoenholtz (2005, 353), the BIA "has been the single most important decision-maker in the immigration system . . . Given that the Supreme Court issues very few decisions concerning asylum law, the BIA essentially interprets immigration law for the nation." Of course, as our next chapters will show, U.S. federal courts also hear cases appealed from the BIA but the workhorse appellate court for immigration decisions is the BIA.

The political influence of the Attorney General on the BIA has proven significant in a couple of instances over the years, two in particular stand out—the "streamlining reforms" during the tenure of John Ashcroft as Attorney General during the first George W. Bush administration, and Jeff Sessions, Attorney General for the first two years of the Trump Administration, overturning BIA precedence. In the late 1990s, Attorney General Janet Reno instituted a series of her own "streamlining reforms" to address the backlog of cases in the immigration courts. These reforms include allowing the BIA chairman to designate certain categories of cases as suitable for single member review, allowing single BIA members to affirm IJ decisions without written opinions, and most significantly, increasing the size of the BIA to 23 members (Miller, Keith, and Holmes 2015b). During John Ashcroft's tenure as Attorney General, he continued with some of the reforms of his predecessor but "fundamentally changed the nature of the BIA's review function . . .

radically changed the composition of the Board" (Schoenholtz 2005, 355). He did this by further "streamlining" of the BIA by making single member decisions the dominant decision-making process and, perhaps contradictorily, reduced the size of the BIA from 23 members to 11 (Miller, Keith, & Holmes 2015b). The pretext for these reforms during Ashcroft tenure was national security—as these reforms were instituted post-9/11, the Bush Administration included reform of the immigration system as part of their "war on terror" (Rana 2009). The reduction in size of the BIA by Ashcroft was done to "increase the coherence of the Board" but critics argued it was a way to remove more liberal BIA judge appointed by Reno (Schoenholtz 2005; Ramji-Nogales, Schoenholtz, and Schrag 2009). In their examination of the BIA, Miller, Keith, and Holmes found that the five BIA members who were removed by Ashcroft were more liberal than the ones who remained on the court (2015b).

Jeff Sessions was the first Attorney General in the Donald Trump administration and was tasked with implementing many features of President Trump's hardline immigration policies. Sessions was a willing participant in this process and was instrumental in implementing the harshest and most criticized immigration policy in the Trump era—zero tolerance and family separations (Shear, Benner, and Schmidt 2020). Sessions also left an indelible mark on the BIA and the immigration court system through the referral process of the Attorney General (Lind 2018c). As stated earlier, the BIA was a creation of the Attorney General's office and as such the Attorney General has the authority to refer BIA cases to themselves for review. Despite the authority that Attorney Generals have to refer cases to themselves the authority is rarely exercised, although former Attorney General Alberto Gonzales has argued that they should use that authority more and likened the referral process to executive orders issued by the President (Gonzalez and Glen 2016).

Attorney General Jeff Session referred several BIA cases to himself which he overturned and had a large impact on the operations of the courts and who was eligible for asylum. One such case was *Matter of Castro-Tum* (2018, 271) where Sessions decided that "Immigration Judges and the Board [BIA] do not have the general authority to suspend indefinitely immigration proceedings by administrative closure." What this meant is that immigration judges could no longer use administrative closure as a case management tool increasing the already long backlog for immigration courts. Another case Sessions referred to himself and decided was the case *Matter of A-B* (2018). Sessions' decision in the *Matter of A-B* vacated the BIA's decision in the *Matter of A-R-C-G* (2014) where they decided that 'married women in Guatemala who are unable to leave their relationship' constitutes a particular social group (Menke 2020). Sessions reversal effectively eliminated asylum to victims of domestic violence. *Matter of A-B* was itself subsequently overturned by

Merrick Garland, the Attorney General in the Biden Administration. These are just two of the cases Sessions referred to himself but they highlight the big impact those referrals have on the immigration system. These decisions were not without criticism, as immigration advocates and legal scholars criticized the outcomes of these specific cases but also the referral process of the Attorney General overall. In a response to former Attorney General Gonzales's plea for Attorney Generals to use their referral power more often, Bijal Shah (2016) argues that the referral power by the Attorney General is not similar to Presidential executive orders as claimed by Gonzales and Glen (2016) because although the Attorney General is appointed by the President and confirmed by the Senate, they are not purely political actors as they must also run a bureaucratic agency—the Justice Department. Additionally, Shah (2016) argues that the referral power does not do what it is allegedly supposed to do—increase uniformity and consistency in immigration courts because as with the matter of Jeff Sessions's referrals they were used to upend longstanding practice and precedence rather than resolve disputes in the law. Furthermore, Julie Menke (2020) argues that the referral authority of the Attorney General may itself be unconstitutional and at the very least an unwelcome political intrusion into the administration of the law.

The ability of the Attorney General to refer cases from the BIA to themselves means that the BIA operates in the shadow of the Attorney General potentially overturning their decisions and therefore makes them attuned to the policy desires of the Attorney General. Both of these stories about Attorney General's Ashcroft and Sessions highlight the potential political influence that permeates the BIA. These anecdotes also give credence to the "Presidential Control Model" of agency administration which argues that it is the White House and its political appointees who drive the action in administrative agencies such as the EOIR (Kim 2018). The heavy influence of the political appointees in shaping immigration courts and law do not prevent institutions such as the BIA from making policy through their decisions but they can shape those decisions through their political influence. Therefore, one would expect to see institutions such as the BIA making different policy-making decisions depending on who is in the White House. This is not to say that the BIA is simply a tool of the President and Attorney General. For example, Koh (2019) describes a scenario in 2008 where the Bush Administration tried to redefine the category of "Crimes Involving Moral Turpitude'" in which the BIA successfully pushed back. Rather it is to highlight the potentially complicated and complex ways politics can influence the policy-making role of the BIA.

BIA and Workload Management

In addition to potential political influence on BIA decisions there is also the demands of the workload that can influence BIA decisions as well. The "streamlining" processes implemented by Attorney Generals Reno and Ashcroft allowed for cases before the BIA to be heard by one judge who could issue an affirmation of the immigration court's decision without an opinion (known as an "AWO"—affirmation without opinion). Of course, this streamlining process was one of the reasons Attorney General Ashcroft used to reduce the size of the BIA from 23 to 11. A review of the immigration court system commissioned by the American Bar Association ("ABA") in 2010 found that the streamlining reforms did reduce the backlog of cases at the BIA but also put pressure on the Board to "issue perfunctory opinions given the press of time, and that the Board faced a significant lack of resources" (Arnold and Porter LLP 2019, 3–6). In an update to the 2010 report issued in 2019 the Law Firm Arnold and Porter LLP (2019), which was commissioned to write both reports, noted that the caseload for the BIA had continued to increase as the caseload for immigration courts in general continued to increase. The increased caseload has led to an increase in the membership of the BIA to 17 in 2015 and up to 21 in 2018 (Arnold and Porter LLP 2019). The BIA now sits at 23 members which is back to its original number prior to the streamlining measures implemented by Attorney General Ashcroft. However, the increase of AWOs that started with Ashcroft's streamlining are still utilized by the current Board despite its current size. This suggests that the workload for the BIA plays an important role in the decisions made by the Board.

RESEARCH DESIGN

To test our propositions regarding decision making by the BIA we utilized the same dataset described in chapter 2. However, the statistical models utilized in this chapter will differ significantly. In chapter 2 we used a multilevel model to account for the various levels of influence in IJ decision making. The BIA is located in Fall Church Virginia so the geographic distribution that was inherent in the decision making of IJs is not present for the BIA. Additionally, to account for the decisions made by the BIA we also need to account for the decision by UACs (and their attorneys) to appeal their case. In other words, there is a selection effect that needs to be addressed to account for the types of cases that get to the BIA for them to rule on. The main model used in this chapter is a Heckman probit model. This is a two-stage model that accounts for the fact that the decisions made by the BIA are only completely observed for a subsample of the total dataset (those that file an appeal) (Breen 1996). The first stage of the model accounts for the decision by UACs to appeal their decision while the second stage accounts for the decisions by the BIA regarding that appeal. Probit modeling is used in our test since both the first stage dependent variable (decision to appeal) and second stage dependent variable (decision to affirm IJs decision) are binary with 1 indicating yes and 0 indicating no (see below for further description).

Before we present the descriptive results of our analysis a quick word about who can appeal a lower court IJ decision is necessary. Since the focus of this project is on unaccompanied minors, we focus on only those instances when UACs decide to appeal the case. It is possible for the U.S. government to appeal a decision from the IJs to the BIA but we do not examine that possibility here. Furthermore, the appeals are weighted heavily toward the UACs appealing cases. In our dataset we have 4,768 cases that were appealed out of a total of 12,826 but only 2,999 of those cases had a decision from the BIA by the end of 2020 which is the last year in our dataset. Of those 4,768 cases that were appealed we surmise that 4,502 of them were appealed by UACs and their lawyers. We know this because in those cases the decision by the IJ was for removal or voluntary removal and since those are negative decisions against the minors, they would be the ones to appeal those decisions. We had to deduce this because unfortunately the data we received from the EOIR did not specify who filed the appeal but only that an appeal was filed. Based on our calculations, approximately 94 percent of the cases appealed were appealed by UACs and their attorneys which is another reason our analysis in this chapter focuses specifically on UACs appeals and not appeals by the government.

Below we present the descriptive results from our analysis. We present here the full results of cases appealed (4,768 cases) while in the results for the Heckman probit model presented later, we only utilize those appealed cases that have a decision by the BIA (2,999).

DESCRIPTIVE RESULTS

Figure 3.1 shows the number of UAC appeals, along with the total number of cases, per year. As one would expect the more cases there are, the more appeals there are and the total number of appeals has increased in the past few years as the total number of cases has increased as well. Although UAC cases only represent a small fraction of the cases heard in immigration courts and in the BIA the increase in cases over the last few years has only increased the workload for both levels of courts.

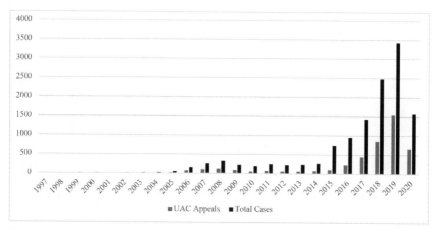

Figure 3.1. UAC Appeals and Total Cases per Year, 1997–2020. Source: Created by the authors.

Figure 3.2 presents the number of appeals and total cases per nationality of the minor appealing the case. We only present those with a minimum of 100 cases for space considerations. Since minors from the Northern Triangle countries comprise the vast majority of total cases they also comprise the vast majority of appeals. Interesting is that the percentage of cases appealed is roughly uniform across the three countries with approximately 30 percent of the cases appealed (35%, 37%, and 34%, respectively). The percentage of cases appealed drops for minors from China, Ecuador, and India with 14 percent, 23 percent, and 24 percent of their cases appealed, respectively.

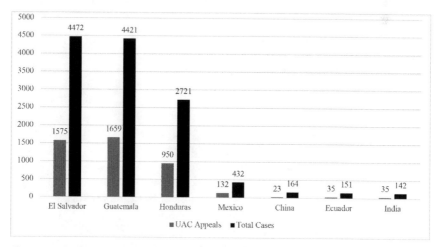

Figure 3.2. UAC Appeals and Total Cases per UAC Nationality with a Minimum of 100 Cases. Source: Created by the authors.

Chapter 3

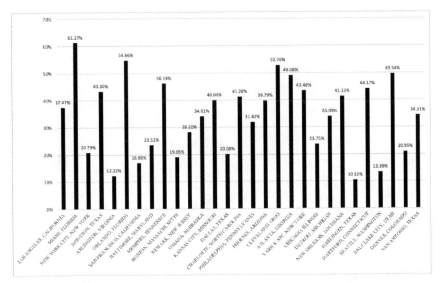

Figure 3.3. Percent of UAC Appeals per Base City with a Minimum of 100 Cases. Source: Created by the authors.

Figure 3.3 presents the number of UAC appeals and total cases per base city with a minimum of 100 cases. Again, the courts with the most cases also generate the most appeals but there is interesting variance in the top cities in terms of the percentage of appeals per cases. For example, in Los Angeles 37 percent of the cases were appealed by UACs but in Miami 61 percent were appealed. In New York City approximately 21 percent of the cases were appealed by UACs but in Houston 43 percent of the cases were appealed. There are a lot of possibilities that may explain this variation and the most obvious is what was discussed in chapter 2 that there is significant variation across jurisdictions regarding the outcomes of cases for unaccompanied minors. Additionally, the decision to appeal a case may be driven by the presence of an attorney for a UAC and some jurisdictions may have more lawyers available than others. Finally, figure 3.4 presents the number of appeals and total cases per Immigration Judges with a minimum of 100 cases.

The variation in cases appealed per immigration judge is even greater than appeals per location of the court. This is not surprising since the negative decisions against UACs vary greatest among immigration judges. However, what figure 3.4 shows us is that the volume of cases heard does not seem to establish a pattern for appeals per immigration judge. For example, the percentage of cases appealed for the four judges with the highest case rate (Ashley A. Tabaddor, John Milo Bryant, Rebecca L. Holt, and Clearase R. Yates) is 41 percent, 10 percent, 45 percent, and 42 percent respectively. While three out of the four have roughly equal percentage of cases appealed, the fourth—John

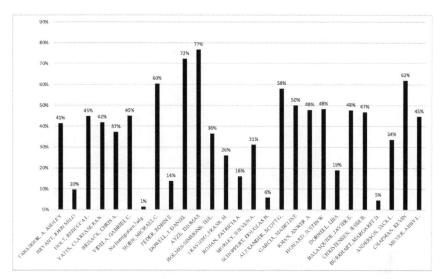

Figure 3.4. UAC Appeals and Total Cases per Immigration Judges with a Minimum of 100 Cases. Source: Created by the authors.

Milo Bryant's significantly low appeal rate shows the variation across judges appellate rate cannot be described as solely a function of scale.

Figure 3.5 presents the number of times the BIA affirmed the ruling of the IJ. To present this result we use the total number of cases appealed by UACs that have a decision in our dataset (2,798).

As can be seen 721 times (26%) the BIA did not affirm the IJs decision on a UAC appealed case. We can count these as positive outcomes for UACs. However, 2,077 times, or 74 percent, of the time the BIA reaffirmed the lower

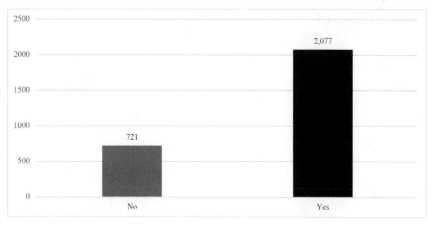

Figure 3.5. BIA Affirms IJ Decision of UAC Appealed Case. Source: Created by the authors.

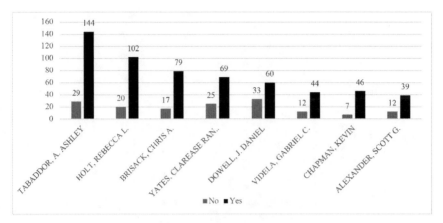

Figure 3.6.   BIA Affirming IJ Decision per IJ with a Minimum of 50 Cases Appealed by UACs. Source: Created by the authors.

court's decision which we can count as a negative outcome for the UAC which appealed the case.

Finally, figure 3.6 shows the number of times the BIA reaffirmed decisions by specific immigration judges with a minimum of 50 cases appealed. The percentage affirmed by the BIA is fairly consistent across the judges with the most cases appealed. The highest level of affirmation is 87 percent and the lowest level of affirmation is 65 percent.

In the next section we will present the results from our Heckman probit model analyzing BIA decisions on cases appealed by unaccompanied minors. First, however, we will describe the dependent variables and independent variables used in the analysis.

DEPENDENT VARIABLE

Our unit of analysis, as in chapter 2, is individual cases but instead of focusing on all cases as in chapter 2 here we are focused on only those cases that have been appealed to the BIA and also those appealed cases for which the BIA has reached a decision. Because of this we utilize a Heckman selection model which first models the decision by UAC and their attorneys to appeal their cases and then in the second stage models the decision by the BIA on those appealed cases. The dependent variable for the first stage of the model is *UM Appeal*; this is a dichotomous variable where 1 is equal to the cases that were appealed by the unaccompanied minor and 0 is the cases that were not appealed. As mentioned above we had to surmise that the case was appealed by the unaccompanied minor because the information we received from the

EOIR did not state that directly. We coded those cases as appealed by the unaccompanied minor if a) they were appealed and b) if the result of the original case was removal or voluntary removal. The dependent variable used in the second stage in the model is *BIA Affirms IJ Decision* which is also a dichotomous variable where 1 indicates that the BIA affirms the lower court's decision and 0 is all other decisions from the BIA. We focus on affirmations of lower court decisions since those are decisions that are against the UAC appealing the case. The BIA affirming the lower court's decision is by far the most frequent decision in our dataset. Of the 2,999 cases with a decision by the BIA in our dataset 2,082 are ones where the BIA affirmed the lower court's decision and dismissed the appeal.

INDEPENDENT VARIABLES

In the stage 1 model we use the same measure for *Human Rights* and *Democracy* that we used in the analysis in chapter 2. We also use the same measures for *Immigration Judge Ideology* and *Immigration Judge Party* that we used in the model in chapter 2. New independent variables included in this model are: *IJ Relief Rate, Dem. Admin., BIA Ideology*, and *BIA Party.*

Relief Rate for Immigration Judges

One assumption behind the decision to appeal a removal order by an unaccompanied minor is that they might have had their case come before a particularly harsh immigration judge. As this study has already shown the rates at which immigration judges rule favorably on asylum claims for unaccompanied minors vary considerably. Therefore, a minor who has their case rejected by a harsh judge may decide that an appeal is more likely to succeed, but conversely a negative ruling from a generous judge may be less likely to be appealed as the minor and their attorney may feel that the case has a lower likelihood of being reversed. Additionally, as Hausman (2016) discussed, error correction is a function of the appellate process so it is necessary to see at what rates harsh and generous immigration judges have their decisions upheld by the BIA. To that end our variable *IJ Relief Rate* is the percentage of asylum cases involving an unaccompanied minor an immigration judge approves out of the total UAC asylum cases they hear each year.

Democratic Administration

Our discussion of the influence of the Attorney General on the form and function of the BIA suggests that the Attorney General can exert pressure (even indirectly) on the decisions of the BIA. With that in mind our variable *Dem. Admin.* is a dichotomous variable where "1" are the years when there was a Democratic President and Attorney General in office and "0" are the years when there is a Republican President and Attorney General in office. The assumption is that the partisan change in the office of the Attorney General would lead to different decisions from the BIA.

Political Ideology of the BIA

As with the judges on immigration courts, understanding the political ideology of the members of the BIA is important to discern the reasoning behind their decisions. One complication for this variable that differs from the Immigration Judge ideological variable is that we do not know which BIA judges (or panel of judges) make which decisions. Therefore, our measure *BIA Mean Ideology* is a measure of the average yearly ideology for the BIA. We construct an ideological measure similar to the one we made for Immigration Judges in chapter 2 for each member of the BIA each year. Then we average the ideology scores for the members of the BIA for each year in our dataset. The average ranges from -1 to -2.315 which shows that overall, the BIA is more conservative than the range of Immigration Judges discussed in chapter 2.

Partisanship of the BIA

Similarly, to the political ideology of the BIA, *BIA Mean Party* is a variable that measures the average partisanship per year of the BIA. To construct the variable, we labeled it as "1" if a BIA member was appointed by a Democratic Attorney General and "0" if appointed by a Republican Attorney General. Then we averaged the score across all BIA members per year. The variable can be read as the percentage of the BIA that was appointed by Democratic Attorney Generals and ranges from 21.7 to 94.1.

In stage 2 of the model, we use the same measure for *Human Rights, Democracy, Immigration Judges Ideology,* and *Immigration Judge Party* that we used in the analysis in chapter 2 and in the first stage of the model used in this chapter. In addition, in stage 2 we also use the same measure for *Military Aid, Volume of Trade, High Undocumented Country,* and *Spanish* that we used in chapter 2. Finally, for model 2 the last independent variables in the model are *IJ Relief Rate, Dem. Admin., BIA Mean Ideology,* and *BIA Mean Party* which are the same measures used in stage 1.

CONTROL VARIABLES

For stage 1 of the model, we use two variables that were also measured the same as the variables used in the analysis in chapter 2—*Attorney* and *Detained*. For stage 2 of the model we also include *Attorney* as a control variable but we also included some specific control variables with regards to the workload of the BIA

Number of BIA Judges

As noted above the size and scope of the BIA has fluctuated over time due to the policy choices of various Attorney Generals. The size of the BIA in our dataset ranges from a low of 7 judges to a high of 23 judges which is the current number. The variable *BIA Judges* is just a count variable of the number of judges on the court per month. We include this as a control variable because the number of BIA judges on the court contributes to the workload of each judge. With fewer judges on the court, in general, those judges will have a larger workload and with more judges then the workload of each judge should be reduced relative to one another. Underlying this is the idea that a higher workload for judges would lead to more deferential attitudes toward the lower courts decisions and therefore more likely to reaffirming the immigration judges decisions.

Time of Immigration Judge Decision to Appeal

Another control variable used in stage 2 of our model deals with the time from the decision made by the Immigration Judge to the date the appeal is filed. The variable *Time Appeal* is a count variable of the number of days between the decision by the Immigration Judge and the appeal filed date. The variable ranges from 0 to 4,025. We are agnostic to the direction this variable may have on BIA decisions but we include it because we believe it captures some important phenomenon that could be at work. First, the length of time between the decision by an IJ and an appeal could reflect the time constraints and workload of the attorney representing the UAC. Second, the length of time to file an appeal could also represent the time UACs spend looking for a lawyer to file their appeal as we know that UACs do go before IJs without attorneys but would need an attorney to file an appeal. Finally, the length of time to file an appeal could represent a strategic move on the part of an attorney where they perhaps wait to file, or conversely file one quickly, based on the composition of the BIA.

Length of Time Appeal Is with the BIA

The fourth control variable used in stage 2 is the length of time the appeal is with the BIA. Similarly, to *Time Appeal*, *BIA Length Appeal* is a count variable of the number of days after an appeal is filed to the date the BIA makes a decision on the appeal. This variable ranges from 1 day to 2,455 days. Again, we include this variable as we consider it a measure that captures the workload on the BIA. We surmise that the longer the appeal is with the BIA the internal pressure to reduce the backlog of cases for the court will increase and the likelihood of reaffirming the IJ decision will also increase,

UAC Appeal Backlog at BIA

Our final control variable for stage 2 of our model analyzed in this chapter is *BIA UAC Cases* which is another count variable of the number of cases appealed by UAC for the previous month. This variable gives us a measure of the workload of the BIA at least with regards to appeals by UACs. Of course, the BIA also hears appeals for a variety of immigration related cases so their workloads are much greater than just making decisions regarding UAC appeals. The variable ranges from 0 to 203. As with *BIA Length Appeal*, we include this variable since it again captures the pressure on the BIA to move through cases quickly. The pressure to move through the cases quickly makes the likelihood of reaffirming the decisions of IJs more likely.

MODEL

As described above we use a Heckman Probit model to analyze the decision by the BIA to reaffirm the decision of the IJ which in this case would be considered a negative outcome for the minor appealing the decision. The analysis requires a selection model because the cases heard by the BIA are not randomly distributed as the decision to appeal is based on many factors. Using a selection model allows us to control for the reasons a case is appealed by UACs and therefore makes the analysis of the BIA decision more valuable. Furthermore, we use a probit model since both of the dependent variables in stages 1 and 2 are dichotomous. Finally, we cluster robust standard errors on Immigration judges as a way of controlling for possible confounders in our analysis.

Stage 1—decision to appeal by UAC—is presented at the bottom of the table. There are many interesting results on why UACs may choose to appeal their decisions from the immigration courts. First, we see that both the *Democracy* and *Human Rights* variables are statistically significant at the .001 level and

RESULTS

Table 3.1

Heckman Probit Model of Affirmations of IJ Decisions by the BIA and Decision to Appeal IJ Decision by UACs

BIA Affirms IJ Decision Probit (Std Error)

Human Rights	.726(.837)
Democracy	1.32***(.358)
Military Aid	-.943(.638)
Volume of Trade (ln)	-.056(.042)
High Undocumented	.050(.207)
Spanish	-.341(.244)
Immigration Judge Ideology	-.005(.024)
Immigration Judge Party	.136(.081)
Immigration Judge Relief Rate	.007**(.002)
Democratic Administration	-.002(.114)
BIA Mean Ideology	-.407(.316)
BIA Mean Party	.014**(.005)
Attorney	.418***(.097)
Number of BIA Judges	.104***(.027)
Time to Appeal	.00006(.0001)
Length of Appeal	.0006***(.0002)
Number of UM Appeals (lagged)	-.003***(.0008)

Appeal IJ Decision of Removal or Voluntary Withdrawal

Human Rights	-3.78***(1.01)
Democracy	-1.77***(.460)
Immigration Judge Ideology	å-.082*(.038)
Immigration Judge Party	-.040(.157)
Immigration Judge Relief Rate	-.041***(.003)
Democratic Administration	.368*(.169)
BIA Mean Ideology	1.97***(.467)
BIA Mean Party	-.004(.007)
Attorney	1.35***(.137)
Detained	.578**(.218)
Observations	3,044
Selected	2,782
Nonselected	262
Log pseudolikelihood	-2,020.24
Wald Chi Square	96.28
Wald Test of Independent Equations	631.97

Created by the authors

both results are negative. The interesting factor here is that although one would expect the level of democracy and the level of human rights abuses in a country to move together (more democratic = less human rights abuses) the results here present a contradiction. The variable *Human Rights* is the Political Terror Scale, which is described in detail in chapter 2, and higher numbers of the scale indicate greater human rights abuses. Meanwhile the *Democracy* variable is the Varieties of Democracy measure, again described in detail in chapter 2, but for this measure higher values indicate a more democratic country. Therefore, both values being negative indicates that UACs from countries that are more democratic are less likely to appeal a negative decision from an Immigration Judge. This is as expected because it indicates the minor in question may not be in as much danger as someone fleeing a non-democratic country. However, our results also indicate that a minor from a country with *greater* human rights abuses is also less likely to appeal a negative decision from an IJ. This is contrary to expectations as one would expect a minor fleeing a country with greater human rights abuses would be more likely to appeal a negative decision because they would have a greater fear of being sent back to their home country.

Continuing with the Stage 1 results, both *Immigration Judge Ideology* and *Immigration Judge Relief Rate* are both statistically significant (at the .05 and .01 levels, respectively) and both signs are negative. Although the sizes of the coeffects are not large they nonetheless present interesting results. With both signs negative it indicates the UACs are less likely to appeal negative decisions from liberal IJs and from IJs with higher relief rates. This is what one would expect as if a more liberal and generous judge rejected a minor's case they might (or their attorney) may feel the likelihood of a positive ruling by the BIA is even less likely. Similarly, the variable *BIA Mean Ideology* is also statistically significant (at the .001 level) but this variable is positive. This is also what one would expect as the more liberal the composition of the BIA is the more likely a UAC would appeal a negative result from an IJ. The belief here is that the BIA represents a greater chance of receiving a positive outcome.

Finally, with regards to Stage 1 results, both control variables *Attorney* and *Detained* are statistically significant (at the .001 and .01 levels respectively) and both variables are positive. This is also expected as UAC with attorneys are more likely to appeal their case (and the size of the coefficient indicates the effect is substantial) and UAC who are (or were at some point) detained are also more likely to appeal their negative result from the lower courts.

The Stage 2 results are also quite interesting for what they show about how the BIA makes decisions regarding the asylum claims of unaccompanied minors. The *Democracy* variable is also statistically significant (at the .001 level) in Stage 2 meaning that the BIA is more likely to affirm an IJs negative decision from an UAC coming from a country that is more democratic. This is in line with expectations as mentioned above one would expect UACs coming from more democratic countries would experience less repression. The *Immigration Judge Relief Rate* variable is also significant in stage 2 of the model (at the .01 level) and the sign is positive but the size of the coefficient is quite small. This result indicates that the greater the relief rate of an IJ (meaning the greater the likelihood that IJ is to grant relief to a UAC) the *greater* the likelihood that the BIA will affirm judges' *negative* decision regarding asylum for UACs. One possible interpretation here is that the BIA is more likely to support negative decisions on UAC asylum claims from IJs more inclined to grant those claims because the assumption is if those IJs reject the claim then the claims lack sufficient validity. Interestingly, this is the opposite of what Hausman (2016) found in his analysis of BIA decisions from more "generous" judges although Hausman's analysis focused on all types of cases not just those appealed by UACs.

Continuing with the results from the Stage 2 model, the *BIA Mean Party* variable is statistically significant (at the .01 level) and positive. This suggests that as the composition of the BIA becomes more Democratic (in that the members of the BIA are appointed Democratic Attorney Generals) the BIA is more likely to affirm the negative decisions from the IJs. This is somewhat contrary to expectations as one may expect that BIA members appointed by Democratic Attorney Generals would be more supportive of asylum claims of UACs.

In terms of the control variables in Stage 2 there are a number of variables that are significant suggesting that the workload of the BIA has an impact on how the BIA makes decisions regarding negative asylum decisions for UACs by IJs. The variables *Number of BIA Judges*, *Length of Appeal*, and *Number of UM Appeals*. All three variables are significant at the .001 level while two out of the three, *Number of BIA Judges*, and *Length of Appeal*, are positive. These two results indicate that as the number of judges on the BIA increases and the length of time the BIA has to consider the appeal the likelihood of the BIA supporting the negative decisions of the IJs increases. The variable *Number of UM Appeals* is negative suggesting that as the cumulative number of UM appeals without a decision increases the BIA is less likely to support the negative decision of the IJs.

Finally, with regards to the last of the control variables that are significant in the stage 2 part of the model, the variable *Attorney* is statistically significant (at the .001) and positive. The positive sign in the coefficient indicates that the BIA is more likely to affirm the negative decision of an IJ if the UAC had an attorney representing them. This suggests that if the UAC did not have an attorney during their case before an IJ, but then appealed the case to the BIA, then the BIA would be more likely to not affirm the lower court's negative decision. On the one hand this is somewhat against expectations because one would assume that if the UAC had an attorney during their hearing before an IJ they would retain the attorney to file the BIA appeal. Also, a more cynical interpretation, would be lawyers do not mind pursuing what they might view as un-meritorious appeals because they will get paid to file the appeal not necessarily to win. However, on the other hand it would also suggest that the negative IJ decision for a case of a minor without an attorney failed to meet certain standards of due process in the eyes of the BIA and they could not affirm the lower court's decision. This would provide some evidence that the BIA as an appellate court does provide some measure of error correction and maintains certain due process standards.

As we did in chapter 2, we also present the predicted probabilities for our model. The results presented here are for stage 2 of the model—the likelihood of the BIA affirming the negative decisions of the lower court IJs. Table 3.2 presents the predicted probabilities for the variables in stage 2 which were statistically significant.

Table 3.2

Predicted Probabilities of BIA Affirming IJ Negative Decisions of UAC Asylum Claims by Statistically Significant Results

Democracy	
1 (.33)	.665

sense. The other variable that does not have 5 categories is *Attorney* which is a dichotomous variable with only 2 categories—UAC has a lawyer or does not have a lawyer.

The results from table 3.2 show the magnitude of the effect of each variable on the likelihood of BIA affirming IJ decisions. The change in predicted probabilities for the variable *Democracy*, going from low level of democracy to high levels of democracy, is .184. The change from *Immigration Judge Relief Rate*, going from low relief rates to high, is .094. The change for *BIA Mean Party*, going from a more Republican BIA to a more Democratic BIA, is .253. The change for not having an attorney to having an attorney increases the probability of the BIA affirming the negative IJ decision by .139. Continuing with the main control variables used in stage 2, the predicted probability for *Number BIA Judges* increases by .337 when moving from 10 judges on the BIA to 22 judges. The predicted probability for *BIA Appeal Length* increases by .176 when going from 1 day the appeal is with the BIA to 940 days the appeal is with the BIA. Finally, the predicted probability for *Number of UM Appeals* decreases by .195 when there is a backlog of 1 case to when there is a backlog of 203 cases.

2 (.45)	.720
3 (.56)	.767
4 (.68)	.813
5 (.79)	.849

Immigration Judge Relief Rate

1 (0)	.758
2 (11.66)	.780
3 (32.49)	.818
4 (53.32)	.852

BIA Mean Party

1 (23.72)	.603
2 (38.18)	.679
3 (52.64)	.746
4 (67.1)	.806
5 (81.56)	.856

Attorney

0 (No)	.650
1 (Yes)	.789

Number of BIA Judges

1 (10)	.595
2 (13)	.710
3 (16)	.807
4 (19)	.881
5 (22)	.932

Length of Appeal

1 (1)	.682
2 (169)	.719
3 (427)	.772
4 (683)	.818
5 (940)	.858

Number of UM Appeals

1 (1)	.824
2 (21)	.808
3 (83)	.754
4 (145)	.692
5 (203)	.629

Created by the authors

Table 3.2 shows the predicted probabilities of the BIA affirming the negative decisions by IJs on UAC asylum cases at 5 levels. The five levels are based on the mean and two standard deviations above and below the mean for each variable. The values for each variable are in parentheses. The exception is the variable *IJ Relief Rates* because the mean is 11.66 percent and the standard deviation is 20.83 percent so one and two standard deviations below the mean would be in negative territory which does not make logical

Overall predicted probabilities provide a more nuanced view of the relationship between the variables by showing what the likelihood of the BIA
affirming the IJs negative decisions against UAC asylum cases is at various
levels of the independent variables.

CONCLUSION

The focus of this chapter was on the decision making of the BIA. The BIA
is the appellate body of the immigration court system and serves an important function in immigration court system. Ideally, appellate courts serve as
error correcting mechanisms and policy-making bodies in terms of issuing
precedence decisions. This chapter examined the error correction process for
the BIA by seeing how IJ relief rates influence BIA decision making, and
while we did not examine the precedent decisions made by the BIA, we did
examine factors that are behind policy-making decisions by judges—politics.
In terms of error-correction we find some marginal evidence that the BIA
engages in error correction with regards to cases appealed by unaccompanied minors. Our Heckman probit model shows that as the relief rate for IJs
increases the BIA is more likely to affirm negative decisions but if the relief
rate is lower for an IJ the BIA is less likely to affirm a negative decision. This
provides some support to the idea of error correction as one could assume
that overly harsh IJs are more likely to make errors in their decision making
and the lower rates of affirmation by the BIA for their decisions indicate a
willingness to correct those errors.

In terms of political influences on the decision making of the BIA we
find some interesting results. One thing of note is not what variables were
significant but ones that were not in our model. We did not find evidence
that immigration judge ideology, partisanship, BIA mean ideology nor the
presence of the Democratic administration significantly influences the decisions of the BIA to affirm negative decisions by IJs. We did find support that
the BIA mean partisanship has an influence on BIA decision making but it is
contradictory of what we would expect. We find that the more Democratic the
BIA the higher the likelihood of the BIA supporting negative decisions from
the BIA, and the predicted probabilities show that the effect is substantial and
increases by .253 when moving from a BIA that is 23 percent Democratic
to one that is 82 percent Democratic. These results call into question the
partisan influence of the Attorney General on the functioning of the BIA at
least with regards to decisions made about appeals from UACs. Additionally,
it questions the extent to which the BIA itself has a strong political agenda
since most of the political variables have little to no effect. What does appear
to influence the BIA decision-making process is its composition in terms of

numbers, how long the appeal is with the BIA, and the backlog of cases (UAC cases specifically). In contrast to chapter 2 which showed a larger political influence in IJ decision making it appears that the BIA is less influenced by politics or willing to pursue a political agenda.

PART II

Chapter 4

Judicial Decision Making at the Micro-Level

Federal Courts' Decision Making on Procedural Rights and Procedural Due Process of Unaccompanied Minors in the U.S.

Alexis Rivera Quintanilla, an unaccompanied alien child from El Salvador who entered the United States without inspection at the age of thirteen, was placed in removal proceedings but released to his godfather in Nassau County, New York (*Quintanilla v. Decker* 2021). As Quintanilla was leaving the Nassau County Court where he pled guilty for the offense of driving on a suspended license, ICE agents arrested and detained him pursuant to its discretionary authority under 8 U.S.C. § 1226(a). The immigration judge denied bond after conducting a bond hearing on December 14, 2020 where Quintanilla was required to prove that he was not a flight risk or a danger to the community. On appeal, U.S. District Judge George B. Daniels of the Southern District of New York ordered the immigration judge to conduct a new bond hearing. He explained that the government should bear the burden through clear and convincing evidence to deny liberty at any Section 1226(a) bond hearing, regardless of the noncitizen's length of detention. This case illustrates how federal courts enforce the procedural due process rights of unaccompanied minors processed through the U.S. immigration enforcement system.

For this chapter, we utilize inductive doctrinal analysis of federal cases to determine how federal judges are constrained by legal precedent, the plain meaning of statutes, and the intent of the framers of statutes. The WESTLAW database contains electronic copies of all published and unpublished court decisions. A keyword search was used to gather cases on UAC decided by all federal courts in the U.S. The advanced search parameters required that the term "unaccompanied alien child" appeared in the main body of the case as of 2022 (N = 293). The authors then read each case individually and determined that not all cases were relevant to the article, either because the case did not involve UAC or did not contain sufficient facts to enable full analysis. Also, some cases were repeated because of the appeal process through the federal courts. This chapter examines federal district and circuit court cases on procedural due process and policy issues raised by unaccompanied alien children in the course of their immigration proceedings. Instead of an empirical, quantitative approach, we organized these decisions around major issues and themes that unaccompanied minors raised at the federal courts. Scrutinizing these decisions are necessary, given that judicial decisions have the force and effect of law and affect the rights of these unaccompanied minors as they go through the U.S. asylum system.

We start by analyzing federal cases that deal with broad government agency policies that affect the procedural rights of unaccompanied minors. Specifically, we discuss federal litigation on the USCIS 2019 Redetermination Memoranda that affected jurisdiction over asylum claims of these minors. We then talk about the rules of the Department of Health and Human Services and the Department of Homeland Security that attempted to end the effectivity of the 1997 *Flores* Settlement Agreement and the outcome of litigation in court. From broad administrative rules, we then focus on government and administrative programs and practice by discussing litigation regarding former President Trump's family separation policy and the effects of DHS's failure to maintain records on family separation. We also discuss litigation surrounding the Center for Disease Control's orders, ICE, and ORR Policies during the COVID-19 pandemic. These policies affect release, detention, and custody of minors. From broad policies, we go into specific procedural rights and issues, namely, how unaccompanied minors can challenge long periods of detention at ICE family residential centers or placement in hotels prior to expulsion under Title 42. We then discuss specific procedural issues during the asylum proceeding. We explain how federal courts have interpreted defects in the Notice to Appear issued to unaccompanied minors and their consequences on the jurisdiction of lower immigration courts. Finally, at the last step of the asylum process, we discuss procedural rights in removal proceedings.

CASE ANALYSIS OF PROCEDURAL
DUE PROCESS RIGHTS

USCIS Memoranda on Determination of Jurisdiction
Over Asylum Claims of Unaccompanied Minors

Recall that there are two processes by which an alien can generally apply for asylum: affirmative and defensive (*J.O.P. v. U.S. Department of Homeland Security* 2020a). The affirmative asylum process occurs when an applicant present in the U.S. for less than a year affirmatively files an asylum application (8 U.S.C. § 1158; *J.O.P. v. U.S. Department of Homeland Security* 2020a). The application is heard by a U.S. Citizenship and Immigration Services asylum officer who conducts a private interview in a nonadversarial manner (8 C.F.R. §208.9(b); *J.O.P. v. U.S. Department of Homeland Security* 2020a). Asylum officers are "specially trained" by USCIS in "international human rights law, nonadversarial interview techniques, and other relevant national and international refugee laws and principles" (8 C.F.R. §208.1(b); *J.O.P. v. U.S. Department of Homeland Security* 2020a, 43). The defensive process, on the other hand, begins when an individual is placed in section 240 removal proceedings in immigration court and raises their asylum claim as a defense to removal (*J.O.P. v. U.S. Department of Homeland Security* 2020a). After aliens are served with a "notice to appear," they are placed in section 240 removal proceedings (8 C.F.R. §1229(a)). Immigration judges, not USCIS, have exclusive jurisdiction over the individual's asylum application during these adversarial immigration court proceedings (8 C.F.R. § 208.2(a), (b)). Immigration courts are operated by the Executive Office for Immigration Review, a Department of Justice component established by regulation (8 C.F.R. §§ 1003.0, 1003.9, 1003.10; *J.O.P. v. U.S. Department of Homeland Security* 2020a).

Under the TVPRA's initial jurisdiction provision, however, USCIS asylum officers instead of immigration judges have initial jurisdiction over unaccompanied minors' asylum applications even when removal proceedings have been initiated. The USCIS asylum process is a "non-adversarial" system "more sensitive to the special needs of children who do not know how to navigate an immigration system designed for adults, and who likely sought safety in the United States without understanding their legal options" (*J.O.P. v. U.S. Department of Homeland Security* 2019, 372; *J.O.P. v. U.S. Department of Homeland Security* 2020, 3). Instead of facing trained government lawyers in adversarial courtroom proceedings, unaccompanied minors engage with USCIS officers trained to apply "child-sensitive and trauma-informed interview techniques" (*J.O.P. v. U.S. Department of Homeland Security* 2019, 372). The TVPRA also directs USCIS to help make counsel available to these children. While asylum applicants generally must file their asylum applications within one year of entering the United States, Section 1158(a)(2)(E) of the TVPRA exempts unaccompanied children from this one-year filing deadline (*Flores-Lobo v. Holder* 2014). Section 1232(d)(8) the TVPRA also delegates authority to adopt regulations governing asylum applications of unaccompanied minors that take into account their specialized needs and that address both procedural and substantive aspects of handling their cases.

To implement the above laws, the USCIS issued several memoranda providing guidelines to its asylum officers on how to assess whether applicants are unaccompanied minors. The first memorandum, issued on March 25, 2009 by USCIS Asylum Division Chief Joseph Langlois ("2009 Langlois Memo"), directed USCIS to assess whether the applicant qualified as an unaccompanied minor both when they received the minor's asylum application and during the applicant's actual interview (*J.O.P. v. U.S. Department of Homeland Security* 2020a, 2020b). On May 28, 2013, USCIS Acting Asylum Division Chief Ted Kim ("2013 Kim Memo") modified the procedures established in the 2009 Langlois Memo. Under the policy adopted by the 2013 Kim Memo, asylum officers were required to accept the findings of the Customs and Border Protection and Immigration and Customs Enforcement regarding the unaccompanied minors' status without needing to redetermine their status, even if they had turned eighteen or been reunited with a parent or guardian by the time they applied for asylum. Under the Kim Memo, when the CPB or ICE had already determined that an applicant was an unaccompanied minor and that determination was still effective on the date the asylum application was filed, USCIS would adopt that determination without inquiring further (*J.O.P. v. U.S. Department of Homeland Security* 2020a, 2020b). The Ninth Circuit in the 2015 case of *Xin Yu He v. Lynch* held that to qualify for the TVPRA's jurisdictional provision, the applicants must qualify as unaccompanied alien children at the time they file an asylum application even if he or she turned eighteen years old thereafter. In the same year, the Fifth Circuit ruled in *Flores-Lobo v. Holder* (2014) that minors who do not qualify as unaccompanied alien children when they file their asylum application were not exempted from the one-year time filing deadline.

On June 14, 2019, USCIS published a memorandum on its website that revised the rules in the 2013 Kim Memo for determining whether a child is eligible for TVPRA protections. The memorandum dated May 31, 2019 became effective on June 30, 2019. The 2019 memorandum ("2019 Redetermination Memo") discussed a decision by the Board of Immigration Appeals in *Matter of M-A-C-O-* (2018) where the BIA concluded that immigration judges have jurisdiction to determine whether an individual previously designated an unaccompanied alien child, but who turned 18 years old before filing an asylum application, no longer qualified as an unaccompanied minor (*J.O.P.*

v. U.S. Department of Homeland Security 2020b). If the immigration judge made such a finding, the BIA held that the TVPRA's initial jurisdiction provision for asylum officers no longer applied and the immigration court had sole jurisdiction over the application (*Matter of M-A-C-O-* 2018). The 2019 Redetermination Memo clarified that *Matter of M-A-C-O-* (2018) does not divest USCIS of its authority to determine whether an application was filed by an unaccompanied minor, which resulted in both immigration judges and USCIS asylum officers having the authority to determine jurisdiction over a given application. The 2019 Redetermination Memo stated that it would return to making independent factual inquiries in all cases in order to determine whether the individual met the unaccompanied alien child definition on the date they filed the asylum application. The memorandum stated in footnote 5 that "if EOIR has explicitly determined that USCIS does not have jurisdiction over an asylum application because it is not one filed by an unaccompanied minor, the asylum officer will defer to that determination" (*J.O.P. v. U.S. Department of Homeland Security* 2020b, 5). Finally, the memorandum stated that its new procedures apply to "any USCIS decision issued on or after the effective date" of the memorandum (*J.O.P. v. U.S. Department of Homeland Security* 2019, 374; *J.O.P. v. U.S. Department of Homeland Security* 2020a, 45).

Under the 2019 Redetermination Memo, an individual originally designated as an unaccompanied alien child who relied on the 2013 Kim Memo could be declined an asylum interview when the USCIS redetermined that the applicant did not qualify as an unaccompanied minor at the time he filed an application. Under the prior rule, individuals determined to be unaccompanied minors by CBP or ICE had two opportunities to present their claims on the merits: first, through the USCIS process and again, if necessary, in an immigration court (*J.O.P. v. U.S. Department of Homeland Security* 2019). Under the new policy, some individuals were no longer eligible to participate in USCIS asylum proceedings because by the time they applied for asylum they had turned eighteen years old or had been reunited with a parent or guardian. Under the new rules also, an individual previously determined to be an unaccompanied alien child and who applied for asylum outside of the one-year filing deadline could also lose all right to asylum because of the one-year bar from which he believed he was exempt.

Litigation on the 2019 Redetermination Memorandum

The 2019 Redetermination Memo was the subject of litigation in three related cases of *J.O.P. v. U.S. Department of Homeland Security* filed in 2019, 2020a, and 2020b. Plaintiffs in that case entered the United States as unaccompanied minors and later filed asylum applications before the USCIS.

At the time they filed their applications, they were 18 years or older or were already reunited with their parents or legal guardian in the U.S. because they relied on the 2013 Kim Memo of not rescinding unaccompanied minor status (*J.O.P. v. U.S. Department of Homeland Security* 2019). They brought a class action against the Department of Homeland Security, alleging that the 2019 Redetermination Memo violated the Administrative Procedure Act and Due Process Clause of the U.S. Constitution (*J.O.P. v. U.S. Department of Homeland Security* 2020a). Plaintiffs also requested a temporary restraining order ("TRO") against its implementation (*J.O.P. v. U.S. Department of Homeland Security* 2019). The court enjoined USCIS from implementing its 2019 Redetermination Memo. The court also restrained USCIS from rejecting jurisdiction over asylum applications of any unaccompanied minor whose application would have been accepted under the 2013 USCIS Kim Memo (*J.O.P. v. U.S. Department of Homeland Security* 2019). The district court later converted the TRO into a preliminary injunction (*J.O.P v. U.S. Dep't of Homeland Sec.* 2019).

USCIS's Deference to Immigration Judges' Jurisdictional Determinations

In *J.O.P. v. U.S. Department of Homeland Security* (2019), the District Court of the District of Maryland granted preliminary injunction to restrain USCIS from deferring to an immigration judge's jurisdictional determinations. The court pointed out that the 2019 Redetermination Memo likely violated the APA because the agency failed to go through "required notice-and-comment procedures" and "failed to consider reliance interests created by the 2013 Kim Memo" (*J.O.P. v. U.S. Department of Homeland Security* 2019, 376). Under the APA, legislative rules must go through notice-and-comment rulemaking before they become effective (*Children's Hosp. of the King's Daughters, Inc. v. Azar* 2018; *J.O.P. v. U.S. Department of Homeland Security* 2020a). This requirement does not apply to interpretive rules (*Children's Hosp. of the King's Daughters, Inc. v. Azar* 2018, 620). A rule is "legislative" or "substantive" and not "interpretive" if it: (1) results in a "substantive change in existing law or policy" (*Children's Hosp. of the King's Daughters, Inc. v. Azar* 2018, 620; *J.O.P. v. U.S. Department of Homeland Security* 2020a, 60); (2) affects "individual rights and obligations" (*Chrysler Corp. v. Brown* 1979, 302; *Morton v. Ruiz* 1974, 232); or (3) are issued by agencies "pursuant to statutory authority and which implement the statute" (*Chen Zhou Chai v. Carroll* 1995, 1340). Because the new policy did not go through a notice-and-comment procedure, the court considered whether the policy was a legislative or interpretive rule.

The court held that the 2019 Redetermination Memo was legislative in nature because the policy was inconsistent with prior agency policy and resulted in a substantive change in existing law or policy (*J.O.P. v. U.S. Department of Homeland Security* 2020a). Under the new policy, USCIS officers must determine whether an individual met the unaccompanied minor definition on the date the individual filed an asylum application instead of adopting the unaccompanied minor status determination made by another federal agency (*J.O.P. v. U.S. Department of Homeland Security* 2019). Also, for USCIS to accept jurisdiction over plaintiffs' asylum applications, they had to file those applications before they turned eighteen years old or before they were reunited with a parent or guardian. The new policy further retroactively affected the rights of plaintiffs by taking away their exemption from the one-year filing deadline. Pursuant to the deferral policy of the 2019 Memo, asylum officers were required to defer to an immigration judge's jurisdictional determination. The rule was also legislative in nature because USCIS issued it pursuant to the agency's statutory authority under the TVPRA to implement the Act (*Chen Zhou Chai v. Carroll* 1995).

The district court in *J.O.P. v. U.S. Department of Homeland Security* (2020b) later granted plaintiffs' motion to convert the TRO into a preliminary injunction. The court also ordered USCIS to "retract any adverse decision already rendered in an individual case" by applying the 2019 Redetermination Memorandum within one week following entry of its order, and reinstate consideration of such a case by applying the 2013 Kim Memorandum (*J.O.P. v. U.S. Department of Homeland Security* 2020, 5).

Final Rule of the Department of Health and Human Services ("HHS") and the Department of Homeland Security ("DHS")

Various other government rules and regulations were not spared from controversy. Aside from the litigation surrounding the 2019 USCIS Redetermination Memorandum, litigation surrounding the *Flores* Settlement Agreement reached federal courts, this time concerning the rules issued by DHS and HHS with the intent to terminate the *Flores* Agreement.

The Final Rule—DHS and HHS Regulations

The 1997 *Flores* Settlement terminates after the government publishes final regulations implementing it. In 2001, the parties modified the Settlement to provide that it would terminate 45 days after defendants' published final regulations implementing it. The government, however, did not publish regulations until August 2019. In August 2019, DHS and HHS jointly issued a final rule entitled "Apprehension, Processing, Care, and Custody of Alien Minors and Unaccompanied Alien Children" ("Final Rule"). The Final Rule aimed to terminate the *Flores* Settlement. It consisted of two sets of regulations issued by DHS and by HHS. The DHS regulations covered the apprehension and processing of both unaccompanied and accompanied minors and the care and custody of accompanied minors. The HHS regulations addressed the care and custody of unaccompanied minors. The new regulations replicated the *Flores* Settlement's protections for unaccompanied minors but significantly reduced the protections for accompanied minors detained with a family member or guardian ("accompanied minors"). While the HHS regulations pertaining to unaccompanied minors complied with the Settlement, the DHS regulations on accompanied minors departed significantly from the Settlement. Although the *Flores* Agreement required that minors who were not released must be transferred to state-licensed programs, the DHS regulations both limited the circumstances for release of accompanied minors and allowed ICE to operate family detention centers under internal standards without state oversight (*Flores v. Rosen* 2020).

The two cases of *Flores v. Barr* (2019) and *Flores v. Rosen* (2020) disputed provisions in the Final Rule. In *Flores v. Barr* (2019), the district court concluded that the Final Rule as a whole was inconsistent with the Agreement, granted plaintiffs' motion to enforce the *Flores* Settlement, and denied the government's motion to terminate the Agreement (*Flores v. Barr* 2019). It also entered a permanent injunction prohibiting enforcement of the entire Final Rule and denied the government's request to "sever the new regulations into valid and invalid portions" (*Flores v. Rosen* 2020, 730). On appeal, the Ninth Circuit in *Flores v. Rosen* (2020) held that the provisions of the new regulations relating to unaccompanied minors were consistent with the *Flores* Agreement and may take effect, with two exceptions. The Ninth Circuit affirmed the district court in part and reversed in part, holding that with respect to the HHS regulations: (1) the provision allowing placement of minors in secure facility upon determining that they were "a danger to self or others" significantly deviated from the *Flores* Agreement; (2) the provision granting minors a bond hearing before an independent HHS hearing officer instead of an immigration judge was not material departure from *Flores* Agreement; and (3) the provision requiring minors to opt-in rather than opt-out the right to a bond hearing was inconsistent with the *Flores* Agreement. The Ninth Circuit also affirmed the district court's order enjoining the provisions relating to accompanied minors that deviated from the Agreement. The Ninth Circuit held, as inconsistent with the Flores Agreement, the DHS regulations regarding release of accompanied noncitizen minors and the licensed facilities where noncitizen minors can be temporarily placed. The Ninth

Circuit concluded that the Agreement was not terminated by the adoption of the regulations (*Flores v. Rosen* 2020).

One of the provisions disputed in the HHS regulations concerned the placement of minors in secure facilities. The *Flores* Settlement provides that a minor may be held in a secure facility (e.g., state or county juvenile detention facility) whenever it determines that a minor: (1) is charged with a crime or is the subject of delinquency proceedings; (2) committed or threatened to commit violence while in government custody; (3) engaged in "unacceptably disruptive conduct" (e.g., drug or alcohol abuse) while in a licensed program; (4) is an escape-risk; or (5) must be held in a secure facility for the minor's own safety (e.g., when the government has reason to believe a particular minor may be abducted by a smuggler") (*Flores v. Rosen* 2020, 732). Mirroring the Settlement, the HHS regulations allowed placement of a minor in a secure facility in the first three circumstances listed in the Agreement. The HHS regulations, however, substituted two additional circumstances in which a minor may be placed in a secure facility: "(4) if a licensed psychologist or psychiatrist determines that the [minor] poses a risk of harm to self or others; or (5) if the minor is a "otherwise a danger to self or others" (*Flores v. Rosen* 2020, 732). The Ninth Circuit agreed with the district court that the fifth circumstance allowing placement of a minor in a secure facility upon an agency determination that the minor is "otherwise a danger to self or others" significantly deviated from and was inconsistent with the *Flores* Settlement.

Another provision related to bond hearings. The *Flores* Settlement provides that a minor in deportation proceedings under government custody shall be granted a bond hearing before an immigration judge, unless the minor indicated on the Notice of Custody Determination form that they refused such a hearing (*Flores v. Sessions* 2017a). The HHS regulations also provided unaccompanied minors with an opportunity for a bond hearing before an HHS adjudicator instead of an immigration judge. The Ninth Circuit held that the HHS regulation granting a bond hearing before an independent HHS hearing office was consistent with the *Flores* Agreement (*Flores v. Rosen* 2020). Shifting bond redetermination hearings for unaccompanied minors from immigration judges under the Department of Justice to independent HHS adjudicators was permissible under the *Flores* Settlement since the transfer did not diminish the minors' due process rights. Another provision in the HHS regulations required unaccompanied minors in secure or staff-secure placements to request a bond hearing instead of automatically providing them a hearing unless they refuse. These were inconsistent with the *Flores* Settlement. The Ninth Circuit in *Flores v. Rosen* (2020) affirmed the district court in declining to terminate those portions of the *Flores* Settlement covered by the HHS regulations. The court held that the *Flores* Settlement remained in effect, notwithstanding the overlapping HHS regulations.

Trump's Family Separation Policy

To deter border crossings from Central America, the Trump Administration implemented a policy of separating families at the United States–Mexico border through a pilot program beginning in July 2017 (*A.P.F. v. United States* 2020). Pursuant to this policy, government officials targeted families for prosecution, separated children from parents, classified the children as UAC, and sent the children across the country without documenting the familial relationship (*A.P.F. v. United States* 2020). On April 6, 2018, the administration of former President Donald J. Trump began implementing a formal "zero tolerance policy" on unauthorized immigration (*Citizens for Responsibility and Ethics in Washington ("CREW") v. U.S. Department of Homeland Security ("DHS")* 2019, 37).

Under the new policy, the administration ended its earlier practice of placing aliens apprehended at the border in civil immigration proceedings. It started "systematically detaining and criminally prosecuting" suspected illegal immigrants for unlawful entry into the country (*CREW v. DHS* 2019, 37). Because minor children could not be held in criminal custody with adults, the DHS also began "systematically separating families apprehended together when attempting to enter the country" (*CREW v. DHS* 2019, 37). While adult family members were placed in criminal custody, DHS deemed the minor children to be UAC and placed them in the custody of ORR using "a poorly-documented interagency process" that resulted in parents and family members being "completely cut off from, and unable to communicate with, their separated children, for weeks—sometimes months—at a time" (*CREW v. DHS* 2019, 37).

Former DHS officials in the agency's Office for Civil Rights and Civil Liberties raised alarm regarding DHS's recordkeeping failures but were ignored (Pelley 2018; Shuchart 2018). The agency conceded in a report that it "was not fully prepared to implement" the policy "or to deal with some of its after-effects" (Dept. of Homeland Security, Office of the Inspector General 2018, 4) ("DHS-OIG Report")—an understatement due to the "significant failures identified in subsequent reports at all levels of the implementation process" (*CREW v. DHS* 2019, 40).

While the Trump administration was implementing its zero tolerance policy, a federal district court enjoined this practice in *Ms. L. v. U.S. Immigration & Customs Enf't* (2018) after recognizing its likely unconstitutionality. The U.S. District Court for the Southern District of California entered a preliminary injunction ordering DHS to stop separately detaining parents and their children, to immediately "facilitate regular communication" between detained parents and their separated children, and to reunite the detained parents with their children within 30 days (*Ms. L. v. U.S. Immigration &*

Customs Enforcement 2018, 1149–1150). DHS was unable to comply with the court's order within 30 days. Reports prepared by the U.S. Government Accountability Office ("GAO") (2018) and DHS's Office of Inspector General (2018) following the end of mandatory separations described a wide range of deficiencies in DHS's implementation of the policy, including in the agency's recordkeeping practices associated with family separations.

The "significant public backlash" to the zero tolerance policy and the thousands of family separations the Trump administration conducted in just a few months eventually led President Trump to issue an executive order on June 20, 2018, directing DHS to stop separating families apprehended at the border (*CREW v. DHS* 2019, 37). In total, the United States separated thousands of families pursuant to this policy. Several cases were filed to hold accountable various government officials implementing Trump's family separation policy under various laws. The 2019 case of *Citizens for Responsibility and Ethics in Washington ("CREW") v. U.S. Department of Homeland Security ("DHS")* was an action filed under the Administrative Procedure Act alleging that the DHS violated the Federal Records Act ("FRA") by maintaining a deficient records management program. The two cases of *Mejia-Mejia v. U.S. ICE* (2019) and *K.O. v. U.S. Immigration and Customs Enforcement* (2020) were filed based on the Supreme Court case of *Bivens v. Six Unknown Fed. Narcotics Agents* (1971) that recognized an implied cause of action for money damages against federal government officials accused of Fourth Amendment constitutional violations. The 2020 case of *A.P.F. v. United States* was a private action under the Federal Tort Claims Act ("FTCA").

DHS's Failure to Maintain Records on Family Separation — Reviewable Actions Under the Administrative Procedure Act

In the case of *CREW v. U.S. DHS* (2019), plaintiff immigrant advocacy groups brought action under Administrative Procedure Act alleging that the DHS violated the Federal Records Act ("FRA") by maintaining "deficient records management program," failing to create records "sufficient to link migrant children to adult companions with whom they were apprehended at border," and failing to create records of agency policy and decisions (*CREW v. DHS* 2019, 37). Plaintiff groups moved for preliminary injunction and the government moved to dismiss. The U.S. District Court for the District of Columbia granted the government's motion to dismiss. The court held, among others, that DHS's alleged failure to: (1) create records, (2) maintain sufficient agency-wide records management program, and (3) create records documenting its decision-making process when implementing and rolling back the zero tolerance immigration policy were not discrete "final agency actions" that can be judicially reviewed under the APA (*CREW v. DHS* 2019,

38). The court explained that the Federal Records Act is a collection of statutes that "govern the creation, management and disposal of federal records"
(*Armstrong v. Bush* 1991, 284). It aims to ensure the proper creation and
preservation of the records of the Federal Government's policies and trans-
actions (44 U.S.C. § 2902; *CREW v. DHS* 2019). The National Archives &
Records Administration ("NARA") (2016, 2018) issued two records management inspection reports on DHS and CBP records management programs that
identified numerous deficiencies in their records management.

The district court described what would be a reviewable agency action
under the APA (5 U.S.C. § 551(13)). When challenging the failure of an
agency to act, a plaintiff must challenge a "discrete agency action" and cannot make "a broad programmatic attack" on an agency's compliance with a
statutory scheme (*Lujan v. Nat'l Wildlife Fed'n* 1990, 891; *Norton v. S. Utah
Wilderness Alliance* 2004, 64). Courts were not authorized by the APA to
"enter general orders compelling compliance with broad statutory mandates"
(*Cobell v. Norton* 2004, 472; *Cobell v. Kempthorne* 2006, 305; *CREW v.
DHS* 2019, 49; *Norton v. S. Utah Wilderness Alliance* 2004, 66). The district
court dismissed the case because the FRA provided only a "broad statutory
mandate" for DHS to follow (*CREW v. DHS* 2004, 51). DHS's failure to
comply with the FRA or its implementing regulations' general requirements
was a deficiency in complying with a broad statutory mandate that "lacked
the specificity requisite for agency action" (*CREW v. DHS* 2004, 51; *Norton
v. S. Utah Wilderness Alliance* 2004, 66).

Propriety of a Bivens Action Based on Trump's Family Separation Policy

The propriety of a lawsuit based on 42 U.S.C. §1983 against federal government officials for specific Constitutional violations was settled in the case
of *Bivens v. Six Unknown Fed. Narcotics Agents* (1971). U.S. Congress
provided a damages remedy to plaintiffs whose constitutional rights were
violated by state officials by enacting 42 U.S.C. §1983 but did not provide
any corresponding remedy for constitutional violations by federal agents
(*Ziglar v. Abassi* 2017). In *Bivens v. Six Unknown Fed. Narcotics Agents*
(1971) ("*Bivens*"), the Supreme Court recognized an implied cause of action
for money damages against federal government officials accused of Fourth
Amendment constitutional violations—those who, acting under color of federal authority, committed an unconstitutional search or seizure. In *Davis v.
Passman* (1979) and *Carlson v. Green* (1980), the Supreme Court extended
the *Bivens* cause of action to allow for money damage claims under the Fifth
and Eighth Amendments. The Supreme Court authorized implied causes of
action for individual damages for only two other species of constitutional

violation: *first,* a claim of gender discrimination in violation of the Fifth Amendment (*Davis v. Passman* 1979); and *second,* a claim of cruel and unusual punishment in violation of the Eighth Amendment (*Carlson v. Green* 1980). To date, the Supreme Court has "never extended its holdings in these two cases beyond their context" (*Mejia-Mejia v. U.S. ICE* 2019, 4). For example, it declined to extend *Davis v. Passman* (1979) to discrimination suits against military officers (*Chappell v. Wallace* 1983), or to extend its Eighth Amendment holding in *Carlson v. Green* (1980) involving federal officials in federal prisons, to include suits against operators of private prisons (*Correctional Servs. Corp. v. Malesko* 2001; *Minneci v. Pollard* 2012). In 30 years of Bivens jurisprudence, the Supreme Court has "extended its holding only twice to different contexts" (*Correctional Servs. Corp. v. Malesko* 2001, 70). Beyond the two exceptions recognized in *Davis v. Passman* (1979) and *Carlson v. Green* (1980), "expanding the Bivens remedy is now considered a disfavored judicial activity" and the Supreme Court "has consistently refused to extend Bivens to any new context or new category of defendants" (*Ziglar v. Abassi* 2017, 1857). Since then, the Court has declined to extend *Bivens* and to find new implied damages remedies ten times (*Hernandez v. Mesa* 2020; *Ziglar v. Abbasi* 2017).

A court faced with a request to extend *Bivens* to a new constitutional cause of action must make a two-step inquiry (*Hernandez v. Mesa* 2020). *First,* the court must inquire whether the request involves a claim that arises in a "new context" or involves a "new category of defendants" distinct from those in any of the three Supreme Court decisions that recognized Bivens actions (*Hernandez v. Mesa* 2020, 743). *Second,* if the claim would extend *Bivens* to a new context, the court must then "ask whether there are any 'special factors that counsel hesitation' about granting the extension" (*Chappell v. Wallace* 1983, 298–299; *Hernandez v. Mesa* 2020, 743; *Ziglar v. Abassi* 2017, 1857). The Supreme Court has rejected the request when one or more "special factors" give "reason to pause before applying *Bivens* in a new context or to a new class of defendants" (*Hernandez v. Mesa* 2020, 743). Although the Supreme Court has not explicitly defined these "special factors," that standard is deferential to Congress—the special factor must cause a court to hesitate before deciding whether it was "well suited" to weigh the net benefits of allowing the damages suit through a *Bivens* action (*Ziglar v. Abassi* 2017, 1858). *Finally,* the Judiciary would likely not allow a new *Bivens* cause of action if there is an alternative remedial cause of action (*Hernandez v. Mesa* 2020; *Ziglar v. Abbasi* 2017). For instance, the District Court for the District of Arizona recognized an alternative remedial action against Trump's family separation policy through a private action based on the Federal Tort Claims Act in *A.P.F. v. United States* (2020).

The issue of whether a *Bivens* money damages action could be filed against officials responsible for implementing Trump's family separation policy were raised in *Mejia-Mejia v. U.S. ICE* (2019) and *K.O. v. U.S. Immigration and Customs Enforcement* (2020).

In *Mejia-Mejia v. U.S. ICE* (2019), Guatemalan citizens Mejia-Mejia and her 7-year-old son, D.M., entered the United States to seek asylum on May 19, 2018. CBP agents immediately detained Ms. Mejia-Mejia and D.M., separated them, and took D.M. to a shelter for unaccompanied minors. Ms. Mejia-Mejia passed her credible fear interview and was released from detention on June 15, 2018. On June 19, Ms. Mejia-Mejia filed both a civil complaint and a motion for a temporary restraining order seeking immediate reunification with D.M. On June 22, 2018, the Office of Refugee Resettlement voluntarily released D.M. to Ms. Mejia-Mejia. The defendants argued that Mejia-Mejia's damages claims require recognition of a new implied constitutional cause of action under *Bivens v. Six Unknown Fed. Narcotics Agents* (1971), and that *Bivens* claims should not be expanded to this context. They also asserted absolute and qualified immunity.

In *K.O. v. U.S. Immigration and Customs Enforcement* (2020), plaintiffs were minor non-United States citizen children who, after arriving in the United States, were forcibly separated from their parents by agents of the DHS, CBP, ICE, or USCIS (*K.O. v. U.S. Immigration and Customs Enforcement ("ICE")* 2020). Siblings 9-year-old K.O. and 17-year-old E.O. Jr. arrived in Texas with L.J., their mother. Upon apprehension by border patrol agents, they were separated from each other and taken to different holding cells. The mother was placed in criminal custody, indicted for illegal entry, and sentenced to time served after pleading guilty. She was then detained in civil immigration custody. The siblings were later released to their father in Massachusetts. In June 2018, after establishing credible fear that the mother would be persecuted if forced to return to Guatemala, she was released and reunited with her family in Massachusetts. The other plaintiff, Guatemalan 11-year-old C.J., entered the United States in 2018 in El Paso, Texas along with his father F.C. Upon apprehension, they sought asylum based on threats from organized crime working with the police in Guatemala. The father was separated from his son and brought to a criminal court and prosecuted for illegal entry. After being separated for over a month, the government later reunited father and son at an immigration facility in Port Isabel, Texas. They brought, through their parents, class action against current and former government employees, in their individual capacities, asserting claims under *Bivens v. Six Unknown Named Agents of Fed. Bureau of Narcotics* (1971) based on alleged violation of their Fourth and Fifth Amendment rights.

In both cases, the District Court of the District of Columbia granted the defendants' motions to dismiss. The court in *Mejia-Mejia v. U.S. ICE* (2019) stated there was no statutory basis for the money damages sought by Mejia-Mejia, that Mejia-Mejia's claims presented a "new context" not recognized by the U.S. Supreme Court, and that "special factors" in Mejia-Mejia's claims "counseled hesitation," precluding the court from recognizing them as new *Bivens* claims (*Mejia-Mejia v. U.S. ICE* 2019, 4). In *K.O. v. ICE* (2020, 366–367), the court also concluded that "special factors" gave the Court "reason to pause." The court in both cases pointed to a number of special factors counseling hesitation in allowing a *Bivens* action. According to the court, *Bivens* suits were not the appropriate mechanism to litigate objections to general government policies (*Correctional Servs. Corp. v. Malesko* 2001; *K.O. v. ICE* 2020; *Mejia-Mejia v. ICE* 2019). *Bivens* claims have historically been brought against individuals—a police officer, a supervisor, or a federal prison guard—who engaged in personal misconduct in a "direct and particularized interaction" with a plaintiff, not against individuals who have applied a general policy that affected plaintiffs (*Mejia-Mejia v. ICE* 2019, 4–5).

The district court surmised that if the courts were to entertain challenges to Executive Branch policies through personal lawsuits against government officials, the discovery required to gain details on individual defendants' motivations could "dampen the candor of conversations and advice" of executive branch officials (*Mejia-Mejia v. U.S. ICE* 2019, 5). Given the thousands of asylum seekers and many others involved in the immigration system, allowing individual capacity damages claims risked "a torrent of new litigation that could burden both the Executive Branch and the judiciary" (*Wilkie v. Robbins* 2007, 562) and prevent officials "from devoting the time and effort required for the proper discharge of their duties" (*Mejia-Mejia v. U.S. ICE* 2019, 5; *Ziglar v. Abassi* 2017, 1860). Due to these potential consequences, courts "rightly hesitate" before "unilaterally creating such broad new categories of liability" (*Mejia-Mejia v. U.S. ICE* 2019, 5). The district court gave two additional reasons why a *Bivens* claim was inappropriate, namely, that the Executive Branch's action in controlling the movement of people and goods across the border between the United States and Mexico implicated an element of national security (*Hernandez v. Mesa* 2020). Also, alternative methods of relief were available to the plaintiffs to challenge the constitutionality of these kinds of government action such as actions for declaratory and injunctive relief against the relevant agencies and government officials in their official capacities, claims under the Administrative Procedure Act or under the Asylum and Withholding of Removal Statutes or the Convention against Torture (*K.O. v. ICE* 2020).

COVID-19 Pandemic, 42 U.S.C. §265, and Centers for Disease Control Orders

Since 1893, federal law has provided federal officials with the authority to stem the spread of contagious diseases from foreign countries by prohibiting the introduction of persons and property from such countries (Act of February 15, 1893). Under 42 U.S.C. §265 ("§265"), whenever the Surgeon General determines that due to the existence of any communicable disease in a foreign country, there is serious danger of its introduction into the U.S. by the entry of persons or goods from that country, the Surgeon General has the power to prohibit entry of persons and property from such countries to avert this danger (*P.J.E.S. by and through Escobar Francisco v. Wolf* 2020). In 1966, the Surgeon General's §265 authority was transferred to HHS, which delegated the authority to the Centers for Disease Control in 2001.

On March 24, 2020, as the COVID-19 virus spread throughout the U.S., the CDC issued a new regulation based on §265, establishing a procedure for suspending the introduction of persons from designated countries (85 Fed. Reg. 16559–01, 2020) ("Interim Rule"). The Interim Rule created Section 71.40 to enable the CDC Director to suspend the introduction of persons into the United States (*P.J.E.S. by and through Escobar Francisco v. Wolf* 2020). The CDC's Interim Rule was made effective immediately without advance notice and comment. The CDC reasoned that the national emergency caused by COVID-19 made it impracticable and contrary to the public health and interest to delay implementation until after a full public notice-and-comment process (85 Fed. Reg. 16565). The CDC also exempted U.S. citizens and lawful permanent residents from the application of the Interim Rule.

Pursuant to the Interim Rule, the CDC Director issued an order effective for 30 days suspending the introduction of persons traveling from Canada or Mexico (regardless of their country of origin) into a land Port of Entry ("POE") or Border Patrol station at U.S. borders with Canada and Mexico (85 Fed. Reg. 17060–02, 2020) ("March Order") (*P.J.E.S. by and through Escobar Francisco v. Wolf* 2020, 504). The CDC Director then requested the DHS to implement the March Order. The March Order was extended for 30 days in April (85 Fed. Reg. 22424–01, 2020) ("April Order") and again in May (85 Fed. Reg. 31503–02, 2020) ("May Order"). The CDC Director requested the DHS to continue to implement the March and April Orders, noting that the CDC Order mitigated the public health risk by significantly reducing the population of covered aliens detained aggregately in POEs and Border Patrol stations (*P.J.E.S. by and through Escobar Francisco v. Wolf* 2020). DHS agents were instructed to transport covered aliens to the nearest POE and immediately return them to their point of transit, whether Mexico or Canada. The CDC Orders did not exempt unaccompanied alien children from forcible expulsion. On September 11, 2020, the CDC published its final rule (85 Fed. Reg. 56424–01, 2020) ("Final Rule").

Litigation on the CDC Orders—*P.J.E.S. By and Through Escobar Francisco v. Wolf (2020)*

In *P.J.E.S. by and through Escobar Francisco v. Wolf* (2020), plaintiff P.J.E.S., a 15-year-old minor from Guatemala who entered the United States as an unaccompanied minor in August 2020, brought action against the Acting Secretary of Homeland Security and various other federal government officials ("Defendants" or the "Government") challenging the legality of the Final Rule and related orders of the CDC described above. Because of the Final Rule and the CDC Orders, unaccompanied minors were detained in hotels or cage-like facilities pending their expulsion from the United States. After entering the U.S. in August 2020 as an unaccompanied minor, P.J.E.S. was apprehended by CBP agents, held in custody in McAllen, Texas, and subjected to expulsion pursuant to the CDC Orders. His father lived in the United States and had a pending immigration case. P.J.E.S. alleged that he "experienced severe persecution in Guatemala" due to his father's political opinions and that his life was threatened due to his refusal to join a gang (*P.J.E.S. by and through Escobar Francisco v. Wolf* 2020, 505).

P.J.E.S. also alleged that DHS detained some unaccompanied alien children longer than the time it would have taken to transfer them to their family members or to an ORR facility. Some minors were held for days or weeks in hotels while waiting for flights back to their home countries, and others were detained in CBP facilities near the border in cage-like settings with other children. These minors also had difficulty accessing legal representation. Their problems were worsened by their unfamiliarity with the process under the CDC Orders, their inability to advocate effectively for themselves, especially when detained in custodial settings by government officers, and the fact that many did not speak English and lacked basic comprehension of the U.S. legal system. P.J.E.S. alleged that at the time he filed his motion for preliminary injunction, DHS had already expelled at least 2,000 unaccompanied alien children pursuant to the CDC Orders and by the end of October, the number of expelled unaccompanied alien children exceeded 13,000. P.J.E.S. filed an action, moving for class certification and class wide preliminary injunction. After he filed the case, the Government exempted him from the CDC Orders.

The District Court of the District of Columbia provisionally granted the motion for class certification and granted the plaintiff's motion for preliminary injunction. The D.C. district court observed that another court in the D.C. District recently examined CBP's new process pursuant to the CDC Orders where the facts were similar to the pending case. In *J.B.B.C. v. Wolf* (2020), the 16-year-old male plaintiff from Honduras, whose father lived in the U.S. with a pending asylum case, was apprehended by CBP when he entered the country near El Paso, Texas and was subject to expulsion based on the CDC Orders. At the time he filed the complaint, the plaintiff in *J.B.B.C.* had been in a hotel for five days while CBP arranged to place him on a flight to Honduras. Since his expulsion was imminent, he filed a motion for temporary restraining order that same day, presenting the same arguments in the pending case. The judge granted the TRO, finding that the plaintiff was likely to succeed on the merits. That court found that Section 265 does not grant the CDC Director the power to return or remove (*J.B.B.C. v. Wolf, et al.* 2020). After the court's ruling, the Government transferred J.B.B.C. to ORR, noting that he would no longer be subject to the CDC Order and claiming that the case was moot. The *J.B.B.C.* plaintiffs then voluntarily dismissed the case.

The D.C. district court in *P.J.E.S. by and through Escobar Francisco v. Wolf* (2020) explained that the authority of the CDC to prohibit introduction of persons does not include expulsion (*P.J.E.S. by and through Escobar Francisco v. Wolf* 2020). Expelling persons was "entirely different" from "interrupting, intercepting, or halting the process of introduction" (*P.J.E.S. by and through Escobar Francisco v. Wolf* 2020, 512). Neither Section 265 nor any of the definitions provided by the Government contained the word expel—they did not even contain synonyms of the word expel, such as eject or evict (*P.J.E.S. by and through Escobar Francisco v. Wolf* 2020; *Rotkiske v. Klemm* 2019). Since current immigration laws explicitly authorized deportation by using words such as remove and return, the court concluded that Section 265 did not include the power to remove or exclude persons who were already present in the U.S. (*P.J.E.S. by and through Escobar Francisco v. Wolf* 2020).

ICE and ORR Policies During the COVID-19 Pandemic- Guidance to Correction and Detention Facilities, Release of Minors, Fingerprinting of Sponsors, Migrant Protection Protocol

During the Coronavirus Disease 2019 ("COVID-19") pandemic that infected up to 200 million people and caused 1.5 million deaths in the United States, the CDC issued "Interim Guidance on Management of Coronavirus Disease 2019 (COVID-19) in Correctional and Detention Facilities" advising these facilities to implement measures to mitigate the risk of transmission and severity of COVID-19 infections ("CDC Guidance") (*Flores v. Barr* 2020b). On March 19, 2020, ORR distributed the "COVID-19 Interim Guidance for ORR Programs" ("ORR Guidance") to its contracted care facilities (*Flores v. Barr* 2020b, 2). ICE's Guidance on COVID-19 suspended social visitation to its three Family Residential Centers ("FRCs") where plaintiffs and their family members were held and offered virtual legal visitation.

Two related cases of *Flores v. Barr* (2020a, 2020b) challenged the policies of ORR and ICE. In *Flores v. Barr* (2020a), plaintiffs requested a preliminary injunction to enforce the *Flores* Settlement. The Central California District Court issued a temporary restraining order and ordered the ORR and ICE ("Defendants") to promptly and safely release class members of unaccompanied minors.

Safe and Sanitary Conditions and Appropriate Medical Care

In *Flores v. Barr* (2020a), the Central California District Court described the obligation of ICE and ORR under Paragraph 12A of the *Flores* Agreement to detain unaccompanied minors in safe and sanitary facilities. Assuring safe and sanitary conditions requires preventing their exposure to illnesses and injuries and providing them with basic hygiene and health needs such as soap, toothbrushes, regulated temperatures, and proper sleeping conditions (*Flores v. Sessions* 2017; *Flores v. Barr* 2019). The *Flores* Agreement also required that minors detained in licensed programs receive "suitable living accommodations," including "appropriate routine medical care, emergency health care services, screening for infectious disease within 48 hours of admission, and immunizations (*Flores v. Barr* 2019, 916; *Flores v. Barr* 2020a, *3).

The court held that plaintiffs did not show a likelihood of success on the merits of their claim against ORR. ORR appeared to substantially comply with the *Flores* Agreement. The Chief Medical Officer of the CDC approved of the ORR Guidance, noting that ORR's COVID-19 procedures actually exceeded the CDC Guidance (*Flores v. Barr* 2020b). ORR showed that it: (1) stopped placements in New York, California, and Washington (states with significant coronavirus outbreaks); (2) limited air travel to local placements; (3) required all care providers to conduct temperature checks twice each day; (4) restricted access to visitors with elevated temperature or flu-like symptoms; (5) had full-time medical staff on site; and (6) isolated anyone who either tested positive or was suspected of exposure to the COVID-19 virus. These updates in policy indicated that ORR provided "safe accommodations and medical care" to plaintiffs in its custody (*Flores v. Barr* 2020b, 5).

The district court, however, found that plaintiffs showed likelihood of success on their claim that ICE breached the *Flores* Agreement. The ICE Guidance appeared deficient because their guidelines did not provide for social distancing, increased personal hygiene, or increased testing and medical care. In ICE family residential centers, social distancing measures were not consistently implemented. Children, family members, and staff continued to spend the time in close physical proximity, and detained minors and family members had conditions that made them vulnerable to COVID-19 and/or already showed symptoms associated with COVID-19, lacked information

about COVID-19, and didn't have access to hand sanitizer, cleaning sup-
plies, personal protective equipment, and medical care (*Flores v. Barr* 2020a,
2020b). Hence, the court required continued heightened monitoring of ICE's
implementation of their health policies.

Release Without Unnecessary Delay and Efforts
Toward Release

As of March 13, 2020, ORR had 3,622 minors in custody, 1,193 of whom
were in congregate settings after having been detained for 30 days or more
(*Flores v. Barr* 2020b). As of December 31, 2019, of the 4,562 minors still in
custody, 50 percent were in custody for less than 20 days, 11.6 percent were
in custody for 31–60 days, and 11.7 percent were in custody for six months
to one year. The court discussed the obligation of ICE and ORR under the
Flores Settlement to release unaccompanied minors from custody and ensure
family reunification (*Flores v. Barr* 2020a). The court held that it was unwise
to rush the release *en masse* of unaccompanied minors—they could possibly
be infected while traveling in public transportation or if placed in homes with
infected family members (*Flores v. Barr* 2020a). The district court noted that
some delays in release by ORR were acceptable (*Flores v. Barr* 2020a).

The court in *Flores v. Barr* (2020a) did not fault ORR for exercising
caution during the initial days of the pandemic by banning the release of
unaccompanied alien children to sponsors in New York, California, and
Washington. The court pointed out that ORR rectified its blanket ban on
releasing minors from facilities in States hardest-hit by COVID-19. Hence,
plaintiffs' requested relief relating to such a ban was moot. The court also
examined the ORR policy banning release of unaccompanied alien children
with exposure to COVID-19 or to sponsor households with confirmed cases
of COVID-19. The court noted that there was no evidence showing that
medical professionals made case-by-case or individualized determinations of
a minor's eligibility for release. The court noted that implementation must be
monitored by the independent monitor and juvenile coordinator to ensure that
the policy "timely facilitates, rather than obstructs," ORR's ability to meet the
Flores Agreement's requirement of release without unnecessary delay (*Flores
v. Barr* 2020a, *7).

The court, however, found that plaintiffs had a strong likelihood of suc-
ceeding on their claim that both ICE and ORR breached the *Flores* Settlement
by failing to release minors to suitable custodians in a prompt manner and to
record their continuous efforts toward minors' release (*Flores v. Barr* 2020b).
In 2019, children in ORR custody remained in custody for an average of 66
days (Office of Refugee Resettlement 2021). ORR did not indicate why it
failed to release these minors or how many of them had sponsors. However,

some of ORR's policies resulting in delays in releasing minors to adult custodians, "appeared to be reasonably calculated" to protect plaintiffs from "harm or neglect" and to "ensure that they have an adequate standard of care" (*Flores v. Barr* 2020b, 6; *Flores v. Sessions* 2018, 18). ICE failed to record their efforts to release the minors and place them in non-secure licensed facilities as required by Paragraphs 14 and 18 of the *Flores* Settlement. In February 2020, about 3,359 minors were detained in ICE family detention facilities. More than half or 1,861 were detained for three months or longer. The district court held that any unexplained delay in releasing a child in ORR and ICE custody violated the *Flores* Settlement (*Flores v. Barr* 2020b).

Withholding Release of Unaccompanied Alien Children with a Pending Migrant Protection Protocol Case or Removal Order

The Migrant Protection Protocols ("MPP") direct the return of asylum applicants who arrive from Mexico as a substitute to the traditional options of detention and parole (*Innovation Law Lab v. McAleenan* 2019). Under the MPP, applicants who arrive from Mexico are processed for standard removal proceedings, instead of expedited removal. They are returned to Mexico and required to wait there until an immigration judge resolves their asylum claims. Immigration officers exercise discretion in returning the applicants they inspect, but the MPP is not applicable to unaccompanied minors, Mexican nationals, applicants who are processed for expedited removal, and any applicant "who is more likely than not to face persecution or torture in Mexico" (*Innovation Law Lab v. McAleenan* 2019, 506).

The district court in *Flores v. Barr* (2020a) held that ORR's policy of withholding release of unaccompanied alien children with a pending MPP case or removal order caused unnecessary delay contrary to its obligations under the *Flores* Settlement. Numerous minors with a pending MPP case or removal order remained in ORR care. Some minors remained in ORR care for months despite pending appeals of their initial removal orders under the MPP. The court stated that if removal was not "ready to take place," there was no reason why ORR should not release minors whose removal orders under the MPP are under appeal (*Flores v. Barr* 2020a, *10).

Detention of Unaccompanied Minors in ICE Family Residential Centers Due to COVID-19 Infections

On June 26, 2020, due to the spike in the rate of COVID-19 infections in ICE's Family Residential Centers and its ongoing breaches of the *Flores* Agreement, the District Court of the Central District of California in the case of *Flores v. Barr* (2020c) ordered ICE to transfer UAC who have resided at an FRC for more than 20 days to non-congregate settings through one of two means: (1) releasing minors to available suitable sponsors or other available COVID-free non-congregate settings with the consent of their parents; or (2) releasing the minors with their parents if ICE exercises its discretion to release the adults (*Flores v. Barr* 2020c, 1). ICE suddenly withdrew from the meet-and-confer process and expressed its unwillingness to "voluntarily agree to any protocol that would potentially provide for the separation of a parent and child who are currently housed together in an ICE FRC" (*Flores v. Barr* 2020c, 1). Plaintiffs filed a motion to enforce the *Flores* Settlement. The district court granted Plaintiffs' motion to enforce the *Flores* Settlement and ordered ICE to disseminate to unaccompanied alien children a Notice of Rights.

Release Without Unnecessary Delay and Maintenance
of Records Regarding Release and Efforts Toward
Family Reunification

Unaccompanied alien children remained at FRCs because of COVID-19 quarantine procedures or because they were detained with a parent who couldn't be released for various reasons (*Flores v. Barr* 2020c). As of August 17, 2020, 83 minors were detained at an FRC for 20 days or more solely because ICE would not release their parents. Non-release of an accompanying parent, however, was not a factor that prohibited a minor's release under the *Flores* Settlement, unless the parent did not consent to such release. Due to ICE's prior disastrous policy of involuntarily separating minors from their parents, the court in *Flores v. Barr* (2020c, 2) issued an injunction prohibiting the practice in its "original chaotic form." In *Ms. L. v. ICE* (2018, 1159), the court enjoined DHS/ICE from detaining parents of minor children separately from their children without determining that the parent was unfit or presented a danger to the child or unless the parent "affirmatively, knowingly, and voluntarily" declined to be reunited with the child in DHS custody. In order to comply with the *Flores* Settlement and the Court's prior orders, ICE was required to have procedures for evaluating the suitability of non-parent custodians for accompanied minors and releasing the minors to those custodians, provided there was parental consent.

The district court noted in *Flores v. Barr* (2020c) that it gave ICE ample opportunity to draft a know-your-rights protocol that would permit affirmative, knowing consent mandated in *Ms. L. v. ICE* (2018). The court explained that a notice of rights under the *Flores* Settlement was necessary to enable families to make informed decisions regarding whether to consent to the minors' release or their right not to be separated. If any minor and their parents sought to make such a choice, ICE was required to have a procedure to process that request, seek potential sponsors, and release the minor (*Flores v. Barr* 2020c). ICE was also required to provide plaintiffs with a "clear, non-coercive notice of rights and a procedure" by which they can "affirmatively, knowingly, and voluntarily" consent to the release of a child to a vetted custodian. (*Flores v. Barr* 2020c, 5).

Placement in Hotels Prior to Expulsion Under Title 42 (Hoteling Program)

On July 22, 2020, the Independent Monitor appointed in *Flores*, Andrea Ordin, and Special Expert, Dr. Paul H. Wise, filed an interim report, notifying the court about DHS's practice of temporarily housing accompanied and unaccompanied minors in hotels for multiple days, pending their expulsion under Title 42 (*Flores v. Barr* 2020d). On August 26, 2020, the Monitor filed another interim report, finding that 25 hotels across three states were used to house 660 minors between the ages of 10 and 17, 577 of whom were unaccompanied. Of the unaccompanied minors, 26 percent (126) were below 15 years old. The minors were housed in hotels an average of five days but 25 percent were detained more than 10 days, with a maximum stay of 28 days. The hoteling program was operated by ICE and its contractor, MVM, Inc. Since the March Order closing the United States' borders with Mexico and Canada to certain persons in response to the COVID-19 pandemic, the hoteling program became a full-scale detention operation for minors and families immediately preceding their expulsion under Title 42. The Independent Monitor recommended that unaccompanied minors be excluded from the hoteling program, finding that there was "no assurance" that it could provide "adequate custodial care for single minors" (*Flores v. Barr* 2020d, *2).

Unaccompanied minor plaintiffs in *Flores v. Barr* (2020d) were detained in hotels by the DHS based on CDC's Title 42 order, pending their expulsion. They asked the district court to order DHS to stop detaining minors in hotels and to comply with the *Flores* Settlement. The United States District Court for the Central District of California granted plaintiffs' Motion to Enforce (*Flores v. Barr* 2020d) and denied the government's motion for stay in *Flores v. Barr* (2020e). On appeal, the Ninth Circuit Court of Appeals also denied the government's motion for stay (*Flores v. Barr* 2020f). Meanwhile in November 2020, the U.S. District Court for the District of Columbia issued a preliminary injunction barring enforcement of the Title 42 Order as to unaccompanied minors (*P.J.E.S. v. Wolf* 2020), but the D.C. Circuit Court of Appeals later stayed the preliminary injunction pending appeal (*P.J.E.S. v. Pekoske* 2021). In February 2021, the CDC issued a notice temporarily exempting unaccompanied alien children from expulsion under Title 42

(Center for Disease Control 2021). The Ninth Circuit Court affirmed the district court's order forbidding DHS from detaining minors in hotels (*Flores v. Garland* 2021).

Placement in a Licensed Program

The district court in *Flores v. Barr* (2020d) stated that defendant government officials materially breached their duty under Paragraphs 12 and 19 of the *Flores* Settlement to place minors in licensed facilities as expeditiously as possible. The court noted that hoteling was not a licensed program because DHS's contractor, MVM, was not licensed by a state agency to provide care for children. The hoteling also did not meet the requirements of licensed programs under the *Flores* Settlement, including providing an "individualized needs assessment, educational services, daily outdoor activity, and counseling sessions" (*Flores v. Barr* 2020d, *3). The court noted that the hoteling program fully replaced licensed programs for minors in Title 42 custody for the period prior to expulsion. The court observed that ORR shelters were 97 percent vacant as the pending case of August 22, 2020, with a capacity of over 10,000 beds. All 197 unaccompanied minors hoteled in July could have been sent to ORR without making a dent in the facilities' capacity. Hoteling also exposed the minors to the dangers of COVID-19.

Safe and Sanitary Conditions

The court found that the conditions were not adequately safe and did not sufficiently account for the vulnerability of unaccompanied minors who were detained (*Flores v. Barr* 2020d). Each minor was supervised by an MVM Transportation Specialist who remained inside the room with the minor or family members. The court, however, raised concerns about the lack of qualified, specialized supervision, especially for younger, unaccompanied children. Minors were left alone with an adult who was not qualified or trained in childcare. There were no formal protocols instructing MVM Specialists on how to provide adequate care for unaccompanied minors, other than that they interact with the children by playing games or turning on the TV (*Flores v. Barr* 2020d). There were no separate standards for minors of different age groups, despite significant developmental differences and vulnerabilities of younger children.

Oversight of the hoteling program was also vague and minimal (*Flores v. Barr* 2020d). Although MVM quality control compliance specialists and ICE personnel were physically present, defendants did not provide information on their formal qualifications or whether they followed specific procedures. The detainees and MVM staff were not regularly tested for COVID-19, except before detainees departed the country. The hotels were open to the public and located in McAllen, El Paso, Phoenix, Houston, and San Antonio, which all experienced high rates of local COVID-19 transmission. ICE and MVM did not have specific protocols in place for when minors or family members who tested positive for COVID-19.

Access to Counsel

Since defendants did not provide notice to plaintiffs' counsel that the minors were being held in hotels, their lawyers only discovered the program when family members called to seek help. Lawyers had difficulty locating minors detained under Title 42 because DHS officials often were unable to provide accurate information as to where a minor was at any given moment. These lawyers often were unable to discover, locate, and contact minors detained in hotels. When attorneys were able to locate a child, ICE physically prevented them from entering the hotel and limited the minors' ability to speak to attorneys by phone. The court noted that defendants did not substantially comply with Paragraph 32 on access to counsel. The *Flores* Settlement contemplated attorneys having "near-unfettered access to minors in custody" provided they meet "certain well-established protocols" (*Flores v. Barr* 2020d, *10).

Long Periods of Detention—Challenging the Legality of Detention or Conditions of Confinement

The Immigration and Nationality Act gives the government discretion to "issue a warrant for the arrest and detention of an alien pending a decision on whether the alien is to be removed from the United States" (*Jennings v. Rodriguez* 2018, 837). The government "may release an alien on bond of at least $1,500 or conditional parole," except those detained pursuant to §1226(c). Under the law, the government is required to take custody of any alien who is inadmissible for having violated "any law or regulation of a State, the United States, or a foreign country relating to a controlled substance" (*Lopez Santos v. Clesceri* 2021, 3). Although the Act permits release on bond under certain circumstances, possession of a controlled substance conviction effectively removes the possibility of bond for a noncitizen in civil detention who is awaiting a final order of removal.

Civil detention of noncitizens for any purpose constitutes a "significant deprivation of liberty" (*Addington v. Texas* 1979, 425; *Reno v. Flores* 1993, 306). Because a statute permitting indefinite detention of an alien raises a "significant constitutional problem," the Supreme Court in *Zadvydas v. Davis* (2001, 699) read an "implicit limitation" into an immigration statute that, on its face, mandated indefinite detention (*Lopez Santos v. Clesceri* 2021, 3). Seventeen years later, the Supreme Court retreated from its earlier reasoning in *Zadvydas v. Davis* (2001). In *Jennings v. Rodriguez* (2018), the Supreme Court rejected the opinion of the Ninth Circuit that due process statutorily required a bond hearing every six months to justify continued detention under §1226(c), concluding instead that mandatory detention under §1226(c) did not have an implied limit.

Due process requires an individualized bond hearing when detention becomes unreasonable (*Lopez Santos v. Clesceri* 2021). Many courts have held that Fifth Amendment Due Process limits unreasonable detention under §1226(c) and the Due Process clause affords the detainee an individualized bond hearing when detention has become unreasonable (*De Oliveira Viegas v. Green* 2019; *German Santos v. Warden Pike Cty. Corr. Facility* 2020; *Hall v. INS* 2003; *Minto v. Decker* 2015; *Smith v. Barr* 2020). Under Seventh Circuit precedent, however, a "noncitizen who has a negligible chance of remaining in the United States" does not possess a right to "remain at large" while immigration proceedings are pending against him or her (*Parra v. Perryman* 1999, 958).

Under the Due Process Clause of the Fifth Amendment, the government has the burden to justify the detention of an immigrant at a bond hearing under §1226(a) (*Cooper v. Oklahoma* 1996; *Garcia v. Decker* 2020; *Medley v. Decker* 2019; *Linares Martinez v. Decker* 2018; *Zadvydas v. Davis* 2001) regardless of the noncitizen's length of detention (*Fernandez Aguirre v. Barr* 2019). In *Quintanilla v. Decker* (2021), the District Court for the Southern District of New York held that the government should bear the burden to deny liberty at any Section 1226(a) bond hearing, regardless of the noncitizen's length of detention. The district court disagreed with existing administrative precedent of the BIA that placed the burden of proof on noncitizens to demonstrate that they are not a danger to the community or a risk of flight in order to merit release on bond (*Joseph v. Decker* 2018).

A handful of cases filed by unaccompanied alien children tackled the issue of whether an action challenging the legality of detention as opposed to conditions of confinement can be brought through either a petition for writ of habeas corpus pursuant to 28 U.S.C. § 2241 or under 42 U.S.C. §1983 or *Bivens v. Six Unknown Named Agents* (1971). Courts in the Third Circuit and the Tenth Circuit varied in their approach. Under Tenth Circuit precedent, a prisoner who challenges the fact or duration of his confinement and seeks immediate release or a shortened period of confinement must do so through an application for habeas corpus (*Godinez v. U.S. ICE* 2020; *Palma-Salazar v. Davis* 2012). For example, a plaintiff can file a habeas corpus petition if he alleges that an immigration agency failed to comply with the law—this is a challenge to the legality of his detention and not the conditions of his confinement (*R.R. v. Orozco* 2020).

In contrast, a prisoner who challenges the conditions of his confinement (e.g., abuse, unsanitary conditions, etc.) as opposed to its fact or duration must do so through a civil rights action pursuant to 42 U.S.C. §1983 or *Bivens v. Six Unknown Named Agents* (1971) and not through federal habeas proceedings (*Betancourt Barco v. Price* 2020; *Codner v. Choate* 2020; *Palma-Salazar v. Davis* 2012; *Standifer v. Ledezma* 2011). A number of district courts in the Tenth Circuit have similarly concluded that a "request for release because of COVID-19 is essentially a challenge to conditions of confinement" and therefore habeas relief is not available under §2241 (*Aguayo v. Martinez* 2020, 2; *Betancourt Barco v. Price* 2020, 6; *Codner v. Choate* 2020, 4; *Rodas Godinez v. ICE* 2020, 2). The Third Circuit and other federal courts, however, have "seemingly condoned conditions of confinement challenges" through a habeas corpus petition (*Aamer v. Obama* 2014, 1032; *Ali v. Gibson* 1978, 975; *Daniel R.-S. v. Anderson* 2020, 4; *Woodall v. Fed. Bureau of Prisons* 2005, 242–244). The Supreme Court has "not foreclosed challenges to conditions of confinement through a petition for a writ of habeas corpus" (*Bell v. Wolfish* 1979, 526; *Preiser v. Rodriguez* 1973, 499; *Ziglar v. Abbasi* 2017, 1863).

Challenge to Conditions of Confinement Due to Possible Exposure to COVID-19

The following two cases illustrate how different district courts arrive at different outcomes in cases involving a challenge to the detained minor's conditions of confinement. In *Rodas Godinez v. United States Immigration and Customs Enforcement ("ICE")* (2020), the District Court for the District of New Mexico (in the Tenth Circuit) denied Godinez's habeas corpus petition that challenged the conditions of his confinement. The district court explained that habeas relief is available where the petitioner "is in custody in violation of the Constitution or laws or treaties of the United States" (*Rodas Godinez v. ICE* 2020, 2). In that case, Godinez, an unaccompanied minor, was transferred to the custody of the Office of Refugee Resettlement and placed in an ORR shelter near El Paso, Texas for unaccompanied migrant children (*Rodas Godinez v. ICE* 2020). When he turned 18, he was transferred to the custody of the DHS and placed in the Otero County Processing Center. In June 2019, an immigration judge terminated removal proceedings against Godinez and DHS appealed to the BIA. While detained, Godinez tested positive for COVID-19 but was asymptomatic. Godinez requested the District Court for the District of New Mexico to issue a writ of habeas corpus releasing him from detention for violation of his Fifth Amendment Due Process rights. He argued that his detention violated his due process rights under the Fifth Amendment because: (1) the conditions placed him at substantial risk of serious illness or death from COVID-19; and (2) the detention facility did not permit social distancing and did not provide for adequate hygiene violates due process (*Rodas Godinez v. ICE* 2020). The District Court for the District of New Mexico denied his writ of habeas corpus action as the inappropriate remedy for an action that challenged the conditions of his confinement, instead of the underlying legal basis for his custody or the duration of his confinement.

In another case however, another district court allowed a habeas corpus proceeding challenging the detainee's conditions of confinement. In *Daniel R.-S. v. Anderson* (2020), the District Court for the District of New Jersey (in the Third Circuit) allowed a challenge to conditions of confinement through a habeas corpus petition, pointing out that the Third Circuit and other federal courts have allowed challenges to conditions of confinement through habeas corpus petitions. In that case, El Salvadorian petitioner Daniel illegally entered the United States in June 2013 at age fifteen as an unaccompanied minor (*Daniel R.-S. v. Anderson* 2020). After his arrest at the border and transfer to ORR, he was released to the custody and care of his mother in New York. After multiple arrests and evidence of MS-13 gang membership, Daniel was taken into immigration custody pursuant to 8 U.S.C. § 1226(a) and placed in removal proceedings when he was 22 years old. Daniel was ordered removed by an immigration judge. Daniel's applications for relief from removal and appeal to the BIA were denied. He then filed a petition for review and a motion for stay of removal before the Second Circuit Court of Appeals. The Second Circuit granted the stay and the petition for review remained pending. After the Second Circuit granted a stay of removal, Daniel's request for bail was denied at a bond hearing because he was a danger to the community because of his criminal history and gang affiliation. Daniel remained detained at Essex County Correctional Facility ("ECCF" or "the jail"). Daniel filed a motion for temporary restraining order seeking immediate release from the jail. He argued that his detention is unlawful and violated his substantive due process because he entered the U.S. as an unaccompanied alien child. He also argued that the court has the inherent power to order his immediate release because he was deprived of "safe conditions and adequate care for his conditions, which cannot be remedied" (*Daniel R.-S. v. Anderson* 2020, 4; *Johnston v. Marsh* 1955, 531; *Leslie v. Holder* 2012, 634–635; *Lucas v. Hadden* 1986, 367–368; *Mapp v. Reno* 2001, 223).

The district court denied Daniel's motion after considering his claim that his exposure to COVID-19 violated his due process rights. The court explained that an immigration detainee's claim for relief based on his medical needs under the Due Process Clause must show both that he has a sufficiently serious medical need and that jail officials were deliberately indifferent to that need (*Andrews v. Camden Cty.* 2000, 228; *Daniel R.-S. v. Anderson* 2020, 4; *Farmer v. Brennan* 1994, 837; *Hairston v. Dir. Bureau of Prisons* 2014, 895;

King v. Cty. of Gloucester 2008, 96; *Natale v. Camden Cty. Corr. Facility*
2003, 581–582; *Parkell v. Morgan* 2017, 159–160; *White v. Napolean* 1990,
110). In determining whether a detainee's conditions of confinement violated
his due process rights, the courts inquire whether those conditions were punitive (*Bell v. Wolfish* 1979). The Third Circuit applies a two-part test for this
inquiry: (1) whether these conditions serve any legitimate purposes; and (2)
whether these conditions are rationally related to these purposes (*Hubbard v.
Taylor* 2008). The court held that Daniel was not entitled to release because
he was not likely to succeed on the merits of his deliberate indifference to
medical needs. Daniel at age twenty-two was not highly susceptible to the
virus and did not have any pre-existing health conditions requiring unique
medical care or special treatment. Respondents did not act with deliberate indifference to his medical needs—Daniel did not have a particularized
medical condition that was not addressed by jail officers. Daniel was properly
detained in jail pursuant and was given multiple bond hearings where he was
denied release based on his past criminal activity and alleged gang ties. The
Government also had a legitimate interest in detaining him and the jail conditions were not excessive.

Unreasonableness of Detention

In *Lopez Santos v. Clesceri* (2021), District Court for the Northern District
of Illinois held that under the totality of the circumstances, Lopez Santos's
detention was unreasonable because he was detained for eighteen months,
there was a "high likelihood of continued detention" for another eighteen
months (at least), the "penal nature" of his confinement, his valid defense
to removal, his "lengthy detention compared to the absence of incarceration
for the marijuana possession," and the "relatively minor criminal offense
for which he was being detained" (*Lopez Santos v. Clesceri* 2021, 7). In that
case, Honduran citizen Lopez Santos entered the U.S. as an unaccompanied
minor when he was 14 years old in December 2014 (*Lopez Santos v. Clesceri*
2021). Upon his arrival, he was placed in detention under the custody of the
Office of Refugee Resettlement. His asylum application was granted twice
by immigration judge Bryant on May 16, 2017 and January 14, 2020. On
appeal, the BIA upheld immigration judge Bryant's findings, but remanded,
for additional fact finding. While waiting for the decision on remand, Lopez
Santos pled guilty to misdemeanor possession of marijuana on July 1, 2019.
He was taken into ICE custody because of his prior conviction for possession
of marijuana. Since September 20, 2019, Lopez Santos was detained in ICE
custody in facilities in Kentucky and Illinois.

Meanwhile, Lopez Santos filed his petition for writ of habeas corpus. He
petitioned the Illinois district court under 28 U.S.C. § 2241 for an immediate

bond hearing pursuant to 8 U.S.C. § 1226(a) arguing that his detention was unreasonable. The district court ordered a bond hearing within thirty days, where the government was required to bear the burden of proof to justify Lopez Santos's continued detention by clear and convincing evidence. The court noted that federal courts have jurisdiction to hear a civil detainee's petition for writ of habeas corpus (*Zadvydas v. Davis* 2001, 687). The Fifth Amendment entitles aliens to due process of law in deportation proceedings (*Rodriguez Galicia v. Gonzales* 2005). Due process requires that these noncitizens have a meaningful opportunity to be heard (*Rodriguez Galicia v. Gonzales* 2005).

The District Court of the Northern District of Illinois distinguished the case of *Parra v. Perryman* (1999) where the Seventh Circuit Court of Appeals stated that a noncitizen who has a slim chance of remaining in the U.S. does not possess a right to remain at large while the immigration proceedings are pending against him or her (*Parra v. Perryman* 1999, 958). The district court adopted the reasoning and analysis of the Third Circuit Court of Appeals in *German Santos v. Warden Pike Cty. Corr. Facility* (2020). In *German Santos v. Warden Pike Cty. Corr. Facility* (2020), the Third Circuit weighed four non-exhaustive factors to determine the reasonableness of detention, namely, the duration of detention, the likelihood of continued detention, the reasons for delay, and the conditions of confinement. The Supreme Court found that detention of up to five or six months is not unreasonable because the noncitizen caused the delay in asking for a continuance (*Demore v. Kim* 2003). However, the longer the detention, the more unreasonable it becomes (*Lopez Santos v. Clesceri* 2021, 5). The Supreme Court did not set a bright-line rule justifying detention under §1226(c) after a certain number of months. Instead, it applies a traditional due process balancing test of factors (*Mathews v. Eldridge* 1976). Noncitizen detainees bear the burden of proof at immigration bond proceedings to establish that they are neither a danger to the community nor a flight risk (*Matter of Urena* 2009). After a noncitizen's detention has become unreasonable, due process requires that the citizen be afforded a meaningful and fair hearing (*Maldonado-Perez v. INS* 1989) where the government must show by clear and convincing evidence that the noncitizen is either a danger or a flight risk (*German Santos v. Warden Pike Cty. Corr. Facility* 2020; *Lopez Santos v. Clesceri* 2021). The court concluded that due process required that Lopez Santos be afforded a bond hearing at which the government bore the burden to show by clear and convincing evidence that he was a danger or a flight risk.

The District Court of the Eastern District of Virginia in *Gutierrez v. Hott* (2020) also granted the writ of habeas corpus petition filed by Guitierrez and required the government to grant him an individualized bond hearing where the government must prove by clear and convincing evidence that he is either a flight risk or a danger to the community (*Gutierrez v. Hott* 2020). In that case, Gutierrez, an unaccompanied minor from El Salvador, filed a petition for writ of habeas corpus pursuant to 28 U.S.C. § 2241, alleging that his prolonged detention in ICE custody violated his right to due process under the Fifth Amendment to the U.S. Constitution (*Gutierrez v. Hott* 2020; *Scott v. Vargo* 2014). In determining whether prolonged detention without a bond hearing violated due process, the Eastern District of Virginia applied a five-factor balancing test, namely: 1) the duration of detention; (2) whether the civil detention exceeds the criminal detention for the underlying offense; (3) "dilatory tactics employed in bad faith" by the parties or adjudicators; (4) legal errors that significantly extend the duration of detention; and (5) the likelihood that the government will obtain a final order of removal (*Bah v. Barr* 2010, 471; *Gutierrez v. Hott* 2020, 496; *Haughton v. Crawford* 2016, 9; *Mauricio-Vasquez v. Crawford* 2017, 4; *Portillo v. Hott* 2018, 708; *Urbina v. Barr* 2020, 6).

Although all five factors must be considered, the first factor is given "significant weight" due to the Supreme Court's well-documented "concerns about prolonged detention" (*Gutierrez v. Hott* 2020, 497). The court concluded that the five factors weighed "strongly in favor" of Gutierrez (*Gutierrez v. Hott* 2020, 497). With respect to the first factor, Gutierrez was detained by ICE for more than 23 months. Although there are no hard or fast parameters, courts agree that the legality of continued detention becomes questionable as it exceeds the one-and-a-half-month average and five-month maximum thresholds cited by the Supreme Court in *Demore v. Kim* (2003) (*Gutierrez v. Hott* 2020, 497). This approach also aligned with the concerns expressed in *Zadvydas v. Davis* (2001) about detention exceeding six months. At least one other court contemplated the outer limit of reasonableness, stating that "a criminal alien's detention without a bond hearing may often become unreasonable by the one-year mark, depending on the facts of the case" (*Portillo v. Hott* 2018, 707). Gutierrez's 23-month detention exceeded the 19-month detention at issue in *Urbina v. Barr* (2020), the 14-month detention at issue in *Portillo v. Hott* (2018), the 15-month detention at issue in *Mauricio-Vasquez v. Crawford* (2017), and the 12-month detention at issue in *Haughton v. Crawford* (2016), where each of the respective courts ruled in favor of the detainee's right a bond hearing. The court concluded that the five factors strongly weighed in Gutierrez's favor, since the government's interest in guarding against flight can be substantially protected even if he is given an individualized bond hearing (*Gutierrez v. Hott* 2020; *Portillo v. Hott* 2018).

Notice to Appear

In the cases of *United States v. Torres Zuniga* (2019) and *B.R. v. Garland* (2021), federal courts considered whether a Notice to Appear that was defective in either content or service affected the jurisdiction of the immigration court. In *United States v. Torres Zuniga* (2019), the District Court for the Eastern District of Virginia concluded that a defective NTA that did not indicate the time and place for hearing did not divest the immigration court of jurisdiction but was cured by the subsequent service of a Notice of Hearing ("NOH") containing the date of the hearing. In *B.R. v. Garland* (2021), the Ninth Circuit held that an improper service of an NTA can be cured if DHS later perfects service before substantive removal proceedings begin. Absent a showing of prejudice, improper service of an NTA can be cured and is not fatal (*B.R. v. Garland* 2021).

In *Pereira v. Sessions* (2018, 2110), the Supreme Court dealt with a "narrow question" of whether an NTA that does not specify either the time or place of the removal proceedings triggers the stop-time rule. The Supreme Court held that a defective NTA that does not designate the specific time or place of the noncitizen's removal proceedings is not a proper NTA under section 1229(a) and so does not trigger the stop-time rule (*Pereira v. Sessions* 2018). The District Court for the Eastern District of Virginia in *United States v. Torres Zuniga* (2019) observed that the "clear minority position" followed by few district courts interpret *Pereira v. Sessions* (2018) so that a defective NTA nullifies the jurisdiction of the immigration court (*United States v. Torres Zuniga* 2019, 659–660). The district court in *United States v. Torres Zuniga* (2019) refuted this interpretation of *Pereira v. Sessions* (2018), pointing out that jurisdiction is established by regulations (*United States v. Torres Zuniga* 2019, 661). The Ninth Circuit also held that regulations determine jurisdiction of courts (*Karingithi v. Whitaker* 2019, 1160).

Both the statute and the regulations list requirements for the contents of an NTA. The regulation requires an NTA to include specified information, such as the "nature of the proceedings," "acts or conduct alleged to be in violation of law," and "notice that the alien may be represented, at no cost to the government, by counsel or other representative" (8 C.F.R. § 1003.15 (b); *United States v. Gomez-Salinas* 2019, 4). The regulation does not require the time and date of proceedings to appear in the initial notice but they need to be included "where practicable" (8 C.F.R. § 1003.18(b). If the date and time is not contained in the NTA, the regulation permits providing notice of the time, place, and date of hearing subsequently. The statute requires inclusion of the time and place at which the proceedings will be held (8 U.S.C. § 1229(a) (1) (G) (i)). The regulations did not require that the 2008 NTA contain the date and time of Torres's hearing.

The Second, Fourth, Sixth, and Ninth Circuit Courts of Appeals, and every district court in the Fourth Circuit rejected jurisdictional attacks on an immigration court based on *Pereira v. Sessions* (2018) (*Banegas Gomez v. Barr* 2019; *Hernandez-Karingithi v. Whitaker* 2019; *Leonard v. Whitaker* 2018; *Perez v. Whitaker* 2018; *United States v. Perez-Arellano* 2018; *United States v. Torres Zuniga* 2019). The Fourth Circuit's unpublished opinions confirm a narrow interpretation of *Pereira v. Sessions* (2018) (*Leonard v. Whitaker* 2018). *Pereira v. Sessions* (2018) did not address the question of an immigration judge's jurisdiction to rule on an alien's removability. Several courts approve of the "two-step notice process," finding that jurisdiction vested in the immigration court upon the immigration court's sending of a subsequent NOH informing the alien of the date and time of his hearing (*United States v. Gomez-Salinas* 2019, 5). After *Pereira v. Sessions* (2018), the Board of Immigration Appeals issued *Matter of Bermudez-Cota* (2018) approving of that approach. The BIA held that an NTA that does not specify the time and place of an alien's initial removal hearing vests an Immigration Judge with jurisdiction over the removal proceedings so long as a notice of hearing specifying this information is later sent to the alien. The Second, Sixth and Ninth Circuit Courts of Appeals expressly approved of the BIA's two-step notice process set forth in *Matter of Bermudez-Cota* (2018) (*Banegas Gomez v. Barr* 2019; *Hernandez-Perez v. Whitaker* 2018; *Karingithi v. Whitaker* 2019).

Removal Proceedings

The following cases deal with the procedural rights and due process of unaccompanied minors placed in immigration proceedings. The federal courts in these cases explained what constituted a voluntary waiver of rights for purposes of the voluntary departure consent form that these minors signed, whether these minors have a right to a bond hearing or to government appointed counsel, what constituted ineffective assistance of counsel in removal proceedings, and what would be considered as exceptional circumstances so as to justify a reopening of immigration proceedings that was decided against an unaccompanied minor.

Rights Before Signing a Voluntary Departure Consent Form

Prior to its abolition in 2003 by the HSA and its replacement by the DHS as a successor agency, INS policies allowed an alien to consent to summary removal from the United States at his or her expense by signing a voluntary departure form (form I-274), waiving the right to a deportation hearing and all other forms of relief. INS policies on voluntary departure[1] for unaccompanied minors varied according to the age, residence, and place of apprehension of the child (*Perez-Funez v. District Director INS* 1985). For unaccompanied minor aged fourteen to sixteen, the INS gathered information on the unaccompanied minor through form I-213, notified the unaccompanied minor of the remedy of voluntary departure, and asked the child to indicate whether he or she wanted voluntary departure or a deportation hearing. For unaccompanied minors who are permanent residents of Mexico and Canada and were arrested near the Mexican or Canadian borders, the INS temporarily detained the unaccompanied minor until a foreign consulate official arrived. The unaccompanied minor was then returned to his or her home country upon requesting voluntary departure.

In *Perez-Funez v. District Director INS* (1985), plaintiff unaccompanied alien children aged 12 to 16 alleged that, upon apprehension, INS asked them to sign a voluntary departure consent form without meaningfully advising them of their rights. The District Court for the Central District of California ruled in favor of plaintiffs and granted a permanent injunction. The district court applied the *Mathews* test to resolve the procedural due process issue (*Mathews v. Eldridge* 1976). The court asserted that an unaccompanied alien child possesses substantial constitutional and statutory rights despite illegally entering the country (*Perez-Funez v. District Director INS* 1985). Under 8 U.S.C. § 1252(b), an alien has the rights to an evidentiary hearing, notice, counsel (at no expense to the government), present evidence, cross-examine witnesses, and to a decision based upon substantial evidence. An unaccompanied alien child has a right to a deportation hearing, which is waived upon signing the voluntary departure form. When unaccompanied minors waive the right to a deportation hearing, they waive the right to various forms of relief, including: (1) adjustment of status (8 U.S.C. § 1254); (2) suspension of deportation (8 U.S.C. § 1254); (3) political asylum (8 U.S.C. § 1158) or withholding of deportation (8 U.S.C. § 1253(h)(1)); and (4) deferred action status (*Perez-Funez v. District Director INS* 1985). Plaintiffs do not possess rights equivalent to those of criminal defendants because deportation proceedings are civil in nature (*INS v. Lopez-Mendoza* 1984). In deportation proceedings, various federal courts have ruled that an unaccompanied minor cannot invoke the exclusionary rule (*Perez-Funez v. District Director INS* 1985), Miranda warnings (*Trias-Hernandez v. INS* 1975), and the right to appointed counsel (*Martin-Mendoza v. INS* 1974).

The District Court for the Central District of California stated that the INS procedures on voluntary departure were "inherently coercive" and did not result in "effective waivers" because the unaccompanied minor did not understand their rights when they signed the voluntary departure form (*Perez-Funez v. District Director INS* 1985, 663). A valid waiver of any right requires that the person "fully understands the right" and "voluntarily intends to relinquish it" (*Edwards v. Arizona* 1981, 477; *Johnson v. Zerbs* 1938, 458). Here, the plaintiffs did not understand the forms and their contents. Their ages, the "stressful situation," the "new and complex" environment and laws, and the "foreign and authoritarian" interrogators made the entire process "inherently coercive" (*Perez-Funez v. District Director INS* 1985, 662).

The court surmised that "access to telephones prior to presentation of the voluntary departure form" was the "only way to ensure a knowing waiver of rights" (*Perez-Funez v. District Director INS* 1985, 664). Case law foreclosed the right of unaccompanied alien children to appointed counsel at government expense (*Martin-Mendoza v. INS* 1974, 992). Instead of providing legal counsel to unaccompanied minors, the government can provide them with the opportunity to contact a parent, close adult relative, or adult friend (*Eddings v. Oklahoma* 1982; Nolasco 2017, 2018). The district court issued a permanent injunction requiring the INS to provide all unaccompanied alien children with an updated free legal services list and a simplified rights advisal approved by the court. Before presenting the voluntary departure form, INS was required to provide all unaccompanied alien children access to telephones and the opportunity to communicate with a parent, close relative, or friend, or to an organization on the free legal services list. INS was also required to obtain a signed acknowledgment showing that it provided the unaccompanied alien child with all required notices and information.

Right to a Bond Hearing Under the Flores Settlement Agreement

One of the issues discussed in court cases pertains to the requirement for a bond hearing under the *Flores* Settlement. Since the mid-2000s, even before the increase of unaccompanied alien children into the U.S. began in 2014, American policymakers were concerned about the role of Central American gangs in forcing unaccompanied alien children out of their respective countries. Congress, along with several executive branch agencies, has spent significant resources to address the role Central American gangs play in their home countries (Seelke 2016). The most notorious of these gangs, MS-13, originated in the U.S. when Salvadoran immigrants formed the organization in the early 1990s. Deportations of suspected MS-13 members exported the problem to El Salvador where the gang operates. MS-13 is transnational in character because it still maintains its connections in the United States. President Trump used the threat posed by Central American gangs, particularly MS-13, as a pretext for a hardline approach to immigration enforcement. This filtered throughout the federal bureaucracy with agencies such as the Immigration and Customs Enforcement using gang affiliation as a justification for deportation even with flimsy to no evidence (Stern 2018). Efforts of

U.S. immigration officials to target unaccompanied alien children based on unfounded allegations of gang membership came under attack in the 2017 case of *Saravia v. Sessions* (2017).

In *Flores v. Sessions* (2017b), the Ninth Circuit considered whether subsequent statutes revoked the *Flores* Settlement, including paragraph 24A which grants every minor in deportation proceedings the right to a bond redetermination hearing before an immigration judge "unless the minor indicates on the Notice of Custody Determination form that he or she refuses such a hearing" (*Flores v. Sessions* 2017b, 869). Plaintiffs alleged that ORR detained unaccompanied alien children "for months, and even years" without providing them any opportunity to challenge the basis for their detention before an independent immigration judge (*Flores v. Sessions* 2017b, 872). The Ninth Circuit noted that the plain texts of the HSA and TVPRA did not explicitly terminate the *Flores* Settlement's bond-hearing requirement. The Ninth Circuit compared the ORR policies to the bond hearing requirement under the *Flores* Agreement (*Flores v. Sessions* 2017b, 877). *First,* ORR policies did not guarantee an unaccompanied alien child the right to present evidence, the right to legal counsel, and did not "identify any standard of proof" including evidentiary requirements (*Flores v. Sessions* 2017b, 878). The bond hearings, however, allowed minors to be represented by legal counsel, provide oral statements, present supporting evidence, and were appealable to the Board of Immigration Appeals. *Second,* the *Flores* Settlement granted minors an automatic bond hearing "unless affirmatively waived" while the ORR review process "must be affirmatively invoked" (*Flores v. Sessions* 2017b, 879).

Another case, *Saravia v. Sessions* (2017), discussed the right to bond hearings of unaccompanied minors who were previously released by ORR but rearrested by ICE. The District Court for the Northern District of California issued in 2017 a preliminary injunction requiring the government to grant a hearing before an immigration judge to any unaccompanied alien child previously placed with a sponsor but rearrested on allegations of gang activity. In this case, ICE agents implementing "Operation Matador" targeted undocumented immigrants in two New York counties (Suffolk and Nassau) allegedly connected to criminal gangs (*Saravia v. Sessions* 2017, 1178). ICE agents rearrested plaintiffs due to allegations of gang involvement from local law enforcement. Plaintiffs were previously arrested as unaccompanied minors, transferred to ORR custody, and released to either parents or sponsors because of the ORR's prior determination that they were not dangerous. Upon rearrest by ICE on suspicion of gang affiliation, they were placed in juvenile detention facilities, the most restrictive secure facility level. The district court required the government to provide the plaintiffs with notice of the basis for rearrest and an opportunity to rebut evidence in a hearing within seven days of arrest (*Saravia v. Sessions* 2017). According to the court, the venue for the hearing must be in the jurisdiction where the minor has been arrested or lives (*Saravia v. Sessions* 2017).

Defendant government officials entered into a Settlement Agreement with the plaintiffs on September 15, 2020 where the government agreed to grant Saravia and all class members a hearing before an immigration judge where they can argue that they should not be detained (*Saravia* Hearing). The *Saravia* Settlement applies to all unaccompanied alien children previously released by ORR to a sponsor but rearrested by DHS due to suspicions of gang involvement. It provides for specific procedures for a *Saravia* Hearing which must occur within ten days of the rearrest such as notice to the minor, right of the minor to select the place of hearing, the government's burden of proof to show that the minor is either a danger to the community or is a flight risk justifying his/her detention, right of the minor to hire a lawyer for that hearing, right to be released if the minor wins the hearing, and right to be placed in an available shelter if not released within three (3) days.

Right to Government Appointed Counsel at Government Expense in Removal Proceedings

One of the issues surrounding unaccompanied minors is the right to counsel at government expense during removal proceedings. The Ninth Circuit Court of Appeals in *CJLG v. Sessions* (2018) held that neither the Due Process Clause nor the INA creates a categorical right to court-appointed counsel at government expense for unaccompanied minors. Immigration judges "at a minimum" must determine: (1) whether the petitioner wants counsel; (2) a reasonable period for obtaining counsel; and (3) assess the voluntariness of any waiver (*Biwot v. Gonzales* 2005, 1094; *United States v. Cisneros-Rodriguez* 2015, 748). The failure of an immigration judge to inquire whether the petitioner wanted or knowingly waived counsel is grounds for reversal (*Nehimaya-Guerra v. Gonzales* 2006; *JEFM v. Lynch* 2016). Claims alleging an unaccompanied minor's right to government-appointed counsel in removal proceedings must exhaust the administrative process before accessing the federal courts (*JEFM v. Lynch* 2016, 1028). Right-to-counsel claims can be raised in petitions for review filed with a federal court of appeals (*Alvarado v. Holder* 2014; *Barron v. Ashcroft* 2004; *JEFM v. Lynch* 2016; *Ram v. Mukasey* 2008; *Sola v. Holder* 2013; *Zepeda-Melendez v. INS* 1984). In one case, however, the District Court for the Northern District of California allowed an unaccompanied minor's motion for attorneys' fees as the prevailing party under the Equal Access to Justice Act (*Primero Garcia v. Barr* 2020).

Sixth Circuit precedent also holds that the Fifth Amendment does not guarantee the right to counsel for aliens at civil removal hearings (*Al-Saka v. Sessions* 2018; *Lassiter v. Dep't of Soc. Servs.* 1981; *United States v.*

Silvestre-Gregorio 2020). Control over matters of immigration is a "sovereign prerogative, largely within the control of the executive and the legislature" (*Landon v. Plasencia* 1982, 34–35). Where the government "holds a hearing, develops the record, provides an interpreter, and explains the rule of law, the alien has received due process" (*United States v. Silvestre-Gregorio* 2020, 856). The Sixth Circuit stated that there is no constitutional right to a government-appointed counsel, regardless of age. If Congress wishes to add additional safeguards, then it has the power to pass legislation and appropriate funds" but the judiciary "cannot—and should not—arbitrarily change the law to achieve certain policy ends" (*United States v. Silvestre-Gregorio* 2020, 856).

Ineffective Assistance of Counsel During Removal Proceedings

In *Cardenas-Martinez v. Garland* (2021), the Fourth Circuit Court of Appeals affirmed the immigration judge's denial of asylum claim of 15-year-old Honduran, Cardenas-Martinez ("Cardenas") despite the failure of his counsel to raise competency issues during his removal proceedings. In that case, Cardenas arrived in the U.S. as an unaccompanied alien child and was released to the custody of his mother (*Cardenas-Martinez v. Garland* 2021). After he was placed in removal proceedings, he applied for asylum. Cardenas was diagnosed with epilepsy in 2014. After arriving in the United States, Cardenas was diagnosed with ADHD, anxiety, and "major neurocognitive defects," especially with respect to his "impulse inhibition, attention, and memory" (*Cardenas-Martinez v. Garland* 2021, 1). Cardenas alleged that he had been beaten in Honduras because of his disorder or disability. The USCIS denied his asylum application because he had failed to demonstrate either past persecution or a likelihood of future persecution on the basis of his membership in a particular social group.

At the removal hearing before the immigration judge, Cardenas appeared with Moss as counsel. The immigration judge conducted a colloquy to determine whether Cardenas understood the purpose of the proceeding, the possible consequences, and the roles of the various participants in the hearing. After determining that Cardenas was competent, she proceeded with the hearing. At the end of the hearing, the immigration judge affirmed his competence, finding him "clearly competent to have testified today without hesitation or doubt" (*Cardenas-Martinez v. Garland* 2021, 3). The immigration judge denied his asylum claim because he failed to demonstrate that "his life or freedom would be threatened on account of a protected ground if returned to Honduras" (*Cardenas-Martinez v. Garland* 2021, 3). Although the immigration judge "was prepared" to accept that "children with disabilities and other forms of special problems" could constitute a "particular social group,"

Cardenas did not show that any abuse he suffered was "on account of" that protected status (*Cardenas-Martinez v. Garland* 2021, 3).

The BIA dismissed his appeal, concluding that Cardenas did not establish deficient performance by his counsel or prejudice from her conduct—both required to make out a claim of ineffective assistance under *Matter of Lozada* (1988). Under *Matter of M-A-M-* (2011, 481, 484), when there are "indicia of incompetency," an immigration judge is required to make "further inquiry" to determine whether a noncitizen is competent to proceed and, if not, to "apply appropriate safeguards" to protect his rights. For example, the immigration judge may order a mental competency evaluation with the noncitizen, asking "questions about where the hearing is taking place, the nature of the proceedings, and [his] state of mind"(*Matter of M-A-M-* 2011, 480–481). On appeal, the Fourth Circuit affirmed the BIA, noting that the immigration judge "stepped into any breach created by counsel, raising the competency question and effectively overriding counsel's disclaimer of the issue" (*Cardenas-Martinez v. Garland* 2021, 6). She proceeded to conduct the very colloquy expressly approved by *Matter of M-A-M-* (2011*)* as one means of testing competency. Regardless of any shortcomings in counsel's performance, the immigration judge undertook the steps required under *Matter of M-A-M-* (2011, 484*)* when there is "indicia of incompetency."

Motion to Reopen Immigration Proceedings Based on Exceptional Circumstances

In *E. A. C. A. v. Rosen* (2021), the Sixth Circuit Court of Appeals held that based on the "totality of the circumstances," there were "exceptional circumstances" that required rescission of the *in absentia* removal order against E.A. *(E. A. C. A. v. Rosen* 2021, 504, 506). Twelve years old E.A., an unaccompanied minor from El Salvador, entered the U.S. illegally in November 2016 and was released by ORR to her mother who lived in New York (*E. A. C. A. v. Rosen* 2021, 501). Their family moved several times—to Arkansas, Memphis, and back to New York. On March 3, 2017, the U.S. DHS mailed a Notice to Appear to E.A. Through the assistance of Catholic Charities, E.A.'s request to change venue to Memphis was approved. After E.A. failed to appear at her June 6, 2018 master-calendar hearing, the immigration judge ordered her removed *in absentia*. On November 30, 2018, E.A., with the assistance of counsel, filed a motion to reopen her immigration proceedings. E.A. asserted that, based on the "totality of circumstances," "exceptional circumstances excused her failure to appear at her immigration hearing" (*E. A. C. A. v. Rosen* 2021, 502).

The immigration judge denied E.A.'s request to reopen her removal proceedings on the ground that she had failed to establish that exceptional circumstances prevented her from appearing at her hearing. On appeal, the BIA affirmed the immigration judge's denial. On petition for review before the Sixth Circuit Court of Appeals, the court held that the BIA abused its discretion when it determined no exceptional circumstances justified applicant's failure to appear at her removal hearing. The court vacated the *in absentia* order of removal and remanded for further proceedings. The Sixth Circuit explained that an immigration judge may rescind an order of removal entered *in absentia* in limited circumstances. In E.A.'s case, an order of removal entered *in absentia* may be rescinded "upon a motion to reopen filed within 180 days after the date of the order of removal if the alien demonstrates that the failure to appear was because of exceptional circumstances" (8 U.S.C. § 1229a(b)(5)(C)(i); *E. A. C. A. v. Rosen* 2021, 504). The statute defines "exceptional circumstances" as those "beyond the control of the" petitioner, such "serious illness of the alien, or serious illness or death of the spouse, child, or parent of the alien" (8 U.S.C. §1229a(e)(1)). When determining whether a petitioner's circumstances meet this standard, the immigration judge considers the "totality of the circumstances" (*Acquaah v. Holder* 2009, 335; *Denko v. INS* 2003, 723).

The Sixth Circuit held that the BIA abused its discretion by finding that E.A. did not establish exceptional circumstances justifying her failure to appear at her immigration hearing. E.A.'s mother's recent childbirth was a "serious medical condition" that supported reopening (*E. A. C. A. v. Rosen* 2021, 504). Childbirth is a serious medical event that necessitates a recovery period (*Touvell v. Ohio Dep't of Mental Retardation & Developmental Disabilities* 2005, 403). Instead of recognizing that childbirth is a serious medical condition, the BIA minimized the seriousness of childbirth and its impact on E.A.'s mother's ability to bring E.A. to Memphis. Parroting the IJ's conclusion, the BIA noted that the mother who was pregnant "knew of the hearing date" in advance and "could have contacted the Immigration Court prior to the hearing" (*E. A. C. A. v. Rosen* 2021, 505). Other circuit courts have recognized that medical conditions that a petitioner is aware of "can constitute exceptional circumstances" (*Singh v. Gonzales* 2007, 100; *Yweil v. INS* 2002, 327).

E.A.'s "young age" also contributed to the court's conclusion that exceptional circumstances exist. Under the totality of the circumstances, E.A.'s young age was an important factor in determining whether exceptional circumstances exist (*Denko v. INS* 2003, 723; *In re Meja-Andino* 2002, 536; *In re Gomez-Gomez* 2002, 528; *Reno v. Flores* 1993, 309). The cases cited by the government in support of the BIA's determination were distinguishable from the present case. In *Jimenez-Castro v. Sessions* (2018), the Sixth Circuit held that the minor petitioner's failure to appear at his hearing because his brother forgot the hearing date was not an exceptional circumstance that merited reopening his immigration case. By contrast, E.A.'s case involved "numerous impediments" that prevented her from attending her immigration hearing, including her "inability to change the location of the hearing, her inability to secure transportation from New York to Memphis, and her mother's recent childbirth" *(E.A.C.A. v. Rosen* 2021, 506).

CONCLUSION

This chapter focused on cases brought in federal courts challenging laws, procedure, and policies that affect the rights of unaccompanied minors navigating the U.S. asylum process. Although the cases do not directly deal with the grant or denial of asylum but issues concomitant to the process of asylum, the issues raised are of vital importance to UAC since these clarify their rights and substantially affect their conditions while awaiting outcomes in their asylum claims. We examine how judges decide on these issues, either expanding or constricting their rights. Analysis of federal court cases indicate that judges are constrained by law and precedent when deciding policy and procedural due process issues that reach their courts. Unaccompanied alien children challenged in federal courts several executive policies and guidelines that affected their procedural due process rights. Examples include the policies of the USCIS on determining who has initial jurisdiction over their asylum applications, regulations issued by the DHS and HHS pertaining to their custody, release, and detention, Trump's family separation policy, and ICE and ORR's policies during the COVID-19 pandemic. Federal courts examined whether legal procedures were followed in issuing these policies, whether broad executive policies should be granted deference when disallowing a damages action against executives who implemented these policies, and whether these policies complied with laws and legal precedent. Other issues related to conditions of their detention such as the availability of a writ of habeas corpus or a *Bivens* action to challenge to their conditions of confinement, their rights during removal proceedings, and whether defects in the notice to appear served on them affected the jurisdiction of the immigration court and subsequent proceedings. Examining these federal court cases provides a comprehensive picture on the range of rights and remedies granted to unaccompanied alien children whose procedural due process rights were violated in the course of their immigration proceedings.

NOTE

1. Voluntary departure is a form of relief for a qualified alien who is apprehended by immigration officials, allowing the alien to depart from the United States without an order of removal (*Perez-Funez v. District Director INS* 1985). An alien allowed to voluntarily depart concedes removability but does not have a bar to seeking admission at a port-of-entry at any time. Section 240B of 8 U.S.C. 1229c authorizes the DHS (prior to the initiation of removal proceedings) or an immigration judge (after the initiation of removal proceedings) to approve an alien's request to be granted the privilege of voluntary departure in lieu of being ordered removed from the United States. The grant of voluntary departure permits the alien to remain in the United States for a maximum of 120 days if voluntary departure is granted prior to the completion of immigration proceedings and a maximum of 60 days if granted at the conclusion of the proceedings before the immigration judge (8 CFR 1240.26(b). Failure to depart within the time granted results in a fine and a ten-year bar to several forms of relief from deportation.

Chapter 5

Judicial Decision Making at the Micro-Level

Federal Court Decisions on Substantive Law and Rights

Responding to the claim of DHS, CBP, and ICE that "Guinean extracts of birth certificates are notoriously suspect," District Judge Janis L. Sammartino, U.S. District Court for the Southern District of California stated that DHS, CBP, and ICE impermissibly relied on the generalization that all Guinean extracts of birth certificate are "notoriously suspect" in determining that N.B. is not a minor and that "the idea that the government can prejudge an entire country's documents as inauthentic *ab initio* is preposterous—it is pernicious discrimination based on a suspect classification of national origin and alienage" (*N.B. v. Barr* 2019, 11). This case illustrates how federal courts can add an additional layer of protection for unaccompanied minors by ensuring that standards and issues decided in immigration courts comply with federal case law and doctrine. However, analysis of federal court cases involving substantive issues raised by unaccompanied minors show that federal judges have at times decided similarly and at other times decided differently on the same litigated issue.

For this chapter, we utilize inductive doctrinal analysis of federal cases to determine how federal district and circuit court judges are constrained by legal precedent, the plain meaning of statutes, and the intent of the framers of statutes. Using the WESTLAW legal database that contains electronic copies of all published and unpublished court decisions, we conducted a keyword search to gather cases on UAC decided by all federal courts in the U.S. The advanced search parameters required that the term "unaccompanied alien child" appeared in the main body of the case as of 2022 (N = 293). Instead of an empirical, quantitative approach, we organized these decisions around

major issues and themes involving substantive legal issues that unaccompanied minors raised at the federal courts concomitant with or subsequent to
their asylum proceedings in immigration courts. Scrutinizing these decisions
are necessary, given that judicial decisions have the force and effect of law
and affect the rights of these unaccompanied minors as they go through the
U.S. asylum system.

We start by discussing cases that resolved the substantive issue of how to
determine the minority status of unaccompanied minors. Some minors age
out of ORR custody and are transferred to DHS. Hence, we proceeded to
discuss cases that resolved which minors who age-out of ORR custody are
eligible for placement in least restrictive settings as required under the 1997
Flores Settlement. From there, we discuss cases that raised issues pertaining
to the detention of these minors. We talk about legal standards for liability
òf officials for abuses they experienced in custodial and detention facilities,
both for sexual abuse and failure to provide them with appropriate medical
care. We also talk about the right of these minors to abortion while in custody.
Finally, we talk about cases that deal directly with asylum claims that were
brought to federal courts through petitions for review of BIA decisions. We
organized these cases based on the grounds for asylum, specifically, what
constitutes parameters of a particular social group to prove persecution or
fear of persecution.

Status as Unaccompanied Minors

One of the issues that arose in federal courts involved the process of determining the minority age of unaccompanied minors who filed asylum applications. Under the TVPRA, unaccompanied alien children should be promptly
placed in the least restrictive setting that is in the best interest of the child (8
U.S.C. § 1232(c)(2)(A)). Congress through the TVPRA also required HHS
and DHS to develop procedures to promptly determine the unaccompanied
minor's age, taking into account multiple forms of evidence, including the
non-exclusive use of radiographs (8 U.S.C. 1232(b)(4); *B.I.C v. Asher* 2016;
N.B. v. Barr 2019; *R.R. v. Orozco* 2020; *V.V. v. Orozco* 2020). Pursuant to this
mandate, HHS developed age determination procedures that allow it to make
age determinations of unaccompanied minors in ORR custody when there is
reasonable suspicion that the child is 18 years or older (*N.B. v. Barr* 2019;
Office of Refugee Resettlement 2022, § 1.6.1).

Section 1.6 of ORR's Children Entering the United States Unaccompanied
("ORR Guide") (Office of Refugee Resettlement 2022) directs ORR case
managers conducting age determinations to seek the following evidence, but
information from each category is not required: (1) documentation, such as
official government-issued documents and other reliable records indicating

date of birth; and (2) statements by individuals, including the unaccompanied alien child, who can credibly attest to the child's age (ORR Policy Guide § 1.6.2). The unaccompanied minor's uncorroborated declaration regarding age cannot be used as the sole basis for an age determination (*C.T.M. v. Moore* 2020). When other information is inconclusive, case managers may use medical age assessment procedures, such as dental maturity assessments through radiographs (*N.B. v. Barr* 2019). Processing as an adult depends on whether the medical age assessment indicates that the individual's estimated probability of being 18 or older is 75 percent or greater in conjunction with the "totality of the evidence" (Office of Refugee Resettlement 2022, §1.6; *R.R. v. Orozco* 2020, 4; *V.V. v. Orozco* 2020, 4; U.S. Immigration and Customs Enforcement 2017, §3.1.2).

Congress's mandate that radiographs not be the only basis for an age determination reflected concern about their reliability (*B.I.C v. Asher* 2016). In 2009, the Office of Inspector General for DHS released a report that recognized that radiographs of a person's bones or teeth cannot determine a specific age due to a "range of factors affecting an individual's growth," including "normal biological variation, cultural and ethnic differences, the timing of puberty, diet, genetics, health, and geography" (*B.I.C v. Asher* 2016, *5; *N.B. v. Barr* 2019, 9). The report also stated that, medical professionals "expressed skepticism" that a radiographic exam could be used to determine whether an individual has specifically attained 18 years of age but "generally agree that radiographic exams could provide a usable age range" (*B.I.C v. Asher* 2016, *5; *N.B. v. Barr* 2019, 9).

The U.S. District Courts that resolved the issue of determining the status of an asylum applicant as an unaccompanied alien child varied in their rulings.

In *C.T.M. v. Moore* (2020), the District Court for the Northern District of Texas dismissed a plaintiff's motion for TRO, explaining that defendant U.S. Customs and Border Protection officials properly considered the totality of evidence in determining that she was an adult and not a minor. In 2014, Congo citizen C.T.M.'s father misrepresented C.T.M.'s age as an adult in a U.S. visa application which was ultimately denied. On June 6, 2019, C.T.M. presented herself as a minor to immigration officials at a California port of entry and requested asylum. On November 20, 2019, ICE conducted an age assessment of C.T.M. by dental radiograph that determined that C.T.M. was an adult, and she remained in ICE custody. After C.T.M.'s counsel asked the immigration court to review her age determination, the immigration judge decided that she was a minor. Although ICE officials attempted to transfer C.T.M. to ORR custody based on the immigration judge's decision, ORR refused custody after concluding that C.T.M. was an adult. C.T.M. filed a petition for a writ of habeas corpus under 28 U.S.C. § 2241, claiming that she was an unaccompanied minor in the custody of ICE pending removal proceedings.

The district court cited the ORR Guide that allowed respondents to make an age determination when there was a "reasonable suspicion" that an unaccompanied alien is over 18 years old (*C.T.M. v. Moore* 2020, *3). The district court found that C.T.M.'s prior U.S. visa application where C.T.M.'s father misrepresented C.T.M.'s age as an adult provided reasonable suspicion to believe she was an adult. CBP officials did not violate the TVPRA or their regulations because they did not rely solely on the dental radiograph to make their age determination. In concluding that C.T.M.'s claim that she was a minor was "likely fraudulent," they relied on various evidence, including school certificates, school records, birth certificate, her U.S. visa application, and travel documents to Nicaragua (*C.T.M. v. Moore* 2020, *4). The court concluded that C.T.M. was not entitled to relief under the *Flores* Settlement because the *Flores* Settlement applied only to minors.

In the 2020 case of *Imon v. Keeton,* the District Court for the District of Arizona similarly stated that ORR validly relied on a dental radiograph that indicated an 88.5 percent probability that petitioner Imon was an adult. In that case, Bangladeshi citizen Imon was apprehended by immigration authorities in July 2018 after entering the United States without authorization. Because he asserted that he was a juvenile and possessed a birth certificate corroborating that claim, Imon was classified as an unaccompanied alien child and placed in a juvenile facility. After an age determination investigation, government officials concluded that Imon was actually an adult. Imon was then transferred to an adult detention facility. On July 16, 2019, an immigration judge ordered him removed from the U.S. and denied his application for asylum. The judge found that Imon was not credible because he submitted a fraudulent birth certificate to immigration officials and misrepresented his age in immigration court. Imon filed a petition for a writ of habeas corpus under 28 U.S.C. § 2241 and a motion for preliminary injunction. The District Court for the District of Arizona denied the motion and dismissed the petition.

The district court explained that ORR did not rely exclusively on evidence that Imon had used a fake identification document when traveling through Central America. Instead, ORR also relied on a dental radiograph, which indicated an 88.5 percent probability that Imon was an adult. The ORR Guide and the TVPRA allowed case managers to consider radiographs on a "non-exclusive basis" when conducting age determinations (*Imon v. Keeton* 2020, *8). ORR did not violate its guidelines by basing its age determination on a combination of Imon's use of false identification documents and a radiograph indicating that Imon was an adult.

In the two cases of *R.R. v. Orozco* (2020) and *N.B. v. Barr* (2019), the respective district courts ruled in favor of the unaccompanied minor seeking asylum. In the 2020 case of *R.R. v. Orozco* (2020), the District Court for the District of New Mexico discredited the reliability of dental radiograph performed on R.R. The case involved an Indian national R.R. who was apprehended by the U.S. Border Patrol after illegally entering the U.S. on April 6, 2020. Upon apprehension, R.R. claimed his date of birth was July 3, 2002. The U.S. Visit and Immigrant Status Indicator Technology ("US VISIT"), a database containing information on entrants to the U.S., documented the birthdate of R.R. as April 25, 2000. Results of a bone density exam completed by Southwest X-ray stated that R.R.'s age is "4 days less than 20 years" and "skeletal age is at least 19 years." Family members provided ICE with a picture of a Government ID card from India ("Aadhar card") and a page out of a passport that indicated R.R.'s birthdate as July 3, 2002. After considering "the totality of the evidence" including a government ID from India and a page out of R.R.'s passport indicating a 2002 birthdate, ICE determined he was an adult. During a videoconference hearing on May 13, 2020 before an immigration judge, R.R. submitted a copy of his birth certificate, the Indian government ID card, and an Income Tax ID. Relying on the bone density exam and the date of birth R.R. had given on three other occasions, the immigration judge found that R.R. was an adult. The immigration judge denied R.R.'s application for asylum and ordered him removed to India. R.R. then filed a Petition for Writ of Habeas Corpus and a Motion for Temporary Restraining Order, asking the Court to: (1) order his immediate transfer from ICE adult detention center to ORR; and (2) enjoin ICE from applying the age determination which prevented him from securing rights as an unaccompanied alien child.

The District Court for the District of New Mexico granted R.R.'s motion in part and ordered him transferred from ICE's adult detention center to ORR. The district court further ordered that R.R. be treated as a juvenile for purposes of detention and immigration proceedings until the court decided whether R.R.'s age determination will be reviewed and enjoined. The district court stated that R.R. was "likely to succeed on the merits of his claim that ICE and the immigration judge did not comply with 8 U.S.C. § 1232(b)(4) and the agencies' Policy Guidelines regarding the use of radiographs" (*R.R. v. Orozco* 2020, 8). Both ICE and the immigration judge relied on the imaging results in making their age determinations. However, the examination did not state whether it was performed by a medical professional experienced in age assessment methods, whether Petitioner's ethnic and genetic background was considered, or the probability percentage that Petitioner was a minor or an adult (*R.R. v. Orozco* 2020).

The District Court for the Southern District of California also discredited the findings of ICE regarding the age of N.B. in the case of *N.B. v. Barr*

(2019). In that case, 16-year-old Guinean citizen N.B. traveled by land to the U.S. to seek asylum as an unaccompanied alien child. Although N.B. did not have legal documents allowing him entrance to the United States, he presented an "extract" from a certified Guinea birth certificate showing his birth date as December 2001. N.B. also presented several official documents showing he was born in December 2001, including a government-issued identification card, a certified extract of a court judgment, and the certified copy of the judgment. N.B. was taken in DHS custody and placed in expedited removal proceedings pursuant to 8 U.S.C. § 1225(b)(1). The ICE Health Services Corps ("IHSC") ordered a dental x-ray examination of N.B. to determine his age. Based on the dental x-ray report, ICE concluded that N.B. would be treated as an adult because "the empirical statistical probability the subject attained 18 years of age is 93.53%." N.B. was detained in group quarters with more than 100 adult men. N.B. filed a petition for habeas corpus with the district court alleging violation of the TVPRA and implementing guidelines, the Administrative Procedure Act, the *Flores* Settlement, and his procedural and substantive due process rights. N.B. sought a preliminary injunction enjoining ICE from unlawfully detaining N.B. in custody with unrelated adults. He alleged that ICE determined that he was an adult based on the exclusive use of a dental radiograph.

The District Court for the Southern District of California granted the petition, concluding that ICE's age determination was based solely on a dental radiograph. The district court concluded that ICE's age determination was based solely on a dental radiograph in violation of the TVPRA. ICE's post hoc justifications also failed properly to consider the "totality of other evidence" probative of N.B.'s minority such as his extract of birth certificate and government-issued student identification card (*N.B. v. Barr* 2019, 10). The court also dismissed respondents' contention that N.B.'s extract of birth certificate was "fraudulent" and suspect (*N.B. v. Barr* 2019, 11). The court noted that ICE claimed that "Guinean extracts of birth certificates are notoriously suspect" without introducing "any evidence that N.B.'s extract of birth certificate in particular is in any way suspect" (*N.B. v. Barr* 2019, 11). According to the court, "the idea that the government can prejudge an entire country's documents as inauthentic *ab initio* is preposterous—it is pernicious discrimination based on a suspect classification of national origin and alienage" (*N.B. v. Barr* 2019, 11). In the absence of any indications that N.B.'s extract of birth certificate in particular was suspect or fraudulent, the court stated that ICE "impermissibly relied on the generalization that *all* Guinean extracts of birth certificate are suspect in determining that N.B. is not a minor" (*N.B. v. Barr* 2019, 11). The court stated that N.B. possessed two forms of identification showing that his date of birth was in December 2001, making him a minor (*N.B. v. Barr* 2019, 12). Not only did N.B. establish a high likelihood that respondents relied exclusively on the dental radiograph in determining his age in violation of the TVPRA, but—based on the totality of the evidence before Respondents—the radiograph itself was likely impermissible. The court concluded that N.B. had a "strong likelihood of success" on his claim that respondents unlawfully placed him in DHS custody (*N.B. v. Barr* 2019, 12).

Eligibility of Age-Outs for Placement in Least Restrictive Settings

One of the recurring issues in court litigation is the eligibility of unaccompanied alien children for placement in the "least restrictive setting" after they are transferred from ORR custody to the custody of the Department of Homeland Security once they reach 18 years old (*Ramirez v. U.S. Immigration and Customs Enforcement* 2020, 94). When noncitizen minors lacking immigration status arrive in the United States without parents or other guardians, they are designated unaccompanied alien children and are placed in the custody of ORR (*Ramirez v. U.S. Immigration and Customs Enforcement* 2021). If they are still in custody of the ORR on their eighteenth birthday, these individuals age out of HHS and ORR custody and are transferred to ICE custody. Immigrants who undergo this transfer from HHS to ORR are referred to as "age-outs" (*Ramirez v. U.S. Immigration and Customs Enforcement* 2021, 1).

Section 1232(c)(2)(B) of the Violence Against Women Act Reauthorization of 2013 ("VAWA") requires that when ICE receives custody of an age-out, it should consider placing them in the least restrictive setting, taking into account the age-out's danger to self and community and their risk of flight (8 U.S.C. § 1232(c)(2)(B); *Alam v. Keeton* 2020; *Jose L.P. v. Whitaker* 2019; *Ramirez v. U.S. Immigration and Customs Enforcement* 2021). All age-outs are eligible under 8 U.S.C. § 1232(c)(2)(B) to participate in alternative to detention programs, utilizing a continuum of alternatives based on the alien's need for supervision, which may include placing them with an individual or an organizational sponsor or in a supervised group home (*Ramirez v. U.S. Immigration and Customs Enforcement* 2020; *R.R. v. Orozco* 2020). An asylum seeker whose status as an unaccompanied minor is later disproved by DHS and who does not qualify as an age-out at the time of transfer to ICE custody is not entitled to the benefits of 8 U.S.C. § 1232(c)(2)(B), including placement in the "least restrictive setting" or alternatives to detention programs (*Alam v. Keeton* 2020, 8). Under the *Flores* Settlement Agreement, unaccompanied minors who later are emancipated by a state court or convicted and incarcerated for a criminal offense as an adult are also not considered minors (*Flores v. Lynch* 2016; *Flores v. Reno* 1997; *U.S. v. Camero-Castaneda* 2021).

DHS is required to conduct an individualized assessment of the age-out and must identify the full range of alternatives to evaluate the available setting that is least restrictive. DHS must determine what settings are actually available and which of these is the least restrictive *(Ramirez v. U.S. Immigration and Customs Enforcement* 2020). DHS and ICE also must make a variety of detention alternatives available for age-outs. Available placement for age-outs are: (1) orders of supervision for those with existing orders of removal and are under immigration court supervision; (2) recognizance for those without removal orders; (3) Immigrations and Customs Enforcement Alternatives to Detention ("ATD") program including tracking by ankle bracelet monitor, by smartphone application, or telephonic reporting; (4) ICE's Intensive Supervision Appearance Program, where outside service providers "conduct office visits, home visits, residence visits, orientation enrollment and other forms of tracking"; (5) ICE bond; and (6) ICE custody, requiring placement of the age-out in an adult detention facility with several different levels of security (low, low-medium, medium, medium high) *(Ramirez v. U.S. Immigration and Customs Enforcement* 2020, 104).

Under Section 1232(c)(2)(B), release of an age-out to an individual/organizational sponsor or supervised group home are viable options. Individual sponsors are required to provide an address where both the age-out and the sponsor will live and where immigration court notices and similar communications can be delivered. Organizational sponsors also provide support for age-outs and help ensure their appearance at any future immigration proceedings. Organizational sponsors do not need to be in an ICE office's area of responsibility ("AOR"), as some shelters accept age-outs from across the country *(Ramirez v. U.S. Immigration and Customs Enforcement* 2020, 103).

A significant number of ICE field offices and officers, however, automatically placed many age-outs in adult detention settings without considering available less-restrictive settings *(Ramirez v. U.S. Immigration and Customs Enforcement* 2020). An age-out, for example, was "more likely to be detained if processed by one of six ICE field offices—Houston, Miami, El Paso, New York, Los Angeles, or Phoenix—than if that age-out's documentation contained evidence of any of the statutory risk factors—danger to community, danger to self, or risk of flight" *(Ramirez v. U.S. Immigration and Customs Enforcement* 2020, 169). The field office where the age-out was processed "mattered significantly to the probability the age-out is detained, even once controlling for risk factors" *(Ramirez v. U.S. Immigration and Customs Enforcement* 2020, 169). Age-outs were 12.7 percent more likely to be detained if they had any one risk factor, and 28.0 percent more likely to be detained if they had all the risk factors. Field offices had greater significant effect—age-outs processed by the Houston office were over 90 percent more likely to be detained than otherwise identical age-outs processed by the San

Antonio office. Age-outs processed in El Paso were over 80 percent more likely to be detained and in New York over 60 percent more likely.

Determining Age-Outs Eligible for Placement in the Least Restrictive Setting

Eligibility for placement in the least restrictive setting was the issue in the cases of *Jose L.P. v. Whitaker* (2019), *Saravia v. Sessions* (2017), *Ramirez v. U.S. Immigrations and Customs Enforcement* (2018), *Rodas Godinez v. ICE* (2020), and *Daniel R.-S. v. Anderson* (2020). Different classes of plaintiff were involved in these cases, namely, unaccompanied minors in ORR custody who were released to either parents or sponsors but later rearrested on allegations of gang involvement while still a minor (*Saravia v. Sessions* 2017), unaccompanied minors previously held in ORR custody but transferred to ICE custody upon turning eighteen years old (*Ramirez v. U.S. Immigrations and Customs Enforcement* 2018; *Rodas Godinez v. ICE* 2020), unaccompanied minor released to the custody of a parent but rearrested upon allegations of gang involvement after becoming an adult (*Daniel R.-S. v. Anderson* 2020; *Jose L.P. v. Whitaker* 2019; *Mendez Ramirez v. Decker* 2020).

The case of *Saravia v. Sessions* (2017) involved an unaccompanied minor who was released to an individual sponsor, but subsequently rearrested while still under 18 years old on suspicion of gang activity. ICE agents implementing "Operation Matador" targeted undocumented immigrants in two New York counties (Suffolk and Nassau) allegedly connected to criminal gangs. ICE agents rearrested plaintiffs due to allegations of gang involvement from local law enforcement. Plaintiffs were previously arrested as unaccompanied minors, transferred to ORR custody, and released to either parents or sponsors because of the ORR's prior determination that they were not dangerous. Upon rearrest by ICE on suspicion of gang affiliation, they were placed in juvenile detention facilities, the most restrictive secure facility level. There, the U.S. District Court for the Northern District of California granted a class-wide preliminary injunction and, on November 20, 2017, ordered the government to provide all "noncitizen minors previously released to a sponsor who were rearrested and are currently in federal custody based on allegations of gang affiliation with a hearing before an immigration judge by no later than November 29, 2017" (*Saravia v. Sessions* 2017, 1205). The Ninth Circuit Court of Appeals affirmed the district court.

The case of *Ramirez v. U.S. Immigrations and Customs Enforcement* (2018) involved plaintiffs who were immigrant teenagers previously held in ORR custody as unaccompanied alien children but transferred to ICE custody when they turned eighteen and placed in adult detention facilities, without being considered for "less restrictive placement options" (*Ramirez v. U.S. Immigrations and Customs Enforcement* 2018, 12). The U.S. District Court for the District of Columbia ruled in plaintiffs' favor. The U.S. District Court for the District of Columbia applied 8 U.S.C. § 1232(c)(2)(B) and required DHS to "consider placement" of the immigrant teenagers who were former unaccompanied minors in the "least restrictive setting" after assessing their "risk of flight" and whether they pose "any danger" to themselves or to the community (*Ramirez v. U.S. Immigrations and Customs Enforcement* 2018, 12).

In *Jose L.P. v. Whitaker* (2019), Jose L.P. ("JLP"), a native and citizen of El Salvador, entered the United States without inspection on October 8, 2014. ICE officials apprehended him and transferred him to the custody of ORR after determining that he was an unaccompanied alien child. On October 17, 2014, the ORR released JLP to the care of his father in New York. On March 28, 2018, Department of Homeland Security agents arrested the now adult JLP as part of an operation targeting suspected gang members and placed him in immigration detention at the Hudson County Jail in New Jersey. JLP challenged his custody status and received a custody determination hearing before an immigration judge on June 22, 2018. The immigration judge denied bond, finding that JLP was a significant flight risk because of his alleged membership in the MS-13 gang and his failure to appear at past immigration hearings. The Board of Immigration Appeals denied JLP's appeal. JLP filed a petition for a writ of habeas corpus. JLP asserted that his detention in county jail violated the APA because the government failed to "consider placement in the least restrictive setting available" under 8 U.S.C. § 1232(c)(2)(B).

The U.S. District Court for the Southern District of New York denied JLP's petition for a writ of habeas corpus, holding that at the time of JLP's detention: (1) he was not unaccompanied alien child and, thus, statutory provision requiring government to consider placement in least restrictive setting available did not apply; and (2) the requirements of 8 U.S.C. § 1232(c)(2)(B) did not apply because JLP was not transferred by ORR to the custody of the Secretary of Homeland Security. The Southern District of New York district court considered the cases of *Saravia v. Sessions* (2017) and *Ramirez v. U.S. Immigrations and Customs Enforcement* (2018) by analogy.

The district court in *Jose L.P. v. Whitaker* (2019) summarized the decisions in *Saravia v. Sessions* (2017) and *Ramirez v. U.S. Immigrations and Customs Enforcement* (2018) as follows: (1) for previously released unaccompanied alien children who are rearrested and detained while still under 18 based on allegations of gang involvement, they must be granted a hearing where the government bears the burden of demonstrating changed circumstances justifying detention; and (2) for unaccompanied alien children who are transferred to DHS custody upon turning 18, the government must consider the least restrictive setting available, including alternatives to detention. The district court explained that 8 U.S.C. § 1232(c)(2)(B) only applied to former unaccompanied minors who turned 18 years old while in ORR custody and were transferred to the custody of the Secretary of Homeland Security. The district court noted that JLP's circumstances did not fit either category. JLP was not an unaccompanied minor because he was already released to the care of his father. He was also not transferred by ORR to the custody of the DHS upon turning 18 years old. Hence the requirement of 8 U.S.C. § 1232(c)(2)(B) that the government consider the least restrictive option did not apply to JLP's detention in March 2018.

The District Court for the District of New Mexico also denied Godinez's motion for temporary restraining order or preliminary injunction in *Rodas Godinez v. ICE* (2020). The case involved Godinez, an unaccompanied minor, who was transferred to the custody of the Office of Refugee Resettlement and placed in an ORR shelter near El Paso, Texas for unaccompanied migrant children. When he turned 18, he was transferred to the custody of the DHS and placed in the Otero County Processing Center. In June of 2019, an immigration judge terminated removal proceedings against Godinez and DHS appealed to the BIA. While detained, Godinez tested positive for COVID-19 but was asymptomatic. Godinez filed a petition for a writ of habeas corpus releasing him from detention for violation of his Fifth Amendment Due Process rights. He argued that he should be released from jail because the government should consider placing him in the least restrictive setting. He requested that the district court issue a temporary restraining order or preliminary injunction directing ICE to release him from the Otero County Processing Center.

The District Court for the District of New Mexico denied Godinez's motion for temporary restraining order or preliminary injunction. The district court stated that DHS in fact considered placing Godinez in the least restrictive setting pursuant to § 1232(c)(2)(B). DHS presented an age-out worksheet that was signed and completed by a Field Office Juvenile Coordinator ("FOJC") and reviewed and signed by a supervisor. The worksheet was contemporaneously completed when DHS considered placing him in the least restrictive setting. The FOJC concluded that Godinez was a danger to himself because: (1) he had no means or knowledge to care for himself without adult supervision; (2) he had a "mental or emotional injury materially impairing [his] growth, developmental and psychological functioning; and (3) he had been abused, neglected, or abandoned by his parents (*Rodas Godinez v. ICE* 2020, 4). The FOJC also found that petitioner who had been in custody for over 269 days was a flight risk because he had no one who could sponsor him—although he had family in the United States, including a brother, uncle, and aunt, they were unwilling to sponsor him.

In two cases of *Daniel R.-S. v. Anderson* (2020) and *Mendez Ramirez v. Decker* (2020), federal district courts denied the right to be placed in the least restrictive setting to former unaccompanied minors who were released to the custody of their parents but were rearrested after they turned 18 years old by ICE. In *Daniel R.-S. v. Anderson* (2020), the U.S. District Court of New Jersey denied Daniel's motion for temporary restraining order seeking immediate release from the jail. The case involved El Salvadorian petitioner Daniel who illegally entered the United States in June 2013 at age fifteen as an unaccompanied minor. After his arrest at the border and transfer to ORR, he was released to the custody and care of his mother in New York. After multiple arrests and evidence of MS-13 gang membership, Daniel was taken into immigration custody pursuant to 8 U.S.C. § 1226(a) and placed in removal proceedings when he was 22 years old. Petitioner was ordered removed by an immigration judge. Petitioner's applications for relief from removal and appeal to the BIA were denied. Petitioner filed a petition for review and a motion for stay of removal before the Second Circuit Court of Appeals. After the Second Circuit granted a stay of removal, Daniel's request for bail was denied at a bond hearing because he was a danger to the community in light of his criminal history and gang affiliation. Daniel remained detained at Essex County Correctional Facility. He filed a motion for temporary restraining order seeking immediate release from the jail. Daniel argued that he should be released from jail because the government should consider placing him in the least restrictive setting.

The U.S. District Court of New Jersey denied Daniel's motion for temporary restraining order seeking immediate release from the jail. The court held that the TVPRA does not apply to Daniel since he ceased to be an unaccompanied alien child once he was transferred into the custody of his mother in the United States prior to his eighteenth birthday (at age fifteen). Daniel therefore was not entitled to placement in the "least restrictive" setting upon his later being taken into custody and placed into removal proceedings, after he turned eighteen in the custody of his mother (*Daniel R.-S. v. Anderson* 2020, 3; *Ramirez v. Decker* 2020, 6–10). Similarly, in *Mendez Ramirez v. Decker* (2020), the U.S. District Court for the Southern District of New York denied plaintiff's petition for habeas corpus, holding that Ramirez was not an unaccompanied minor after he was released to the custody of his mother but was rearrested after he turned 18 years old by ICE pending removal proceedings. Therefore, he is not entitled to the legal protections afforded to them under the TVPRA and was not entitled to placement in the least restrictive setting.

In two related cases of *Ramirez v. U.S. Immigration and Customs Enforcement* filed in 2020, 2021, unaccompanied minors previously held in ORR custody but transferred to ICE custody upon turning eighteen years old brought class action against the DHS and its Secretary, ICE, and its Acting Director, contending that DHS and ICE ("defendants") violated Administrative Procedure Act (APA) by systematically failing to consider their placement in the least restrictive setting available. The District Court for the District of Columbia granted limited structural injunction due to the defendants' "resistance in complying with the statute throughout the course of litigation" (*Ramirez v. U.S. Immigration and Customs Enforcement* 2021, 1).

The court held that a limited injunctive relief was appropriate. The court noted that ICE's conduct throughout the litigation "further emphasized the need for injunctive relief" (*Ramirez v. U.S. Immigration and Customs Enforcement* 2021, 7). Both the U.S. Supreme Court and the D.C. circuit have held that a "comprehensive [injunctive] order" is "particularly justified" when the government has had "repeated opportunities to remedy" violations and where the history of litigation has been extensive (*DL v. District of Columbia* 2017, 105; *Hutto v. Finney* 1978, 687). According to the court, defendants' efforts to implement the court's prior orders were "minimal at best" (*Ramirez v. U.S. Immigration and Customs Enforcement* 2021, 7). For example, the Court noted that the ORR should and does have more onerous sponsorship requirements than ICE, but that ICE was not bound by these standards when making determinations under the statute. However, ICE continued to reject proposed sponsors for age-outs throughout 2018 and 2019 because the potential sponsors had not met ORR-specific sponsorship requirements.

Although the court identified problems in ICE's decision-making processes and not just its officers' documentation of their decisions, ICE responded to the court's injunction only by developing a new Age Out Review Worksheet ("AORW") documentation system instead of reexamining the substance of its actual decision-making processes. The court also remained "troubled by ICE's conduct during the pendency of this case" (*Ramirez v. U.S. Immigration and Customs Enforcement* 2021, 8). While the litigation was ongoing, ICE attempted to circumvent its "newly instituted reporting requirement" by completing many AORW forms *after* custody determinations had actually been made, often times "even having officers who were entirely uninvolved in the original custody determination complete and sign off on the documentation" (*Ramirez v. U.S. Immigration and Customs Enforcement* 2021, 8). Contrary to ICE's representations to the court, it had failed to document a significant portion of age-outs on AORW forms and had misrepresented these statistics. Between April 1, 2016 and March 31, 2019, ICE had failed to make records for 1,473 age-outs. Additionally, 88 individuals had aged out between March 31, 2019 and May 24, 2019 without being recorded in the SharePoint site (*Ramirez v. U.S. Immigration and Customs Enforcement* 2021). The above conduct constituted a pattern "of agency recalcitrance and resistance to the fulfillment of its legal duties" that "strongly" supported the imposition of injunctive relief (*Ramirez v. U.S. Immigration and Customs Enforcement* 2021, 8).

Detention of Unaccompanied Minors

In a number of cases, federal courts discussed the various rights of unaccompanied alien children in the custody of ORR or DHS. In the 1993 case of *Reno v. Flores*, the U.S. Supreme Court considered whether a detained unaccompanied alien child who does not have any available parent, close relative, or legal guardian has the right to be released to the custody of any other "willing-and-able private custodian" instead of being confined to a "government-operated or government-selected child-care institution" (*Reno v. Flores* 1993, 302). The Court held that the INS regulations permitting release of unaccompanied minors only to his or her parents, close relatives, or legal guardians did not "facially violate substantive due process" (*Reno v. Flores* 1993, 302). Governmental custody of a juvenile who did not have any available parent, close relative or legal guardian was rationally related to the government's interest in "preserving and promoting the welfare of the child" (*Reno v. Flores* 1993, 303; *Santosky v. Kramer* 1982, 766).

The Fourth Circuit also considered the nature and extent of unaccompanied alien children's due process rights in placement decisions in the two related 2016 cases of *DB v. Cardall* (2016) and *Beltran v. Cardall* (2016). In *DB v. Cardall* (2016), the issue was whether the ORR had continued authority to detain unaccompanied alien children who could not be released to a suitable custodian when deportation proceedings were terminated against them. RMB and his mother Beltran illegally entered the U.S. in 2005 but were separated for nearly three years. While in the custody of the ORR, RMB was held in juvenile detention facilities, the most restrictive placement. The mother submitted a family reunification request to the ORR, asking for RMB's release to her custody. The ORR denied the request based on a home study recommending against release due to RMB's criminal history and high risk of recidivism. The Fourth Circuit held that RMB was an unaccompanied alien child based on the ORR's assessment that his mother was incapable of providing for his physical and mental well-being (*DB v. Cardall* 2016). According to the court, the authority of ORR to detain RMB did not cease upon termination of removal proceedings against him because ORR was specifically required by law to determine whether a proposed custodian can provide for the unaccompanied alien child's physical and mental well-being.

On remand, the district court in *Beltran v. Cardall* (2016), concluded that the ORR's family reunification procedures did not provide RMB and his mother Beltran due process of law. The district ordered RMB's release to care and custody of his mother Beltran. The district court then examined the adequacy of ORR procedures for placement of unaccompanied alien children with suitable custodians (*Beltran v. Cardall* 2016). Here, the ORR ordered a home study upon submission of the family reunification form by the mother. The home study recommended against releasing RMB to his mother's care because of RMB's behavioral problems instead of the mother's parental fitness. A month after the home study, petitioner received a short letter stating that her request was denied because RMB required an environment with a "high level of supervision and structure" (*Beltran v. Cardall* 2016, 485). The district court concluded that the ORR process was deficient because the proceedings were unilateral and the mother was not informed of the evidence or the facts relied upon. The court concluded that ORR deprived the mother of a meaningful opportunity to present her case because it made the subjective judgment without any form of hearing. All the procedures of the ORR for placement consisted of "internal evaluation and unilateral investigation" (*Beltran v. Cardall* 2016, 476). The ORR's deficient procedures "created a significant risk" that the mother and RMB would be "erroneously deprived of their right to family integrity" (*Beltran v. Cardall* 2016, 476).

In *Santos v. Smith* (2017), the United States District Court for the Western District of Virginia in 2017 determined whether an unaccompanied alien child was deprived of due process when the ORR denied his mother's request for release to her custody. When he was 14 years old, OGLS fled Honduras and entered the United States to be reunited with his mother. He was apprehended, determined to be an unaccompanied alien child and transferred to ORR custody. After OGLS disclosed his participation in criminal gang activities, ORR placed him at the Shenandoah Valley Juvenile Center ("SVJC"), a secure facility in Staunton, Virginia. After the mother filed a petition with ORR asking to be reunified with her son, ORR conducted a home study that recommended reunification (*Santos v. Smith* 2017). The ORR issued a decision more than 14 months after the home study was completed and denied the application for family reunification. The mother filed a petition for writ of habeas corpus alleging that ORR violated her due process rights and sought OGLS's immediate release to her custody. The district court held that the detention of OGLS for more than 29 months violated procedural due process and ordered his immediate release to the custody of Santos. The district court stated that due process consists of "notice and the opportunity to be heard" at a "meaningful" time and manner (*Armstrong v. Manzo* 1965, 545; *Santos v. Smith* 2017, 611).

Legal Standard for Abuses Experienced in Facilities

Another issue confronted by federal courts involved the appropriate legal standard to use when unaccompanied alien children detained in ORR facilities alleged abuses and inadequate medical care. Since federal courts are bound by U.S. Supreme Court precedents, they deliberated on whether to apply the legal standard of deliberate indifference in *Farmer v. Brennan* (1994) or the Youngberg standard for medical care in *Youngberg v. Romeo* (1982).

Deliberate Indifference Standard in Farmer v. Brennan (1994)

The Supreme Court in *Farmer v. Brennan* (1994) prescribed the legal standard of deliberate indifference to determine whether a government official's "episodic act or omission" violated plaintiffs' Fifth Amendment due process right to protection from harm (*EAFF v. Gonzalez* 2015, 210; *Hare v. City of Corinth Miss.* 1996, 647). A government official is liable if he or she: (1) had "subjective knowledge of a substantial risk of harm" to the plaintiff ("subjective awareness"); and (2) did not respond in an "objectively reasonable" manner "in light of clearly established law" ("objectively reasonable response") (*Farmer v. Brennan* 1994, 884). To prove subjective awareness, defendant officials must have "actual notice of an existing risk" or must have inferred the obvious risk based on facts known to him, including circumstantial evidence (*Farmer v. Brennan* 1994, 837). Defendant officials who had subjective awareness may be found liable only if they did not respond in an "objectively reasonable manner even if the harm ultimately was not averted" (*Farmer v. Brennan* 1994, 884). The government may raise the defense of "qualified immunity from monetary damages" against claims of deliberate indifference (*Doe v. Robertson* 2014, 387). The defense of qualified immunity requires a two-step analysis: (1) whether defendants violated a "clearly established right" of the plaintiff; and (2) whether defendants' conduct was "objectively reasonable in light of clearly established law at the time of the incident" (*EAFF v. Gonzalez* 2015, 209; *Hernandez ex rel. Hernandez v. Tex. Dep't of Protective & Regulatory Servs.* 2004, 879).

The Fifth Circuit applied the deliberate indifference standard in the 2015 case of *EAFF v. Gonzalez,* involving eleven unaccompanied Central American minors arrested by Texas Border Patrol agents and placed by the ORR in a Nixon, Texas detention facility pending immigration proceedings. They filed an action against defendant ORR officials in their individual capacities under *Bivens v. Six Unknown Named Agents of Federal Bureau of Narcotics* (1971) ("*Bivens* action"), claiming monetary damages for violation of their constitutional rights. They alleged that they were physically or sexually abused while detained in the Nixon facility. The Fifth Circuit held that the plaintiffs failed to prove that defendants were deliberately indifferent to their Fifth Amendment due process rights to be protected from harm because defendants did not have "subjective awareness of the risk"—they did not have "actual knowledge" or the risk was not obvious (*EAFF v. Gonzalez* 2015, 205). In *Farmer v. Brennan* (1994, 842), the U.S. Supreme Court explained that a risk "may be obvious" when inmate attacks were "longstanding, pervasive, well-documented, or expressly noted by prison officials in the past." There was no pattern of abuse that made the risk obvious to the defendant officials because there was "only one confirmed case of sexual abuse and one confirmed case of physical abuse" which led to the suspension or termination of the perpetrators (*EAFF v. Gonzalez* 2015, 213). The Fifth Circuit concluded that the government officials were entitled to qualified immunity because they responded reasonably to the perceived risk. Upon learning of the isolated incidents, defendants implemented policies to ensure more frequent monitoring of staff and preventing staff from entering bathrooms and bedrooms without an escort, reviewed staffing procedures, and scheduled additional staff training.

Standard of Medical Care While Detained in ORR Facilities

In the case of *Doe 4 by and through Lopez v. Shenandoah Valley Juvenile Center Commission* (2021), the Fourth Circuit Court of Appeals decided on the legal standard to impose liability on employees of ORR facilities for failure to provide adequate care to detained unaccompanied minors. Appellants were unaccompanied minors who fled their native countries of Honduras, Guatemala, Mexico, and El Salvador after experiencing persecution and violence. Detained at Shenandoah Valley Juvenile Center, these minors struggled with severe mental illnesses, resulting in frequent self-harm and attempted suicide. As a secure juvenile detention facility, SVJC imposed various forms of discipline and sanctions ranging from verbal reprimands to removal from daily programming and room confinement. As a last resort, SVJC permitted staff to engage in the use of force to enforce these sanctions. Physical restraint techniques included physically grabbing the child in a "full nelson" hold, use of handcuffs or shackles, and strapping minors onto an "emergency restraint chair" (*Doe 4 v. Shenandoah* 2021, 331). Plaintiffs filed a class action suit under 42 U.S.C. § 1983, alleging, among other things, that the Shenandoah Valley Juvenile Center Commission ("Shenandoah") failed to provide a constitutionally adequate level of mental health care due to its punitive practices and failure to implement trauma-informed care (*Doe 4 v. Shenandoah* 2021). The U.S. District Court for the Western District of Virginia entered summary judgment in Shenandoah's favor after finding that it provided adequate care by offering access to counseling and medication (*Doe v. Shenandoah Valley Juvenile Ctr. Comm'n* 2018).

The Fourth Circuit Court of Appeals reversed the district court and remanded, holding that summary judgment was not proper because the district court incorrectly applied a standard of deliberate indifference when it should have applied the standard in *Youngberg v. Romeo* (1982) by determining whether Shenandoah substantially departed from accepted standards of professional judgment (the "Youngberg Standard") (*Doe 4 v. Shenandoah* 2021). Because the Youngberg Standard governs Appellants' claim, the district court erred by applying the standard of deliberate indifference. The district court excluded evidence relevant under *Youngberg v. Romeo* (1982), including Dr. Lewis's opinions concerning trauma-informed care and Dr. Weisman's opinions.

Youngberg Standard in Youngberg v. Romeo (1982)

The Fourth Circuit Court decided that the standard for medical liability in *Youngberg v. Romeo* (1982) applied when determining the adequacy of mental health care provided to a detained immigrant child, including an unaccompanied minor. In *Youngberg v. Romeo* (1982), the Supreme Court considered the Fourteenth Amendment protections guaranteed to a mentally disabled person involuntarily committed to a state institution. The Court held that liability may be imposed only when the decision by the professional represented a "substantial departure from accepted professional judgment" (*Youngberg* 1982, 320–323)

The Fourth Circuit explained that a facility caring for an unaccompanied minor fails to provide a constitutionally adequate level of mental health care if it "substantially departs from accepted professional standards" (*Doe 4 v. Shenandoah* 2021, 342). The *Youngberg* standard required more than negligence. Evidence establishing "mere departures" from the applicable standard of care were "insufficient" to show a constitutional violation (*Patten v. Nichols* 2001, 845). The evidence must show a "substantial departure" from accepted professional judgment, practice, or standards indicating that the person responsible actually did not base the decision on accepted professional judgment (*Doe 4 v. Shenandoah* 2021, 343; *Youngberg v. Romeo* 1982, 323). Under the *Youngberg v. Romeo* (1982) standard ("Youngberg Standard"), courts do not determine the correct or most appropriate medical decision (*Patten v. Nichols* 2001). The proper inquiry was whether the decision was "so completely out of professional bounds" so that it can only be explained as arbitrary and nonprofessional (*Patten v. Nichols* 2001, 845). By applying this standard, a court deferred to the "necessarily subjective aspects" of the decision making of medical professionals and accorded those decisions the "presumption of validity" (*Doe 4 v. Shenandoah* 2021, 343; *Patten v. Nichols* 2001, 845). A decision earned this deference only if it reflected an actual exercise of medical judgment (*Inmates of Allegheny Cnty. Jail v. Pierce* 1979).

According to the Fourth Circuit, the trial court incorrectly applied the standard of deliberate indifference described in *Farmer v. Brennan* (1994) to SVJC. Under this standard, a plaintiff must prove: (1) that the detainee had an objectively serious medical need; and (2) that the official subjectively knew of the need and disregarded it (*Brown v. Harris* 2001; *Farmer v. Brennan* 1994; *Martin v. Gentile* 1988). One difference between the *Youngberg* Standard of professional judgment and deliberate indifference is that the *Youngberg* Standard does not require proof of subjective intent. Thus, the Youngberg Standard "presents a lower standard of culpability" compared to the Eighth Amendment standard for deliberate indifference (*Doe 4 v. Shenandoah* 2021, 343). To apply the *Youngberg* Standard to a claim of inadequate medical care, a court must determine whether the treatment provided is adequate to address a person's needs under a relevant standard of professional judgment (*Doe 4 v. Shenandoah* 2021).

After determining that the *Youngberg* Standard applied to the unaccompanied minors' claim, the court held that trauma-informed care was "part of the landscape of relevant evidence" that should be considered by the trial court when determining the relevant standard of professional judgment (*Doe 4 v. Shenandoah* 2021, 346). A trauma-informed system of care was one that provided an environment where "youth feel safe," were assisted in coping when past traumatic experiences were triggered, and where exposure to "potentially retraumatizing reminders or events" were reduced (*Doe 4 v. Shenandoah* 2021, 344). For minors, trauma-informed care was "already in widespread use in juvenile detention systems" and was considered the appropriate standard of professional care for juvenile justice, including detained minors by the Department of Justice (U.S. Dep't of Justice 2012) and by multiple national organizations including the Substance Abuse and Mental Health Services Administration, the National Council of Juvenile and Family Court Judges, and the National Center for Mental Health and Juvenile Justice (*Doe 4 v. Shenandoah* 2021, 345; Stoffel et al. 2019).

Detention of Unaccompanied Minors in Unsafe and Unsanitary CBP Border Patrol Stations

The 1997 *Flores* Settlement established a nationwide policy for the detention, release, and treatment of minors in the custody of the INS (*Flores v. Barr* 2019). It required the government to place each detained minor in the least restrictive setting based on the minor's age and special needs while ensuring the minor's timely appearance before the INS and the immigration courts

(*Flores v. Barr* 2019). Under the *Flores* Settlement, minors not released for various reasons must be placed in licensed, non-secure facilities that meet certain standards (*Flores v. Lynch* 2016). Under paragraph 12A of the agreement, after arrest, the INS was required to hold minors in "safe and sanitary" facilities, considering the "particular vulnerability of minors" (*Flores v. Barr* 2019, 913). The Settlement required facilities to provide access to toilets and sinks, drinking water and food, medical assistance if needed, adequate temperature control and ventilation, adequate supervision to protect minors from others, and contact with family members who were arrested with the minor (*Flores v. Barr* 2019). Paragraph 28A requires an INS Juvenile Coordinator to monitor compliance with the agreement and maintain an up-to-date record of all minors placed in proceedings and who remained in INS custody for longer than 72 hours (*Flores v. Barr* 2019).

In *Flores v. Barr* (2019), plaintiff unaccompanied minors detained by immigration authorities moved to enforce the 1997 *Flores* Settlement, alleging that they were detained in unsafe and unsanitary conditions and in secure, unlicensed facilities. The District Court for the Central District of California, partially granted their motion. The district court found that the government violated the *Flores* Settlement by detaining minors in unsanitary and unsafe conditions at Border Patrol stations where they were deprived of adequate sleep and not provided adequate access to food, clean water, and basic hygiene items (*Flores v. Barr* 2019). Many minors in Border Patrol custody were forced to sleep on concrete floors, with no bedding aside from pieces of thin polyester foil and subjected to cold temperatures, overcrowding, and constant lighting (*Flores v. Barr* 2019). The district court also found that the government violated the *Flores* Settlement by failing to consider the minors for release and by detaining minors in detention facilities not licensed for the care of minors (*Flores v. Barr* 2019). The district court ordered defendants to enforce its obligations and also directed the government to appoint an internal "Juvenile Coordinator" to monitor the government's compliance with the agreement and report to the court. The government appealed to the Ninth Circuit Court of Appeals in *Flores v. Barr* (2019).

On appeal, the Ninth Circuit Court of Appeals first considered whether it had jurisdiction over the case, noting that it had appellate jurisdiction over interlocutory district court orders modifying a consent order (*Flores v. Barr* 2019, 914). The Ninth Circuit dismissed the appeal for lack of jurisdiction because the district court's order did not modify the *Flores* Settlement. The district court found, among other things, that minors (1) were "not receiving hot, edible, or a sufficient number of meals during a given day," (2) "had no adequate access to clean drinking water," (3) experienced "unsanitary conditions with respect to the holding cells and bathroom facilities," (4) lacked "access to clean bedding, and access to hygiene products (i.e., toothbrushes, soap, towels)," and (5) endured "sleep deprivation" as a result of "cold temperatures, overcrowding, lack of proper bedding (i.e., blankets, mats), [and] constant lighting" (*Flores v. Barr* 2019, 915). These conditions did not satisfy paragraph 12A's requirement that facilities be "safe and sanitary," given "the particular vulnerability of minors" (*Flores v. Barr* 2019, 915–916). The Ninth Circuit explained that the district court's conclusion "reflect a commonsense understanding of what the quoted language requires" (*Flores v. Barr* 2019, 916). Assuring that children "eat enough edible food, drink clean water, are housed in hygienic facilities with sanitary bathrooms, have soap and toothpaste, and are not sleep-deprived" were essential to the children's safety (*Flores v. Barr* 2019, 916). The district court properly construed the *Flores* Settlement as requiring such conditions rather than allowing the government discretion to decide whether to provide them.

Continued Retention by ORR Due to Imminent Removal by ICE

The district court of the District of Maryland held that ORR cannot retain custody or detain an unaccompanied minor who was not a safety or flight risk simply because of a pending removal by ICE (*J.S.G. ex rel. Hernandez v. Stirrup* 2020). J.S.G., a seventeen-year-old Guatemalan unaccompanied minor who experienced threats of violence and death from Guatemalan gang members, was held in detention by ORR but was later released to his brother in South Carolina (*J.S.G. ex rel. Hernandez v. Stirrup* 2020). After J.S.G. failed to appear in immigration court, he was ordered deported in absentia. Due to the pending deportation order, J.S.G. was transferred from a juvenile detention center to an ORR facility in Baltimore, Maryland after he was determined to be an unaccompanied minor. On March 13, 2020, J.S.G.'s immigration counsel filed a Motion to Rescind and Reopen J.S.G.'s immigration proceedings in the Charlotte Immigration Court, triggering an automatic stay of deportation until the immigration judge made a ruling. Five days later, on March 18, 2020, immigration judge denied relief. J.S.G. appealed the judges' ruling on April 21, 2020.

Meanwhile, ORR in February 2020, began processing paperwork to reunify J.S.G. with his paternal grandfather, Hernandez as an alternative to keeping J.S.G. in ORR detention. Hernandez completed the application for reunification and received a positive home study recommendation in early April 2020. Pending Hernandez's application, ORR Case Manager Rosales informed J.S.G.'s immigration counsel that ICE had instructed ORR staff "not to let [J.S.G.] leave" (*J.S.G. ex rel. Hernandez v. Stirrup* 2020, 2). J.S.G.'s immigration counsel, unaware that the immigration judge had denied her motion to reopen J.S.G.'s immigration proceedings, informed Rosales of the automatic stay of removal order. Upon learning that ICE intended to remove J.S.G. from the United States within two weeks and despite the suitability of J.S.G.'s grandfather as a custodian of J.S.G. who was cleared for release by ORR health authorities, ORR decided to retain custody of J.S.G (*J.S.G. ex rel. Hernandez v. Stirrup* 2020, 3). By and through his grandfather Hernandez, J.S.G. filed a petition for Judicial Review of Placement Pursuant to *Flores* Settlement Agreement, Complaint for Injunctive and Declaratory Relief, and Petition for a Writ of Habeas Corpus ("the Petition") on April 20, 2020. The Maryland District Court granted J.S.G.'s Motion for a Temporary Restraining Order.

The district court found that J.S.G. established that he was entitled to injunctive relief because he was likely to succeed on the merits of his claims. Specifically, ORR's failure to release J.S.G. to his grandfather violated the *Flores* Settlement and the Trafficking Victims Protection Reauthorization Act of 2008. Although ORR decided that J.S.G. could safely be released to his grandfather, it denied J.S.G.'s reunification application when it learned from ICE of its intent to remove J.S.G. from the country. The district court noted that it was "not aware of any cases" holding that a minor's imminent removal by ICE automatically makes him a flight risk (*J.S.G. ex rel. Hernandez v. Stirrup* 2020, *6). Assuming that ORR may deny reunification based solely on an imminent removal, J.S.G. cannot be considered a flight risk because his removal was not "actually imminent"—Guatemala no longer accepted removals from the U.S. due to the COVID-19 outbreak. Unless Guatemala accepted removals from the U.S., ORR would possibly hold J.S.G. in perpetuity.

Right to Abortion

In fiscal year 2018, almost 50,000 unaccompanied minors were referred to ORR (*J.D. v. Azar* 2019). Pursuant to the requirement under federal law (8 U.S.C. § 1232[c][2][A]) to promptly place unaccompanied alien children "in the least restrictive setting that is in the best interest of the child," ORR places these minors in one of 100 federally funded shelters across the country (*J.D. v. Azar* 2019, 1301). Approximately 30 percent of the unaccompanied minors who recently arrived in the United States have been female (U.S. Dep't of Health & Human Servs. 2019). Each year, ORR has several hundred pregnant unaccompanied minors in its custody (*J.D. v. Azar* 2019). At least 21 shelters, in states such as Texas, Arizona, Virginia, and Washington, have housed pregnant unaccompanied alien children. In fiscal year 2017, the only year where there is recorded data concerning abortion requests, 18 pregnant unaccompanied minors in ORR custody requested an abortion. In March 2017, ORR announced that shelters "are prohibited from taking any action that facilitates an abortion without direction and approval from the Director of ORR" (Memorandum from Kenneth Tota 2017). Previously, a shelter did not have to secure the Director's approval before assisting a minor with accessing abortion services unless federal funds were used directly for the procedure.

Under the new policy's requirement to secure the ORR Director's approval before permitting abortion access, ORR Director Scott Lloyd denied every abortion request presented to him during his tenure. He refused every request regardless of the circumstances, including when the pregnancy resulted from rape (*J.D. v. Azar* 2019). The requirement to obtain the Director's approval thus functioned as a blanket ban on abortion. The ban applied only to those unaccompanied minors who are in ORR custody. The following unaccompanied minors were not subject to the ban: (1) those released to a sponsor; (2) minors who obtained lawful immigration status; or (3) minors who turned 18 and were transferred to DHS custody which allows pregnant women in its custody to obtain abortions (Immigration & Customs Enforcement Guidelines 2016).

A 2017 case involved the right of an unaccompanied alien child to terminate her pregnancy while in custody of the ORR. In *Garza v. Hargan* (2017), unaccompanied minor Jane Doe was eight weeks pregnant when she entered the United States without inspection. She was detained, transferred to the custody of the ORR, and placed in a federally funded shelter in Texas. The ORR refused Doe's request for permission to go to an abortion clinic because of ORR policies (*Azar v. Garza* 2018, 1791). Rochelle Garza, Doe's guardian *ad litem*, filed a class action on behalf of Doe and "all other pregnant unaccompanied minors in ORR custody" challenging the constitutionality of ORR's policy (*Azar v. Garza* 2018, 1791). On October 18, 2017, the District Court issued a temporary restraining order allowing Doe to obtain an abortion immediately. On October 20, 2017, a panel of the Court of Appeals for the District of Columbia Circuit vacated the relevant portions of the temporary restraining order. Four days later, the District of Columbia Circuit Court of Appeals, sitting *en banc*, vacated the panel order and remanded the case to the District Court. The government then filed a petition for *certiorari* which the Supreme Court granted in 2018 in *Azar v. Garza* (2018, 1792). The Supreme Court vacated the *en banc* order, and remanded the case to the District of Columbia Circuit Court of Appeals with instructions to direct the District Court to dismiss the individual claim for injunctive relief as moot after the abortion (*Azar v. Garza* 2018).

Another case, *J.D. v. Azar* (2019), also involved the right of unaccompanied minors to obtain abortion while in ORR custody. Four plaintiff unaccompanied minors in ORR custody and whose requests for an abortion were denied under the new ORR policy of Director Lloyd brought class action challenging it. Seventeen-year-old plaintiff Jane Doe was pregnant when apprehended at the border and transferred to the custody of an ORR shelter in Texas. She requested access to an abortion after securing the judicial bypass required under Texas law. Although Doe secured her own private funding and transportation for the abortion services, and although she satisfied the conditions under Texas law to obtain an abortion, ORR Director Lloyd refused to authorize her release from the shelter for the procedure.

On October 18, 2017, the District Court of the District of Columbia granted Jane Doe a temporary restraining order, enjoining the government from preventing her transport to an abortion facility or from otherwise interfering with her decision to terminate her pregnancy. A panel of the D.C. Circuit Court vacated that decision on October 20 (*Garza v. Hargan* 2017), but four days later, the court, *en banc,* vacated the panel order and reinstated the district court's temporary restraining order (*Garza v. Hargan* 2017). Jane Doe obtained an abortion the next day (*Azar v. Garza* 2017). At the time, she was 14 weeks pregnant. Almost three months later, before Doe turned 18 years old, ORR released her to a sponsor. On June 1, 2018, the Supreme Court vacated the *en banc* order because Doe's claim had become moot (*United States v. Munsingwear, Inc.* 1950).

The second plaintiff in *J.D. v. Azar* (2019) was 17 years old Jane Poe who was pregnant as a result from rape when apprehended at the border in November 2017. Poe repeatedly requested an abortion even though her mother (in her country of origin) and a potential sponsor (in the United States) threatened to beat her if she attempted to terminate her pregnancy. ORR's Deputy Director for Children's Programs wrote a memorandum to Director Lloyd explaining the circumstances surrounding Poe's request for an abortion (Memorandum from Jonathan White 2017). The Deputy Director further explained that Poe "does not have any viable sponsors" and that her pregnancy had reached 21 weeks, so that the state-law deadline for an abortion was "fast approaching" (*J.D. v. Azar* 2019, 1304; Memorandum from Jonathan White 2017, 16–17). According to the Deputy Director, it was "critical that a decision to approve or deny her request" be made "as soon as possible" (*J.D. v. Azar* 2019, 1305; Memorandum from Jonathan White 2017, 17). Director Lloyd, however, denied Poe's request for permission to obtain an abortion, explaining that the request asked ORR to "participate in killing a human being in [ORR's] care," and "[ORR] ought to choose [to] protect life rather than to destroy it" (*J.D. v. Azar* 2019, 1305; Memorandum from Jonathan White 2017, 23). One day later, the district court granted Poe's motion for a temporary restraining order over the government's opposition. Poe then obtained an abortion. On December 13, 2018, counsel informed the court that Poe had been granted asylum and was no longer in ORR custody.

The final two named plaintiffs in *J.D. v. Azar* (2019) were Jane Roe and Jane Moe who were both released from ORR custody before terminating their pregnancies. After the government discovered Roe was not a minor, she was transferred to DHS custody which allowed immigration detainees to obtain an abortion. On the other hand, Moe was released to a sponsor. The four named plaintiffs moved for preliminary injunction, claiming that ORR maintained a blanket ban on abortion access, a parental-notification-and-consent requirement, and compelled religious counseling, violating the Fifth and First Amendments. The D.C. Circuit Court affirmed the district court's grant of preliminary injunction for the plaintiffs. Under Supreme Court precedents, the Constitution "offers basic protection to the woman's right to choose" (*Stenberg v. Carhart* 2000, 921; *Planned Parenthood v. Casey* 1992, 833; *Roe v. Wade* 1973, 93). Before viability, the woman has a right to choose to terminate her pregnancy (*Stenberg v. Carhart* 2000, 921; *Planned Parenthood v. Casey* 1992, 870). The government may not "impose an undue burden on the woman's decision before fetal viability" (*Stenberg v. Carhart* 2000, 921; *Planned Parenthood v. Casey* 1992, 877). An "undue burden" is "shorthand" for the conclusion that a state regulation has the purpose or effect of "placing a substantial obstacle in the path of a woman seeking a pre-viability abortion" (*Stenberg v. Carhart* 2000, 921; *Planned Parenthood v. Casey* 1992, 877).

The government argued that Supreme Court decisions upholding an individual's right to obtain an abortion do not include a right to have the government fund it (*Harris v. McRae* 1980, 317–318; *Maher v. Roe* 1977, 475–477; *Poelker v. Doe* 1977, 519–521; *Rust v. Sullivan* 1991, 201–203; *Webster v. Reproductive Health Servs.* 1989, 509). They argued that ORR's policy is not a ban on access to an abortion but rather is a refusal to subsidize abortion. Thus, the government can fund and provide medical services incident to childbirth but not abortions (*Webster v. Reproductive Health Servs.* 1989, 509–510) and can prohibit recipients of federal funding from using the funds for abortion-related activities, *Rust v. Sullivan* 1991, 201–203). The D.C. Circuit Court agreed that preexisting ORR policy prohibits ORR funding for abortion services (except with the Director's approval in cases of rape, incest, or danger to the pregnant minor's life) (Memorandum from David Siegel 2008). However, the court countered that the government's reliance on that line of precedents is "misconceived" because the current case "does not involve government funding of abortions" (*J.D. v. Azar* 2019, 1327). Jane Doe, for example, secured private funding and transportation for the abortion she sought to access but was still denied ORR approval for her to leave the shelter to get the procedure. The court stated that "[this] is not a refusal to *fund* an abortion; it is a refusal to *allow* it" (*J.D. v. Azar* 2019, 1327). Reconciling the Supreme Court's funding decisions with its decisions establishing a constitutional right to terminate a pregnancy pre-viability, the government cannot "compel a minor to carry her pregnancy to term against her wishes so that the government can be relieved of a self-imposed administrative requirement" (*J.D. v. Azar* 2019, 1327). The court pointed out that pregnant adults in immigration custody detained by the DHS and federal inmates in the Bureau of Prisons for federal inmates were allowed access to abortion. The incongruous result is that a 17-year-old unaccompanied minor in ORR custody was compelled to carry her pregnancy to term against her wishes (*Doe v. ORR* 2018) whereas an 18-year-old in DHS custody or federal inmates could choose otherwise.

The government next argued that an unaccompanied minor could avoid the ban through voluntary departure from the United States. The court refuted this, saying that voluntary departure is a form of immigration relief granted "only at the discretion of the government" (*J.D. v. Azar* 2019, 1330). It is not a "freely available escape hatch from a government veto on abortion" but is instead a "second government veto" (*J.D. v. Azar* 2019, 1330). The process of voluntary departure may also take considerable time in situations wherein "time is of the essence" (*J.D. v. Azar* 2019, 1330). The voluntary departure process for Jane Doe, for example, had not progressed far, indicating that voluntary departure was not immediately available. The fact that a person could freely go elsewhere did not negate the abortion ban as an undue burden because abortion may not be available in the place of destination. Even if plaintiff minors were granted voluntary departure and could return to their country of origin, they may not be able to obtain an abortion there. More than 90 percent of all minors in ORR custody come from Honduras, Guatemala, or El Salvador, where abortion is criminalized. Due to the unavailability of abortion in their countries of origin, voluntary departure did not alleviate the burden imposed by ORR's ban. Finally, even if voluntary departure allowed a minor to obtain an abortion in her country of origin, it came at a "significant cost" (*J.D. v. Azar* 2019, 1330). Voluntary departure required withdrawing any claims for other forms of immigration relief such as asylum, special visas, or adjustment of status.

The significance of the above rulings, however, may be impacted by the U.S. Supreme Court's recent decision in *Dobbs v. Jackson Women's Health Organization* (2021) which overruled *Roe v. Wade* (1973) and *Planned Parenthood of Southeastern Pa. v. Casey* (1992). The majority opinion held that abortion was not a protected Constitutional right and returned the decision regarding abortion regulations back to the states. Although the overturning of *Roe v. Wade* (1973) did not make abortion illegal nationwide, abortion became illegal in states with trigger laws to restrict abortion after *Roe v. Wade* (1973) and *Planned Parenthood of Southeastern Pa. v. Casey* (1992) were overturned. Thirteen states have trigger laws that ban most abortions in the first and second trimesters, namely, Arkansas, Idaho, Kentucky, Louisiana,

Mississippi, Missouri, North Dakota, Oklahoma, South Dakota, Tennessee, Texas, Utah, and Wyoming.

Asylum Proceedings

Some of the issues that arose in federal courts involved jurisdiction over asylum proceedings, third party custody of unaccompanied alien children, and the authority to grant consent to a state juvenile court's jurisdiction for special immigrant juvenile status.

In *Garcia v. Barr* (2020), the Sixth Circuit Court of Appeals held that an immigration judge, rather than the USCIS, had jurisdiction to decide the asylum claim of a former unaccompanied alien child who filed an asylum application when he was nineteen years old. According to the court, the initial jurisdiction of the asylum officers of USCIS applies only when the applicant still meets the definition of an unaccompanied alien child when he applies for asylum—it's not enough that the alien was an unaccompanied alien child when he "first entered the country" (*Cortez-Vasquez v. Holder* 2011, 298; *Garcia v. Barr* 2020, 895; *Harmon v. Holder* 2014, 733–735; *In re M-A-C-O-* 2018, 480; *Mazariegos-Diaz v. Lynch* 2015, 675–676; *Salmeron-Salmeron v. Spivey* 2019, 1287–1289).

An asylum application cannot be filed by a six-year-old unaccompanied minor or his relative who did not have legal custody, if the parent of the unaccompanied alien child opposed the application (*Gonzalez v. Reno* 2000). Third parties who are not related to the unaccompanied alien child cannot gain custody of the minor or be appointed as custodians by a state juvenile court without the consent of the Secretary of the DHS (*United States ex. rel. the minor child K.E.R.G.* et al. *v. Burwell* 2014). In *Gonzalez v. Reno* (2000), six-year-old Elian Gonzalez arrived in the United States alone, after his mother died during their trip aboard a small boat from Cuba to Florida. Gonzalez, on his own and through his uncle, filed an asylum application that was denied by the INS as legally void. The INS declined to hear the case on the merits based on its policies under which: (1) six-year-old aliens lacked capacity to file asylum claims and must be represented by an adult in applying for asylum; (2) in the absence of special circumstances, only a parent can represent a six-year-old child in asylum proceedings, even if the parent is outside country; and (3) the parent's residence in communist-totalitarian country such as Cuba was not a "special circumstance" that justified consideration of an asylum claim by the six-year-old child (*Gonzalez v. Reno* 2000, 1350). The U.S. District Court for the Southern District of Florida dismissed Elian's claim of violation of due process. The Eleventh Circuit affirmed, holding that INS did not violate the alien's due process rights and that INS policies were reasonable interpretations of immigration law. The court also stated that INS was entitled to deference given the "well-established principles of statutory construction, judicial restraint, and deference to executive agencies" (*Gonzalez v. Reno* 2000, 1346).

Foreign nationals may be eligible for classification as special immigrants and seek adjustment to lawful permanent resident status based on such classification. The classification of Special Immigrant Juvenile status is available to certain children who, as determined through state juvenile court proceedings, cannot reunify with one or both parents because of "abuse, neglect, abandonment, or a similar basis under state law" (8 U.S.C. § 1101(a)(27)(J)). Under Section 1101(a)(27)(J) of the INA (1997), acquisition of a declaration of dependency from a state court is a prerequisite to applying for an SIJ visa, available to certain unmarried aliens under the age of twenty-one. The law also requires that the Secretary of Homeland Security consent to the grant of special immigrant juvenile status. A juvenile court does not have jurisdiction to determine the custody status or placement of an alien in the custody of the Secretary of Health and Human Services unless the Secretary of Health and Human Services specifically consents to such jurisdiction.

In the two cases of *F.L. v. Thompson* and *Yeboah v. U.S. Dept. of Justice* decided in 2003 before the current version of the law on SIJ status, the Circuit Courts construed the consent requirement for the grant for SIJ status to unaccompanied alien children. The D.C. Circuit Court ruled in the 2003 case of *F.L. v. Thompson* that the DHS and not the ORR has authority to grant an unaccompanied alien child's request for consent to a state juvenile court's jurisdiction. The Third Circuit in *Yeboah v. U.S. Dept. of Justice* (2003) reiterated that the defunct INS (now the DHS) has broad discretion to allow or deny consent to a state court's jurisdiction in a dependency hearing to grant SIJ status (*Yeboah v. U.S. Dept. of Justice* 2003).

Basis for Asylum

Federal courts are guided in their review of the decisions of the BIA by various immigration laws and policies pertaining to unaccompanied alien children. One of these laws is the Immigration and Nationality Act which gives the United States discretion to grant asylum to persons considered to be refugees (8 U.S.C. § 1158(b)(1)(A)). To qualify as a refugee, an applicant must show that he or she is "unable or unwilling to return to, and is unable or unwilling to avail himself or herself of the protection of" his or her home country "because of persecution or a well-founded fear of persecution on account of race, religion, nationality, membership in a particular social group, or political opinion" (8 U.S.C. § 1101(a)(42)(A); *Amanfi v. Ashcroft* 2003, 726; *Bolainez-Vargas v. Garland* 2021, 162; *I.N.S. v. Elias-Zacarias* 1992, 481–482; *Rodas-Orellana v. Holder* 2015, 986). Failure to establish persecution on account of any of these categories is fatal to a petitioner's asylum and withholding claims (*Sepulveda v. U.S. Att'y Gen.* 2005, 1232).

A well-founded fear of persecution requires the applicant to show both a genuine, subjective fear of persecution, and an objective reasonable fear of persecution supported by credible, direct, and specific evidence (*Karki v. Holder* 2013; *Shehu v. Attorney General of U.S.* 2007). Persecution is the infliction of suffering or harm upon those who differ in race, religion, or political opinion in a way regarded as offensive, and requires more than just restrictions or threats to life and liberty (*Karki v. Holder* 2013; *Thap v. Mukasey* 2008). Persecution does not include every type of treatment regarded by society as unfair, unjust, unlawful, or unconstitutional (*Marikasi v. Lynch* 2016) or offensive (*Ali v. Ashcroft* 2004; *Japarkulova v. Holder* 2010). Only impending and menacing threats possibly qualify as past persecution (*Japarkulova v. Holder* 2010; *Mikhailevitch v. INS* 1998). To establish a well-founded fear of persecution, the applicant must provide specific information showing a real threat of individual persecution. They cannot rely on speculative conclusions or mere assertions of fear of possible persecution (*Harchenko v. INS* 2004).

A "nexus" exists when the applicant shows that at least one of the five characteristics listed in the law was or will be at least "one central reason" for persecution (8 U.S.C. § 1158(b)(1)(B)(i); *Ndayshimiye v. Att'y Gen.* 2009, 129). In 2005, Congress passed the REAL ID Act, Pub. L. No. 109-13, 199 Stat. 302 (2005), which clarified the standard for evaluating mixed-motive asylum cases—in cases where the persecutor has more than one motive, an applicant must prove that the protected characteristic "was or will be at least one central reason for persecuting the applicant" (*Lopez-Cruz v. Attorney General United States* 2019, 710). The Sixth Circuit in *Maraziegos-Morales v. Garland* (2021), abrogated the "one central reason" standard for withholding of removal claims under the INA and replaced it with a less stringent "a reason" test in accordance with the REAL ID Act (*Guzman-Vazquez* v. Barr 2020). The protected ground need not be the primary motivation for persecution, but asylum cannot be granted if a protected ground is only an "incidental, tangential, or superficial" reason for persecution of an asylum applicant (*Ndayshimiye v. Att'y Gen.* 2009, 130). Conflicts of a "personal nature" and "isolated criminal acts" are not persecution based on a protected characteristic (*Amaya-Amaya v. Attorney General United States* 2020, 769).

The requirement of "membership in a particular social group" requires that the group has "immutability, particularity, and social distinction" within the society (*Abarca-Fuentes v. Garland* 2021, 1023; *Betancourt-Aplicano v. Sessions* 2018, 282; *Cruz-Guzman v. Barr* 2019, 1036; *Reyes v. Lynch* 2016, 1131). Immutability requires that the group "either cannot change, or should not be required to change" because it is fundamental to their individual identities or consciences (*Umana-Ramos v. Holder* 2013, 671). Particularity refers to whether an accurate description of the proposed group can be made to sufficiently distinguish it in the particular society as a discrete class of persons (*Al-Ghorbani v. Holder* 2009). Social distinction requires that the individuals with the shared characteristic be perceived as a group by society (*Umana-Ramos v. Holder* 2013).

If an asylum claim is based on the conduct of non-governmental actors, the petitioner must demonstrate that the persecutors are either associated with the government or that the government is unwilling or unable to control them (*José-Tomás v. Barr* 2020; *Juan Antonio v. Barr* 2020). An applicant meets this burden when she shows that she cannot reasonably expect the government to assist her in controlling her perpetrator's actions (*Al-Ghorbani v. Holder* 2009; *Juan Antonio v. Barr* 2020) or that the government was unable or unwilling to control the persecutors (*K.H. v. Barr* 2019).

Parameters of Particular Social Group

The Third Circuit Court of Appeals defined the parameters of the particular social group in *Leiva-Barrios v. Attorney General United States* (2021). Guatemalan Leiva-Barrios entered the United States as a 16-year-old unaccompanied alien child in 2014. He filed an application for asylum, alleging that his sister's husband and father-in-law were murdered, his sister was threatened and was in hiding, and that unknown people had attacked his school and killed six students. An immigration judge denied his application for asylum and ordered him removed. On appeal, the Third Circuit denied his petition for review. The Third Circuit explained that to be eligible for asylum, Leiva-Barrios must show that he is unable or unwilling to return to Guatemala "because of persecution or a well-founded fear of persecution on account of race, religion, nationality, membership in a particular social group, or political opinion" (8 U.S.C. § 1101(a)(42)(A)). Although the BIA assumed that Leiva-Barrios's family was his "particular social group" for asylum purposes, families do not constitute a "particular social group" unless they are "socially distinct," a requirement that Leiva-Barrios failed to show (*Leiva-Barrios v. Attorney General United States* 2021, 2; *Romero v. Att'y Gen.* 2020, 342). Leiva-Barrios's fear of persecution was not objectively reasonable because Leiva-Barrios, his parents, and his siblings were never threatened or harmed and the identities and motives of the people who murdered his sister's husband and father-in-law were unknown. Leiva-Barrios's fear of "the mob" was insufficient to demonstrate an objectively reasonable fear of persecution (*Leiva-Barrios v. Attorney General United States* 2021, 3). The mob was not active in his hometown and never interacted with him or his family.

Asylum Based on Proposed Social Group of Young Men
Opposed to Gang Membership

In the following cases, the Sixth, Ninth, Tenth, and Eleventh Circuit Court of Appeals denied asylum based on the proposed social group of young men opposed to gang membership (*Gomez-Rodas v. Barr* 2019; *Bolainez-Vargas v. Garland* 2021; *Perez v. Garland* 2021; *Zapata-Matute v. U.S. Attorney General* 2019).

The Sixth Circuit Court of Appeals in *Perez v. Garland* (2021) held that Perez's proposed group of "young Guatemalan men between the ages of 15 and 25 who have opposed gang activity and lack protection" was too vague and indeterminate to qualify as a particular social group (*Perez v. Garland* 2021, 1). Perez-Ramirez, a Guatemalan citizen, claimed that gang members assaulted him on three separate occasions when he refused to join them. He fled to the U.S. as an unaccompanied alien child in 2015 and sought asylum. The BIA affirmed the immigration judge's denial of Perez's asylum application, holding that Perez's proposed social group of "young Guatemalan men between 15 and 25 who oppose gang recruitment and lack adequate protection" was not immutable, particular, or distinct (*Perez v. Garland* 2021, 2).

The Sixth Circuit denied Perez-Ramirez's appeal. Perez's proposed group did not have a "clear boundary that separates it from the rest of society" because gangs in Guatemala target a wide variety of people for recruitment, including children under age 15 and women (*Perez v. Garland* 2021, 3). Similarly, the Sixth Circuit declined to recognize the following as social groups qualifying for asylum: (1) young Salvadorans who were threatened because they refused to join the MS gang (*Umana-Ramos v. Holder* 2013); (2)"women who oppose gangs in Guatemala" (*Juan-Mateo v. Sessions* 2018, 448–449); and (3) "Salvadoran teenage girl[s]" targeted for recruitment by the Maras (*Escobar-Batres v. Holder* 2010, 447).

The Ninth Circuit Court Appeals in *Gomez-Rodas v. Barr* (2019) affirmed the Board of Immigration Appeals ("BIA") decision denying asylum to an El Salvadorian unaccompanied minor. The Ninth Circuit held that *Gomez-Rodas*'s proposed social group of "young Salvadoran men who are opposed to gang membership and do not have tattoos" cannot be a basis for asylum (*Gomez-Rodas v. Barr* 2019, 62). The court conceded that evidence on country conditions describe tattoos as "one of the most distinctive traits of the violent gang Mara Salvatrucha," that children in areas of El Salvador controlled by the Mara were "subjected to forced recruitment, and that those who oppose recruitment risk harassment, extortion, or death" (*Gomez-Rodas v. Barr* 2019, 62). This evidence "though tragic," did not compel the conclusion that Gomez's proposed social group was "sufficiently discrete or recognized by society as a distinct group" (*Gomez-Rodas v. Barr* 2019, 62).

The Tenth Circuit Court of Appeals also rejected asylum applications based on the proposed social group of males who resisted gang membership in *Bolainez-Vargas v. Garland* (2021) and *Rodas-Orellana v. Holder* (2015). In *Rodas-Orellana v. Holder* (2015, 991), the Tenth Circuit held that the proposed group of "El Salvadoran males threatened and actively recruited by gangs, who resist joining because they oppose the gangs" was not cognizable because it lacked social distinction. Social distinction requires a proposed group to be perceived as a group by society. In evaluating social distinction, the BIA considers whether citizens of the applicant's country would consider individuals with the pertinent trait to constitute a "distinct social group," and whether the applicant's community can identify an individual as belonging to the group (*Rodas-Orellana v. Holder* 2015, 991).

In *Bolainez-Vargas v. Garland* (2021), El Salvadoran native Bolainez-Vargas entered the United States in 2013 as a 16-year-old unaccompanied minor. At a hearing before the immigration judge, he and his uncle described gang violence that their family experienced in El Salvador. In 2007, his parents were attacked by the MS-13 gang because they failed to move their small business out of a rival gang's territory. His father was killed and his mother was shot nine times, although she survived. The family contacted the police about the shooting but the police did nothing because they did not want to get shot or killed themselves. After the shooting, Mr. Bolainez-Vargas and his siblings moved two hours away to live with an uncle but the threats from gang members continued. Bolainez claimed persecution as a member of two particular social groups: (1) teenagers recruited by criminal gangs who rejected membership; and (2) children of families targeted by criminal gangs for retaliation. The immigration judge rejected his claims and ordered him removed to El Salvador, stating that the gang's recruitment efforts did not qualify as persecution and the attack on his parents were not directed at him personally. The immigration judge also determined that neither of his proposed social groups was legally cognizable. Even if the second group was cognizable, there was no nexus between the gang's recruitment activities and the attack on his family members because there was no evidence that he was targeted for retaliation as a family member of either his mother or his father. The Tenth Circuit similarly explained that the harm to Bolainez-Vargas's parents did not constitute persecution directed at him because he was not individually targeted or physically harmed in the attack (*Ritonga v. Holder* 2011, 976). Regarding the threats from gang members, the Tenth Circuit held that "it is well-established that this sort of threatening activity does not constitute persecution" (*Vatulev v. Ashcroft* 2003, 1210). Bolainez also failed to establish that the alleged persecution was because of his membership in a cognizable particular social group. His first proffered group of "teenagers recruited by criminal gangs who have rejected membership" lacked social distinction (*Bolainez-Vargas v.*

Garland 2021, 163). As for the second proposed group of "children of families targeted by criminal gangs for retaliation," Bolainez failed to establish the necessary causal connection between the gang activity and his membership in the second social group (*Bolainez-Vargas v. Garland* 2021, 163). For persecution to be "on account of" a statutorily protected ground, the victim's protected characteristic must be "central to the persecutor's decision to act against the victim" (*Rivera-Barrientos v. Holder* 2012, 646). According to the Tenth Circuit, the gang's activities were motivated by its criminal interests and not by Bolainez's family ties.

The Eleventh Circuit held in *Zapata-Matute v. U.S. Attorney General* (2019) that Zapata-Matute was not entitled to asylum or withholding of removal based on membership in a particular social group. In that case, Honduran native Zapata-Matute fled to the U.S. as a 14-year-old unaccompanied alien child in 2013 after gang members threatened to kill his uncle Gerardo who quit the Honduran gang (*Zapata-Matute v. U.S. Attorney General* 2019). After his illegal entry, DHS initiated removal proceedings against him and eventually released him into his mother's custody in Florida. While removal proceedings were pending against Zapata-Matute, he was informed that his uncle Gerardo was murdered when he was deported back to Honduras. He filed an application for asylum with the USCIS on August 24, 2015. This filing had the effect of closing his removal proceedings before the immigration judge. DHS reopened removal proceedings on August 8, 2016 after USCIS denied the application, and Mr. Zapata-Matute's removal hearing took place on May 16, 2017. The immigration judge denied his application for asylum because his proposed group of "young men and women who may be subjected to recruitment efforts by the gangs and who may reject or resist membership in such gangs" was not cognizable under the BIA's past precedent. Zapata-Matute appealed the IJ's decision to the BIA, which affirmed the removal order. The Eleventh Circuit Court Appeals denied the petition for review of the Board of Immigration Appeals' decision. The Eleventh Circuit stated that the immigration judge correctly applied binding BIA precedent in concluding that his proposed social group of "young men and women who may be subjected to recruitment efforts by the gangs and who may reject or resist membership in such gangs" was not cognizable under the INA (*Matter of S-E-G-,* 2008).

Asylum Based on Proposed Social Group—Fear of Persecution on Account of Protected Ground

In the following cases, federal circuit courts elaborated on the requirement that persecution must be on account of a protected ground and on the nexus requirement to establish fear of persecution.

The Third Circuit Court of Appeals denied the appeal of asylum applicant Guzman-Garcia in *Guzman-Garcia v. Attorney General United States* (2021) because of evidence that Guzman-Garcia could relocate to another part of Guatemala to avoid persecution of gang members like his similarly situated family members who remained in Guatemala without physical harm. Guatemalan Guzman-Garcia entered the United States in December 2014 as an unaccompanied minor. Guzman-Garcia applied for asylum, claiming he was persecuted as a member of a particular social group ("PSG"). He alleged that gang members threatened to kidnap him and then seek ransom money from his father, who owned a cattle ranch. He also claimed that they intended to kill him. The threats were made in letters and in person over "several years" but Guzman-Garcia was never physically harmed, nor did his father ever pay money to any gang members (*Guzman-Garcia v. Attorney General United States* 2021, 236). His father and sister continued to live, without incident, in Guatemala. The IJ denied his application for asylum, because he did not prove past persecution or an objective fear of future persecution—his family continued to live without harm in Guatemala. After the BIA denied his appeal, he filed a petition for review with the Third Circuit. The Third Circuit denied the appeal.

In the case of *Lopez-Cruz v. Attorney General United States* (2019), the Third Circuit Court of Appeals held that Lopez-Cruz failed to demonstrate that her status as a young female head of household was at least "one central reason" for the persecution she feared (*Gonzalez-Posados v. Att'y Gen.* 2015, 685). The Third Circuit affirmed the BIA, holding that Lopez-Cruz failed to establish a nexus between harassment and threats she received from men and her membership in social group of "young female heads of household" (*Lopez-Cruz v. Attorney General United States* 2019, 708). The evidence suggested that Lopez-Cruz's status as a "young female head of household" provided an *opportunity* for her alleged persecutors to take advantage of her– it did not establish that such status was relevant to their *motivation*. The facts that Lopez-Cruz's father was absent and her mother was ill indicated her social vulnerability but did not prove the motive of her persecutors. Country reports indicating that female heads of household were considered a vulnerable population also did not relate to the particular motives of Lopez-Cruz's persecutors. The only evidence relating to the motives of Lopez-Cruz's persecutors—that one wanted to "make [her] the 'woman of the house" and that she would "take [her] sister's place"—did not suggest that they were motivated by Lopez-Cruz's status as a young female head of household (*Lopez-Cruz v. Attorney General United States* 2019, 710). It was not unreasonable for the BIA to conclude that, even if Lopez-Cruz belonged to a protected group, she did not satisfy her burden of establishing that her membership in that group was more than an "incidental, tangential, or superficial" reason for the persecution she feared (*Lopez-Cruz v. Attorney General United States* 2019, 712; *Ndayshimiye v. Att'y Gen.* 2009, 130).

The Sixth Circuit also denied the application for asylum of Corrales-Herrera in *Corrales-Herrera v. Garland* (2021). In that case, Honduran native, Corrales-Herrera, entered the United States as an unaccompanied minor in February 2014. He applied for asylum, claiming that he feared persecution by gangs because he was recruited, beaten, threatened, and robbed by gangs, and he witnessed violence involving his family by gang members. The immigration judge ordered him removed to Honduras and the BIA dismissed his appeal. On appeal, the Sixth Circuit explained that general conditions of rampant gang violence alone were insufficient to support a claim for asylum (*Patel v. Gonzales* 2005; *Umana-Ramos v. Holder* 2013, 670–671). Instead, the asylum applicant must show that he was targeted for abuse based on his membership in a protected category (*Umana-Ramos v. Holder* 2013). Corrales-Herrera argued that he was a member of two social groups targeted for abuse: (1) Honduran males between ages 14 and 18 with no parental protection and (2) family members of his father. The court concluded that the first group did not "share a common immutable characteristic," was not defined with particularity, and was not "socially distinct within Honduran society" (*Corrales-Herrera v. Garland* 2021, 2). There was also no evidence that his parents in the United States could not accompany him back to Honduras to provide parental protection. Although the second group was cognizable and sufficiently particularized, there was no evidence he had been or would be targeted on account of his membership in that particular group.

The Sixth Circuit in *Abarca-Fuentes v. Garland* (2021) also affirmed the BIA's findings, noting that petitioner Abarca-Fuentes was unable to show a nexus between his physical and mental disabilities and the gang recruitment he faced in El Salvador. There, an El Salvadorian national named Abarca-Fuentes entered the U.S. as an unaccompanied minor in 2014. Upon apprehension, he was charged with removability. After being released from custody, he went to live with his mother in Michigan. He then petitioned for asylum, alleging that he repeatedly refused the recruitment attempts of the MS-13 gang. He was often teased in school and his neighborhood due to his mental retardation. The MS-13 gang threatened to kill his aunt if he did not join their ranks. Although the threats to the police, they were never resolved. In 2018, the immigration judge denied his application to stay in the United States. The BIA affirmed the immigration's decision to deny him relief from removability. The Sixth Circuit explained that Abarca did not establish persecution before the immigration judge because he was never physically harmed and only suffered ridicule from neighbors. He was also not a member of a cognizable group of "young males aged 14 to 21 with no family in El Salvador who have noticeable mental and physical disabilities" (*Abarca-Fuentes v. Garland* 2021, 1024). Being the target of gang recruitment was "too broad of a category" to meet the "social visibility requirement" under the INA (*Abarca-Fuentes v. Garland* 2021, 1024). Also, the gang indiscriminately targeted "most if not all segments of society as opposed to the persecution of a specific group" (*Abarca-Fuentes v. Garland* 2021, 1024; *Castro v. Holder* 2013, 513).

The Sixth Circuit Court of Appeals in *Maraziegos-Morales v. Garland* (2021) held that Maraziegos did not establish a nexus between the persecution and her membership in "the Maraziegos family" and her "Charismatic Catholic" religion (*Maraziegos-Morales v. Garland* 2021, 4). In that case, 17-year-old Guatemalan Maraziegos-Morales ("Maraziegos") entered the U.S. illegally as an unaccompanied minor. Upon apprehension by CBP agents, she was released to the custody of her older brother in Tennessee to await formal removal proceedings. She applied for asylum claiming that she faced persecution from MS-13 gang members. A gang leader threatened her when she was nine years old and verbally harassed her over the years. Gang members also persecuted Maraziegos-Morales and her family because of their Charismatic Catholic religion. Gang members stole their church's instruments, ransacked the church, and threatened members with physical violence. The immigration judge denied her asylum. The BIA affirmed the immigration judge, concluding that neither membership in a particular social group nor religious animus constituted one "central reason" for Maraziegos's alleged persecution (*Matter of C-T-L-* 2010).

The Sixth Circuit denied her petition for review. The Sixth Circuit noted that although MS-13 gang members threatened Maraziegos, her family, and members of her church, they did not act on those threats. Maraziegos had "just one physical altercation" with the gang leader over an eight-year span. These acts were not sufficient to rise to the level of persecution because they were not "extreme" systematic mistreatment (*Maraziegos-Morales v. Garland* 2021, 3; *Thapa v. Holder* 2014, 320–321). Maraziegos also did not demonstrate a well-founded fear of future harm. She must show a "real threat of *individual* persecution" that is "subjectively genuine and objectively reasonable" (*Dieng v. Holder* 2012, 873; *Maraziegos-Morales v. Garland* 2021, 3) beyond a "general, speculative assertion of fear" (*Marikasi v. Lynch* 2016, 291–292). The Sixth Circuit did not consider "young Guatemalan women who oppose sexual demands by gang members" as a qualifying social group because it "lacks discrete and socially perceptible characteristics that distinguish the group from all other Guatemalan women" (*Maraziegos-Morales v. Garland* 2021, 4; *Rreshpja v. Gonzales* 2005, 555). The group's "only seemingly unifying characteristic" was that each member faced the "same persecution for rejecting gang advances" (*Maraziegos-Morales v. Garland*

2021, 4). The Sixth Circuit held that this feature did not satisfy the INA's particularity requirement (*Kante v. Holder* 2011). There was no evidence that the mistreatment she experienced from the gang was "on account of" her protected status (*Zaldana Menijar v. Lynch* 2015). It was "unclear" whether the gang's harassment occurred as a result of animus toward the Maraziegos family, Charismatic Catholics, or for some other reason (*Delgado-Ortiz v. Holder* 2010, 1151).

In *Rivars-Garcia v. Garland* (2021), the Tenth Circuit affirmed the BIA's determination that abuse suffered by the unaccompanied minors at hands of their father and uncle were not due to their membership in the family as required for asylum. In that case, sibling brothers from Guatemala who illegally entered the U.S. as unaccompanied minors were placed in removal proceedings where they filed applications for asylum, withholding of removal, protection under the CAT, and humanitarian asylum (*Rivars-Garcia v. Garland* 2021). During their removal hearing, they testified that they suffered physical and emotional abuse from their father and uncle. Their father often abused them but also fought with his friends and new wife when he was drunk or high on drugs. They lived with their aunt Zully for four months before they traveled to the United States to join their mother. They claimed that they were persecuted and feared future persecution on account of their membership in the particular social groups of (1) the immediate members of the Rivars and Garcia families and (2) Guatemalan youth without adequate familial support. Jairo also sought relief based on his membership in the particular social group of Guatemalan youth with disabilities. The BIA affirmed the immigration judge's denial of their petition.

On petition for review, the Tenth Circuit Court of Appeals affirmed the BIA. The Tenth Circuit held that petitioners had the burden of proving they were eligible for asylum and withholding of removal (*Rodas-Orellana v. Holder* 2015). The immigration judge found that the proposed social group of immediate members of the Rivars and Garcia families was a "cognizable particular social group" and that petitioners "suffered harm at the hands of their father and their uncle" (*Rivars-Garcia v. Garland* 2021, 170). However, the immigration judge found that the violence against them was not perpetrated "because of their family ties"—their father and uncle "looked for victims of convenience" when they were "drunk or high" (*Rivars-Garcia v. Garland* 2021, 170). Their fears of gang recruitment also did not rise to the level of persecution and did not have anything to do with their membership in the Rivars and Garcia families (*Rivars-Garcia v. Garland* 2021, 171).

CONCLUSION

This chapter analyzed how federal district and circuit court judges decided on substantive issues raised in asylum cases involving unaccompanied minors that have reached their courts. On the issue of status determination as an unaccompanied alien child, the courts applied the provisions of the TVPRA and ORR Guidelines to evaluate the credibility of evidence showing that the asylum applicant was or was not a minor at the time of apprehension by immigration officials. Under current laws, immigration officials are required to consider multiple forms of evidence, including the non-exclusive use of radiographs, to determine the age of the asylum seeker. Federal courts considered the totality of evidence and the factual circumstances to determine whether immigration officials solely relied on the dental radiograph or considered evidence presented by the asylum seeker to determine the status of the child as an adult or a minor.

One issue relevant to eligibility under asylum laws for placement in least restrictive settings is whether the petitioner is an age-out or a former unaccompanied alien child transferred from ORR to DHS custody. The courts made various distinctions among unaccompanied minors in ORR custody who were released to either parents or sponsors but later rearrested on allegations of gang involvement while still a minor, unaccompanied minors previously held in ORR custody but transferred to ICE custody upon turning eighteen years old (age-outs), unaccompanied minor released to the custody of a parent but rearrested upon allegations of gang involvement after becoming an adult. Only the second category are considered age-outs eligible to placement in least restrictive settings as an alternative to detention. Other issues discussed in this chapter include the rights of unaccompanied alien children while detained, parameters of persecution and basis for the grant of asylum, and the right to abortion while in federal custody. Doctrinal analysis of jurisprudence that federal judges arrived at similar outcomes on some substantive issues but arrived at disparate outcomes at other times, depending on the forum of the asylum application. Applying the law to the facts of the case has led some federal courts to arrive at divergent outcomes on the same litigated issue.

Conclusion

In June 2018, Carlos Holguin gave an interview to National Public Radio ("NPR") regarding the attempts by the Trump administration to modify the terms of the *Flores* Agreement to allow the administration to detain children and their families longer than the time prescribed by the agreement. It was notable for Holguin to be commenting on this process as he was the original lawyer who represented Jenny Flores challenging the conditions of her detention. Mr. Holguin has continued to defend the *Flores Agreement* in court. When asked by the reporter if he thought 33 years ago when he first brought the case, he would still be defending the agreement in court he said:

> (Laughter) I had no idea, no. This is—this has been something that has come as a complete surprise. There is a clause in the original Flores settlement that would have sunset-ended the agreement after five years, but it required the government to implement the terms of the settlement as a federal regulation. The government never did that. And they've still never done that. So the government has had the ability for many, many years to extricate themselves from the requirements of the Flores settlement, but they've never had the wherewithal to simply promulgate the rules that are necessary for it to do so. (Cornish 2018).

Holguin's response captures so much of the U.S. government's response to how it processes and adjudicates asylum claims by UACs in the U.S. As he notes this process has been ongoing for decades. Although the humanitarian crisis of 2014 captured people's attention, and since then media focus and political posturing has kept the issue of unaccompanied minors migration to the U.S. in the national consciousness, as Holguin's quote above notes the U.S. government has been unable and unwilling to appropriately manage the situation. As we have shown throughout this book the U.S. government's response to unaccompanied minors seeking asylum has been haphazard, subject to dramatic shifts in politics, and ultimately not in the best interest of the child. From the 'zero tolerance' policies of the Trump administration to the policy of allowing unaccompanied minors to appear before immigration judges without an attorney, the United States government has not produced a consistent and humane policy of handling asylum claims from UACs.

MAIN THEMES

A few main themes emerge from our analysis of the judicial proceedings, from immigration courts to Federal courts, of UACs seeking asylum. First is the haphazard or inconsistencies in the decision-making across immigration judges. Chapter 2 examined the social, economic, and political factors that influence immigration judges' decisions on granting asylum to UACs or not. In examining 12,826 cases of UACs claiming asylum in immigration courts from 1997 to 2020 we found many examples of inconsistencies in the decision making of immigration judges. By simply looking at the distribution of case outcomes across geographical entities one can see huge disparities. For example, positive outcomes on asylum applications for UACs varied greatly across hearing location, base city, county, and state in which the case was heard. More importantly they varied greatly across immigration judges themselves. This is inline with previous studies which examine the variation in asylum approval across all cases (Miller et al. 2015, Ramji-Nogales et al. 2009). We proceed further, however, to examine what factors may be behind this great divergence in asylum outcomes for UACs. We find some support for the country characteristics of where minors are fleeing from impacting their asylum claims. This is what one would expect if asylum law was universally followed and implemented by immigration judges. We particularly find that the level of democracy in the home country of a UAC is determinative meaning the more democratic the country the less likely the UAC is to receive asylum in the U.S. However, we do not find similar support for the level of human rights repression in a state.

In terms of politics driving the large disparity in asylum outcomes for UACs we answer in the affirmative. We present evidence that the ideology of the immigration judge, the partisanship of the immigration judge, and even the county level support for Presidential candidates all factor into the disparity rate for UACs seeking asylum. For social factors we find that UACs coming from a country where Spanish is the main language are significantly less likely to receive asylum than those coming from non-Spanish speaking countries. Finally, in due process terms we see that UAC who go before an immigration judge without a lawyer are much less likely to receive asylum than those who do have a lawyer. From this analysis we can conclude that many factors outside the control of the minor and outside the applicable law factor into unaccompanied minors receiving asylum in America. In fact for UACs to receive asylum in the U.S. it is perhaps better to be "lucky" in terms of which judge you go before than having an airtight case of asylum.

Chapter 3 takes a look at the first stage of the appellate process for asylum claims by unaccompanied minors—The Board of Immigration Appeals. The

BIA serves as the main appellate body for the immigration legal system. We examine in Chapter 3 what factors determine whether the BIA is likely to support the negative decisions by immigration judges on UAC asylum cases. Here again we found inconsistencies in the application of asylum law and the influence of politics on the decision-making of the Board. However, those forces were not as strong on the BIA as they are for the body of immigration judges itself. What seems to matter more for the BIA is the workload and the workflow.

Overall we see that the BIA overwhelmingly approves of the lower courts negative decisions against unaccompanied minors. More often than not, UACs are not finding a path to receiving asylum in the U.S. by appealing their cases to the BIA. There are some exceptions of course and those exceptions do align with the larger themes of this book. For example, in terms of political influence on the BIA the Attorney General can influence the operations of this institution in significant ways. Not just through the appointment process, the process of expanding or contracting the size of the Board, but also through the referral process where the AG can assign themselves cases from the BIA. This power of the AG shows that the BIA operates in the shadow of the Attorney General and so one can expect that the BIA would rule in alignment with the politics of the AG in office. More precisely one would expect the BIA to be "harsher" towards UACs during Republican administrations but more "generous" during Democratic ones. We however find the opposite, at least with regards to the mean partisan composition of the BIA. If the BIA is more Democratic their likelihood of supporting the opinions of immigration judges rejecting asylum claims from UACs increases.

As in Chapter 2, we also find that the level of democracy in the country the minor was feeling from influenced the BIA's decision as they were more likely to support the rulings from IJs denying asylum from minors fleeing countries with higher levels of democracy. As with chapter 2 again we do not find a similar influence for the level of human rights repression. In terms of due process, we also find that the Attorney variable was significant but interestingly the results were that if UACs had an attorney during their trial with IJs the BIA was more likely to support the IJs negative ruling. What this shows is that the BIA is willing to rectify situations where UACs are going before IJs without lawyers by rejecting those negative decisions by IJs. This shows the BIA is able to serve due process somewhat by recognizing UACs without attorneys before IJs is not a situation where they can adequately make their case. Additionally, we find that the BIA is more likely to affirm the negative rulings on asylum for UACs from judges who are overall more "generous" in their asylum decisions. Conversely the Board is less likely to affirm the negative decisions from judges who are overall more "harsh" in their decisions regarding asylum for UACs. This finding also suggests that the BIA can serve as a check on potential due process violations which occur at the immigration judge decision level.

Finally, we also find that workload management has an effect on BIA rulings. The number of judges, the length of time the case is before the Board and the number of cases appealed by UACs have an impact on whether the Board is more supportive of the negative decisions made by IJs towards UAC asylum claims or not. Overall we find that the BIA is not immune to political influence but it is perhaps more immune than the immigration judges themselves which is interesting considering the AGs ability to refer cases from the Board to themselves. Additionally, we see the BIA is able to correct for some of the due process deficiencies that happen at the immigration court level.

Chapters 4 and 5 examine closely federal court decisions regarding asylum claims by unaccompanied minors. These chapters shift us from the macro-level analysis in chapters 2 and 3 to a micro-level analysis where we examine the specific facts and legal principles of federal cases involving unaccompanied minors. Chapter 4 examines procedural due process rights for UACs while chapter 5 examines the substantive rights of UACs. Both of these chapters shift from the political lens used in chapters 2 and 3 to a legal one using the legal model of judicial decision making to understand the outcomes of federal judges' decision making on asylum claims for unaccompanied minors.

Chapter 4 highlights the genuine importance of the *Flores* Agreement in protecting the procedural rights of unaccompanied minors. Multiple federal cases, using the *Flores* agreement, pushed back against many of the hardline measures pursued by the Trump administration and even some of the policies pursued by the Obama administration. The Trump administration even attempted to neutralize the *Flores* agreement by issuing a final rule implementing its procedures. However, multiple federal courts determined that the administration's implementation was inconsistent with the original agreement. More specifically, the courts determined that the Trump administration's final rule deviated significantly from the original agreement on when UACs could be held in a secure facility and on bond hearing requests. The Trump administration wanted to be able to hold minors in secure facilities when they were considered "otherwise a danger to self or others" and also wanted to change the bond hearing request to one where the minor would need to affirmatively request it as opposed to being automatically offered one. These are the two main provisions the Federal courts objected to and they highlight the importance of the *Flores* agreement in safeguarding procedural rights for unaccompanied minors. The *Flores* agreement was also essential in holding the executive branch accountable in its holding of UACs during the COVID-19 pandemic ensuring that the pandemic was not used as an excuse for indefinite detention or detaining minors in unsanitary conditions.

Additional laws and policies are important for safeguarding the procedural rights for unaccompanied minors. The Administrative Procedures Act was essential in stopping the Trump administration's family separation policy. Additionally, some UACs were able to challenge their detention (and release and re-detention as the case may be) under *Habeas Corpus* petitions. Although the Federal Courts have served as a bulwark in protecting some of the rights of UACs, especially against some of the most extreme measures of the executive branch, they did not act completely in favor of unaccompanied children. For example, the courts routinely rejected attempts by individuals subject to the family separation policy to bring *Bivens* claims against officials implementing the policies. Furthermore, and more significantly, the federal courts have re-enforced the policy that the government is not required to provide counsel to unaccompanied minors in immigration court proceedings despite the fact that failure by IJs to inform UACs of legal services available to them can be grounds for reversal of their case.

Chapter 5 focusing on the substantive rights of unaccompanied minors as determined by federal court cases highlights again the importance of the *Flores* agreement in protecting the rights of UACs as well as the importance of the TVPRA in doing the same. The TVPRA requires UACs to be placed in "the least restrictive setting that is in the best interest of the child" (8 U.S.C. § 1232(c)(2)(A)), and for HHS and DHS to develop procedures to make a "prompt determination" of the unaccompanied alien child's age, taking into account "multiple forms of evidence, including the non-exclusive use of radiographs" (8 U.S.C. 1232(b)(4); *R.R. v. Orozco* 2020, 4; *V.V. v. Orozco* 2020, 4). This latter requirement has proven an important check on government agencies such as ICE who, as the cases described in Chapter 5 show, were over reliant on radiographs to try and determine the age of UACs. Additionally, in Chapter 5 we saw how courts used the *Flores* agreement to ensure that the ORR was following "the best interest of the child" in determining placement for UACs and also holding the CBP accountable for holding these children in unsafe and unsanitary conditions when they first encountered and detained them.

In terms of Constitutional protections, there was a mixed result for UACs in federal courts. One the one hand the courts uniformly found that the ORR was violating the right of female UACs to seek abortions. During the Trump Administration, Scott Lloyd, then director of ORR, required that he personally approve any requests by female UACs to seek abortions which he promptly denied (Siegel 2017). On the other hand, however, the federal courts generally found in favor of the government in cases where UACs claimed that during their detention they were subject to abuse. The courts applied the narrow "deliberate indifference" standard stating that government officials were not liable for failing to prevent the abuse by other detainees.

Finally, and most importantly, the federal courts routinely rejected claims from UACs that being persecuted for resisting efforts to join a gang did not qualify the UAC for asylum in the United States. Using the standards established by the INA, the federal courts argued that being a minor and subject tb threats from gangs because they would not join, although "tragic," do not constitute grounds for asylum because that is too broad a category and thus does not make them a protected group. This strong affirmation by multiple federal courts has had a significant impact on the asylum claims for many UACs since what is driving most of them to flee the Northern Triangle countries is persecution from gangs.

THE BEST INTEREST OF THE CHILD AND
THE GLOBAL REFUGEE SYSTEM

In her book *Child Migration & Human Rights in a Global Age* (2014) Jacqueline Bhabha makes a striking but obvious point

> Children fleeing persecution would seem to have a peculiarly strong claim to protection, placed as they are at the intersection of two distinctly vulnerable populations, refugees and children, and faced with alternatives likely to irreparably harm their life prospects. Prevention of violence at a minimum would seem to mandate protective intervention (2014: 205).

Bhabha goes on to note that although child migrants, and unaccompanied minors in particular, should be the easiest cases for granting asylum they are often denied such rights and not just in the United States, but in many other countries as well. She asks a rhetorical question that beggars belief that it even needs to be asked, "why is it that children migrating away from severe adversity . . . encounter hostility and a climate of suspicion despite a broad international consensus supportive of their right to protection." (2014: 205)

Those international standards that she is referencing are the Refugee Convention (1951) and the United Nations Convention on the Rights of the Child (1989). The Convention on the Rights of the Child establishes what is known as the "best interest of the child" standard which states, among other things, that this standard should be the "primary consideration" in all actions involving children (UN CRC 1989). Additionally, the "best interests of the child" principle holds the State "ultimately responsible" in meeting and protecting the "basic needs" and "fundamental rights" of children (USCIS Asylum Division 2009, 8). Although the U.S. is not a member of the Convention on the Rights of the Child, as we show in Chapter 1 the U.S. has incorporated a "best interest of the child standard" in various laws and policies from the TVPRA to the *Flores* agreement, to various guidelines issued by the Office of Chief Immigration Judge among others. However, as we also show in subsequent chapters, especially Chapter 5 the U.S. immigration and federal courts have not incorporated a "best interest of the child" standard as substantive grounds for asylum.

Many of the cases of unaccompanied minors seeking asylum covered in this book are of children fleeing from three countries—El Salvador, Guatemala, and Honduras with many of them fleeing gang violence and the threat of gang recruitment. Both the immigration courts and the Federal courts have decided that this level of persecution is not grounds for asylum in the U.S. In a strict legal sense the courts are probably correct but on common sense and humanitarian grounds it seems hard to see how deporting a child back to a country to be subject to gang violence is in any way in the "best interest of the child." This dual nature of the "best interest of the child" standard in U.S. immigration law highlights the overall inconsistency with which the U.S. treats asylum claims from unaccompanied minors. For instance, under the TVPRA the U.S. government is required to place unaccompanied minors it detains in "the least restrictive setting that is in the best interest of the child" (8 U.S.C. § 1232(c)(2)(A)), but that same minor may also be subject to deportation back to their home country because persecution by a gang does not meet the narrow standards for asylum under the law.

Fundamentally, this is not just an issue for unaccompanied minors. The entire asylum system, or immigration matrix as termed by Helen Boursier (2019), is chock full of inconsistencies, contradictions, and barriers that structurally make it very difficult for people (adults and minors) who have a well-founded fear of persecution to receive asylum. As Boursier notes the "immigration matrix" includes everyone and everything from the laws establishing the grounds for asylum to the judges that enforce those laws, the ORR employee who conducts a home visit to determine if the environment is safe for the detained child to stay in, to the Border Patrol agent who first encounters the child as they enter the U.S. Through this mass of people and policies it is easy for legitimate claims to get denied.

The denial of legitimate asylum claims is not just a problem for unaccompanied minors and it is also not just a problem in the United States. As Serena Parekh (2020) notes, there are actually two refugee crises in the world today. The second is the enormous amount of people who are fleeing persecution in their home countries but the first is the policies and procedures set up by wealthy countries in the West (such as the U.S.) that prevent people from reaching them to avail themselves of their rights to asylum. She argues that the heart of the first crisis is:

"that refugees around the world are largely unable to get refuge." (2020: 3). This is because "most states consider it a legitimate exercise of their national sovereignty to implement deterrence policies that make it difficult, and danger-ous, for refugees to claim asylum in the first place. This is why asylum has come to resemble a cat-and-mouse game—refugees seek their human rights, while Western states try to prevent them from doing so." (2020: 10)

The refugee system established after World War II exemplified by the Refugee Convention of 1951 is broken. Created during the Cold War the global refu-gee system reflected the politics of the time with its emphasis on individual persecution and priority given to dissidents fleeing the Soviet Union and other Communist countries (Micinski 2021). The collapse of Communism and the end of the Cold War deprived the U.S. and the Western world of its main rival and its ability to score political points by accepting refugees from its antagonist. More recently, the rise of "demagogic nationalism" (Braaten 2021) exemplified by reactionary political movements in the United States, Europe and other countries such as Brazil has turned countries that at one time were open to accepting asylum seekers to close their borders and build walls to keep people out. With the potential catastrophic disruption to peoples lives caused by climate change already emerging, people fleeing for refuge to safe places is only going to increase. The United States and the rest of the world need to recognize this new reality and create new standards of asylum that include persecution by private actors such as gangs and disruption caused by climate change if we want a world where human rights are respected and people can live lives of dignity, especially children.

Bibliography

Aamer v. Obama, 742 F.3d 1023 (D.C. Cir. 2014).

Abarca-Fuentes v. Garland, 852 Fed.Appx. 1021 (6th Cir 2021).

Abrajano, Marisa, and Zoltan L. Hajnal. 2015. *White Backlash: Immigration, Race, and American Politics.* Princeton University Press.

Acquaah v. Holder, 589 F.3d 332 (6th Cir. 2009).

Act of February 15, 1893, ch. 114, § 7, 27 Stat. 449, 452, ECF No. 15-5 at 5.

Addington v. Texas, 441 U.S. 418, 99 S.Ct. 1804, 60 L.Ed.2d 323 (1979).

Administrative Procedure Act ("APA"), 5 U.S.C. § 701 et seq.

Aguayo v. Martinez, No. 120CV00825DDDKMT, 2020 WL 2395638 (D. Colo. May 12, 2020).

Aguilera-Enriquez v. INS, 516 F.2d 565 (6th Cir. 1975).

Alam v. Keeton, Slip Copy, 2020 WL 5439513 (D. Arizona, 2020).

Al-Ghorbani v. Holder, 585 F.3d 980 (6th Cir. 2009).

Ali v. Ashcroft, 366 F.3d 407 (6th Cir. 2004).

Ali v. Gibson, 572 F.2d 971 (3d Cir. 1978).

Al-Saka v. Sessions, 904 F.3d 427 (6th Cir. 2018).

Alvarado v. Holder, 759 F.3d 1121 (9th Cir. 2014).

Alvarez, Priscilla. 2021a. "Biden Administration Tells Facilities for Migrant Children to Reopen to Pre-Pandemic Levels." *CNN,* March 5. https://www.cnn.com/2021/03/05/politics/immigration-border-crowding-covid/index.html.

Alvarez, Priscilla. 2021b. "Government Watchdog Launches Review Into Troubled Fort Bliss Facility for Migrant Children." *CNN,* August 2. https://www.cnn.com/2021/08/02/politics/fort-bliss-migrants-ig/index.html.

Amanfi v. Ashcroft, 328 F.3d 719 (3d Cir. 2003).

Amaya-Amaya v. Attorney General United States, 811 Fed.Appx. 764 (3rd Cir. 2020).

Amendment and Extension of Order Under Sections 362 and 365 of the Public Health Service Act: Order Suspending Introduction of Certain Persons from Countries Where a Communicable Disease Exists, 85 Fed. Reg. 31503, 2020 WL 2619696 (May 26, 2020) ("May Order").

American Bar Association Commission on Immigration. 2015. "A Humanitarian Call to Action: Unaccompanied Children in Removal Proceedings Present a Critical Need for Legal Representation." Last modified April 15, 2015. https:

//www.americanbar.org/content/dam/aba/administrative/immigration/trainings/representing_uacs_neworleans_2015.pdf.

Amnesty International. 2021. "Facts and Figures: Deportations of Unaccompanied Migrant Children by the USA and Mexico." Last modified June 11, 2021. https://www.amnesty.org/en/latest/news/2021/06/facts-figures-deportations-children-usa-mexico/.

Amuedo-Dorantes, Catalina, and Thitima Puttitanun. 2016. "DACA and the Surge in Unaccompanied Minors at the US-Mexico Border." *International Migration* 54 (4): 102–117.

Amuedo-Dorantes, Catalina, and Thitima Puttitanun. 2018. "Undocumented Youth in Limbo: The Impact of America's Immigration Enforcement Policy on Juvenile Deportations." *Journal of Population Economics* 31: 597–626.

Andersson, Hilary, and Anne Laurent. 2021. "Children Tell of Neglect, Filth and Fear in US Asylum Camps." *BBC News*, May 23, 2021. https://www.bbc.com/news/world-us-canada-57149721.

Andrews v. Camden Cty., 95 F. Supp. 2d 217 (D.N.J. 2000).

Anker, Deborah, and Michael Posner. 1981. "The Forty Year Crisis: A Legislative History of the Refugee Act of 1980." *San Diego Law Review* 19 (9): 1–89.

A.P.F. v. United States, 492 F.Supp.3d 989 (D. Arizona 2020).

Apprehension, Processing, Care, and Custody of Alien Minors and Unaccompanied Alien Children, 84 Fed. Reg. 44 (August 23, 2019) ("Final Rule").

Aquino, Alyssa. 2021. "DC Circ. Lifts Block on Migrant Children Expulsion Policy." *Law360*, January 29. https://www.law360.com/articles/1350276/dc-circ-lifts-block-on-migrant-children-expulsion-policy.

Aref v. Lynch, 833 F.3d 242 (D.C. Cir. 2016).

Argueta, Carla. 2016. "Border Security: Immigration Enforcement Between Ports of Entry." *Congressional Research Service Report R42138*, April 19. https://sgp.fas.org/crs/homesec/R42138.pdf.

Armstrong v. Bush, 924 F.2d 282 (D.C. Cir. 1991).

Armstrong v. Manzo 380 U.S. 545 (1965).

Arnold and Porter LLP. 2019. "Reforming the Immigration System Updated Report." *American Bar Association.* Washington, D.C.

Arthur, Andrew. 2021. "Reports Suggest HHS Is Cutting Corners in Vetting Sponsors of Migrant Children." *Center for Migration Studies*, May 6, 2021. https://cis.org/Arthur/Reports-Suggest-HHS-Cutting-Corners-Vetting-Sponsors-Migrant-Children.

Azar v. Garza, ⸺ U.S. ⸺, 138 S. Ct. 1790, 201 L.Ed.2d 118 (2018) (per curiam).

Bah v. Barr, 409 F. Supp. 3d 464 (E.D. Va. 2019).

Ballas v. Tedesco, 41 F. Supp. 2d 531 (D.N.J. 1999).

Banegas Gomez v. Barr, 922 F.3d 101 (2d Cir. 2019).

Barron v. Ashcroft 358 F.3d 674 (9th Cir. 2004).

Bartels, Brandon. 2010. "Top-Down and Bottom-Up Models of Judicial Reasoning." In *The Psychology of Judicial Decision Making*, edited by David Klein and Gregory Mitchell. New York: Oxford University Press.

Barthold v. INS, 517 F.2d 689 (5th Cir. 1975).

Basri v. Barr, 469 F. Supp. 3d 1063 (D. Colo. 2020).

Bean, Tammy, Elisabeth Eurelings-Bontekoe, and Philip Spinhoven. 2017. "Course and Predictors of Mental Health of Unaccompanied Refugee Minors in the Netherlands: One-year Follow-up." *Social Science & Medicine* 64 (6): 1204–1215.

Bell v. Wolfish, 441 U.S. 520 (1979).

Beltran v. Cardall, 222 F.Supp.3d 476 (E.D. Virginia 2016).

Berman v. Young, 291 F.3d 976 (7th Cir. 2002).

Betancourt-Aplicano v. Sessions, 747 F. App'x 279 (6th Cir. 2018).

Betancourt Barco v. Price, No. 2:20-CV-350-WJ-CG, 2020 WL 2099890 (D.N.M. May 1, 2020).

Bhabha, Jacqueline. 2014. *Child Migration & Human Rights in a Global Age.* Princeton: Princeton University Press.

B.I.C v. Asher, 2016 WL 8672760 (W.D. Washington, 2016).

Bivens v. Six Unknown Federal Narcotics Agents, 403 U.S. 388, 91 S.Ct. 1999, 29 L.Ed.2d 619 (1971).

Biwot v. Gonzales 403 F.3d 1094 (9th Cir. 2005).

Bi Xia Qu v. Holder, 618 F.3d 602 (6th Cir. 2010).

Blue, Sarah, Alisa Hartsell, Rebecca Torres, and Paul Flynn. 2020. "The Uneven Geography of Asylum and Humanitarian Relief: Place-Based Precarity for Central American Migrant Youth in the United States Judicial System." *Journal of Ethnic and Migration Studies*: 47 (20): 4631–4650.

Bolainez-Vargas v. Garland, 2021 U.S. App. LEXIS 16959 (10th Cir. 2021).

Bonilla-Morales v. Holder, 607 F.3d 1132 (6th Cir. 2010).

Boursier, Helen T. 2019. *Desperately Seeking Asylum: Testimonies of Trauma, Courage, and Love.* Lanham, MD: Rowman & Littlefield.

B.R. v. Garland, 4 F.4th 783 (Ninth Circuit 2021).

Braaten, Daniel. 2021. "Human Rights: What Does the Future Hold?" *International Studies Review* 23 (3): 1164–1178.

Braaten, Daniel, and Claire Braaten. 2021. "Children Seeking Asylum: Determinants of Asylum Claims by Unaccompanied Minors in the U.S. from 2013–2017." *Law and Policy* 43 (2): 97–125.

Breen, Richard. 1996. *Regression Models: Censored, Sample Selected, or Truncated Data.* Thousand Oaks, CA: Sage Publications.

Bronstein, Israel, and Paul Montgomery. 2011. "Psychological Distress in Refugee Children: A Systematic Review." *Clinical Child and Family Psychology Review* 14 (1): 44–56.

Brown v. Harris, 240 F.3d 383 (4th Cir. 2001).

Brown v. Plata, 563 U.S. 493, 131 S.Ct. 1910, 179 L.Ed.2d 969 (2011).

Brownfield, William. 2012. "Gangs, Youth, and Drugs—Breaking the Cycle of Violence." *U.S. Department of State*, October 1, 2012. https://2009-2017.state.gov /j/inl/rls/rm/199133.htm.

Bruno, Andorra. 2015. "In-Country Refugee Processing: In Brief." *Congressional Research Service Report R44020*, May 7, 2015. https://sgp.fas.org/crs/homesec/ R44020.pdf.

Bruno, Andorra. 2015. "Unauthorized Alien Students: Issues and 'DREAM Act' Legislation." *Congressional Research Service Report RL33863*, January 20. https://crsreports.congress.gov/product/pdf/RL/RL33863.

Bruno, Andorra. 2019. "Immigration: U.S. Asylum Policy. *Congressional Research Service Report 45539.* February 19. https://fas.org/sgp/crs/homesec/R45539.pdf.

Buckhannon Bd. & Care Home, Inc. v. West Virginia Dep't of Health & Human Res., 532 U.S. 598, 121 S.Ct. 1835, 149 L.Ed.2d 855 (2001).

Byrne, Olga, and Elise Miller. 2012. "The Flow of Unaccompanied Children Through the Immigration System. *Vera Institute of Justice,* March. https://www.vera.org/downloads/publications/the-flow-of-unaccompanied-children-through-the-immigration-system.pdf.

Caldwell, Alicia, and Michelle Hackman. 2021. "Border Crossings by Migrant Children to Rise Sharply, U.S. Estimates Show." *Wall Street Journal*, March 26. https://www.wsj.com/articles/border-crossings-by-migrant-children-to-rise-sharply-according-to-internal-u-s-government-estimates-11616800942.

Call, Charles. 2021. "The Imperative to Address the Root Causes of Migration From Central America." *Brookings Institution*, January 29. https://www.brookings.edu/blog/order-from-chaos/2021/01/29/the-imperative-to-address-the-root-causes-of-migration-from-central-america/.

Carbonell v. I.N.S., 429 F.3d 894 (9th Cir. 2005).

Cardenas-Martinez v. Garland, Not Reported in Fed. Rptr., 2021 WL 3138593 (4th Circuit 2021).

Cardona, Alexi. 2021. "Recapping the Five Biggest Controversies at the Homestead Migrant Children's Camp." *Miami New Times*, February 26. https://www.miaminewtimes.com/news/abuse-allegations-at-homestead-shelter-for-migrant-children-11886996.

Carlson v. Green, 446 U.S. 14, 100 S.Ct. 1468, 64 L.Ed.2d 15 (1980).

Carlson v. Landon, 342 U.S. 524 (1952).

Casas-Castrillon v. DHS, 535 F.3d 942 (9th. Cir. 2008).

Castillo Sanchez v. U.S. Attorney General, 523 Fed. App'x 682 (11th Cir. 2013).

Castro v. Holder, 530 F. App'x 513 (6th Cir. 2013).

Catholic Relief Services. 2021. "Between Rootedness and the Decision to Migrate." Last modified October 2020. https://reliefweb.int/sites/reliefweb.int/files/resources/between_rootedness_and_the_decision_to_migrate.pdf.

Cavendish, Betsy, and Maru Cortazar. 2011. "Children at the Border: The Screening, Protection And Repatriation of Unaccompanied Mexican Minors." *Appleseed,*. https://www.issuelab.org/resources/14642/14642.pdf

Centers for Disease Control and Prevention. 2020a. "Control of Communicable Diseases; Foreign Quarantine: Suspension of Introduction of Persons into United States From Designated Foreign Countries or Places for Public Health Purposes." 85 Federal Register 16559. March 24. https://www.govinfo.gov/content/pkg/FR-2020-03-24/pdf/2020-06238.pdf.

Center for Disease Control and Prevention. 2020b. "Notice of Order Under Sections 362 and 365 of the Public Health Service Act Suspending Introduction of Certain Persons From Countries Where a Communicable Disease Exists." 85 Federal

Register 17060. March 26. https://www.govinfo.gov/content/pkg/FR-2020-03-26 /pdf/2020-06327.pdf.

Centers for Disease Control and Prevention. 2021a. "Notice of Temporary Exception from Expulsion of Unaccompanied Noncitizen Children Encountered in the United States Pending Forthcoming Public Health Determination." 86 Federal Register 9942. February 17. https://www.govinfo.gov/content/pkg/FR-2021-02-17 /pdf/2021-03227.pdf.

Chand, Daniel, and William Schreckhise. 2015. "Secure Communities and Community Values: Local Context and Discretionary Immigration Law Enforcement." *Journal of Ethnic and Migration Studies* 41 (10): 1621–1643.

Chand, Daniel, and William Schreckhise. 2020. "Independence in Administrative Adjudications: When and Why Agency Judges Are Subject to Deference and Influence." *Administration & Society* 52 (2): 171–206.

Chand, Daniel, William Schreckhise, and Marianne Bowers. 2017. "Dynamics of State and Local Context and Immigration Asylum Hearing Decisions." *Journal of Public Administration Research and Theory* 27 (1): 182–196.

Chaplin, Angelina. 2019. "Florida Detention Center Expands, Packing in Migrant Children Like Sardines." *Huffington Post*, February 12. https://www.huffpost.com/ entry/florida-detention-center-immigrant-children_n_5c5e1a64e4b0910c63f071e1.

Chappell v. Wallace, 462 U.S. 296 (1983).

Chavez, Lilian, and Cecilia Menjívar. 2010. "Children Without Borders: A Mapping of the Literature on Unaccompanied Migrant Children to the United States." *Migraciones Internacionales* 5 (3): 71–111.

Chen Zhou Chai v. Carroll, 48 F.3d 1331 (4th Cir. 1995).

Chiedi, Joanne. 2019. "Care Provider Facilities Described Challenges Addressing Mental Health Needs of Children in HHS Custody." *U.S. Office of Inspector General OEI-09-18-00431*, September. https://oig.hhs.gov/oei/reports/oei-09-18 -00431.pdf.

Children and Families Administration. 2014. "Announcement of the Award of Two Single-Source Program Expansion Supplement Grants to Support Legal Services to Refugees Under the Unaccompanied Alien Children's Program." Last modified October 16, 2014. https://www.federalregister.gov/documents/2014/10/16/2014 -24555/announcement-of-the-award-of-two-single-source-program-expansion -supplement-grants-to-support-legal.

Children's Hosp. of the King's Daughters, Inc. v. Azar, 896 F.3d 615 (4th Cir. 2018).

Chishti, Muzaffar, and Faye Hipsman. 2014. "Dramatic Surge in the Arrival of Unaccompanied Children has Deep Roots and No Simple Solutions." *Migration Information Source*, June 13, 2014. https://www.migrationpolicy.org/article/ dramatic-surge-arrival-unaccompanied-children-has-deep-roots-and-no-simple -solutions.

Chrysler Corp. v. Brown, 441 U.S. 281, 99 S.Ct. 1705, 60 L.Ed.2d 208 (1979).

Citizens for Responsibility and Ethics in Washington ("CREW") v U.S. Department of Homeland Security, 387 F.Supp.3d 33 (D. Columbia, 2019).

CJLG v. Sessions, 880 F.3d 1122 (2018).

Cobell v. Kempthorne, 455 F.3d 301 (D.C. Cir. 2006).

Cobell v. Norton, 392 F.3d 461 (D.C. Cir. 2004).

Cobell v. Norton, 428 F.3d 1070 (D.C. Cir. 2005).

Codner v. Choate, No. 20-CV-01050-PAB, 2020 WL 2769938 (D. Colo. May 27, 2020).

Control of Communicable Diseases. 2020. "Foreign Quarantine: Suspension of Introduction of Persons Into United States from Designated Foreign Countries or Places for Public Health Purposes." 85 Fed. Reg. 16559, 2020 WL 1330968. March 24.

Control of Communicable Diseases. 2020. "Foreign Quarantine: Suspension of the Right to Introduce and Prohibition of Introduction of Persons into United States From Designated Foreign Countries or Places for Public Health Purposes." 85 Fed. Reg. 56424, 2020 WL 5439721. September 11 ("Final Rule").

Control of Communicable Diseases. 2020. "Order Suspending Introduction of Certain Persons from Countries where a Communicable Disease Exists." 85 Fed. Reg. 17060, March 26.

Cooper v. Oklahoma, 517 U.S. 348 (1996).

Coppedge, Michael, John Gerring, Carl Henrik Knutsen, Staffan I. Lindberg, Jan Teorell, Nazifa

Alizada, David Altman, Michael Bernhard, Agnes Cornell, M. Steven Fish, Lisa Gastaldi,

Haakon Gjerløw, Adam Glynn, Sandra Grahn, Allen Hicken, Garry Hindle, Nina Ilchenko, Katrin Kinzelbach, Joshua K[rusell, Kyle L. Marquardt, Kelly McMann, Valeriya Mechkova, Juraj Medzihorsky, Pamela Paxton, Daniel Pemstein, Josefine Pernes, Oskar Ryd´en, Johannes von Römer, Brigitte Seim, Rachel Sigman, Svend-Erik Skaaning, Jeffrey Staton, Aksel Sundstrrom, Eitan Tzelgov, Yi-ting Wang, Tore Wig, Steven Wilson and Daniel Ziblatt. 2022. "VDem [Country–Year/Country–Date] Dataset v12/" Varieties of Democracy (V-Dem) Project. https://doi.org/10.23696/vdemds22.

Cornelius, Wayne, and Marc R. Rosenblum. 2005. "Immigration and Politics." *Annual Review of Political Science* 8: 99–119.

Cornish, Audie. 2018. "Interview with Carlos Holguin." *NPR*, June 22. https://www.npr.org/2018/06/22/622678753/the-history-of-the-flores-settlement-and-its-effects-on-immigration.

Corona, Eliana. 2017. "The Reception and Processing of Minors in the United States in Comparison to That of Australia and Canada: Would Being a Party to the UN Convention on the Right of the Child Make a Difference in U.S. Courts?" *Hastings International and Comparative Law Review* 40 (2): 205–229.

Corrales-Herrera v. Garland, Not Reported in Fed. Rptr., 21-3332 (6th Cir. 2021).

Correctional Servs. Corp. v. Malesko, 534 U.S. 61 (2001).

Cortez-Vasquez v. Holder, 440 F. App'x 295 (5th Cir. 2011) (per curiam).

Coulehan, Erin. 2021. "Report: Number of Unaccompanied Migrant Children at CBP Facilities Drops, Daily Apprehensions Persist." *Border Report*, April 30. https://www.borderreport.com/hot-topics/immigration/report-number-of-unaccompanied-migrant-children-at-cbp-facilities-drops-daily-apprehensions-persist/.

Crespin-Valladares v. Holder, 632 F.3d 117 (4th Cir. 2011).

Cruz-Guzman v. Barr, 920 F.3d 1033 (6th Cir. 2019).

C.T.M. v. Moore, Slip Copy 2020 WL 5919737 (D. C., N.D. Texas 2020).

Dada v. Mukasey, 554 U.S. 1, 128 S.Ct. 2307, 171 L.Ed.2d 178 (2008).

Dallakoti v. Holder, 619 F.3d 1264 (10th Cir. 2010).

Daniel R.-S. v. Anderson, Slip Copy, 2020 WL 2301445 (D. New Jersey 2020).

Daniels, Jeff. 2018. "Trump Administration's 'Zero Tolerance' Border Enforcement Policy to Separate More Families." *CNBC*, May 7. https://www.cnbc.com/2018/05/07/tougher-us-border-enforcement-policy-to-separate-more-families.html.

Davis v. Passman, 442 U.S. 228, 99 S.Ct. 2264, 60 L.Ed.2d 846 (1979).

Davis v. Pension Benefit Guar. Corp., 571 F.3d 1288 (D.C. Cir. 2009).

DB v. Cardall, 826 F.3d 721 (4th Cir. 2016).

De Oliveira Viegas v. Green, 370 F. Supp. 3d 443 (D.N.J. 2019).

Delgado-Ortiz v. Holder, 600 F.3d 1148 (9th Cir. 2010).

Demore v. Kim, 538 U.S. 510, 123 S.Ct. 1708, 155 L.Ed.2d 724 (2003).

Denko v. INS, 351 F.3d 717 (6th Cir. 2003).

Dept. of Homeland Security, Office of the Inspector General. 2018. "Special Review—Initial Observations Regarding Family Separation Issues Under The Zero Tolerance Policy." Last modified September 27, 2018. https://www.oig.dhs.gov/sites/default/files/assets/2018-10/OIG-18-84-Sep18.pdf ("DHS OIG Report").

Diaz, Tom. 2011. *No Boundaries: Transnational Latino Gangs and American Law Enforcement.* Ann Arbor: University of Michigan Press.

Dickson, Caitlin. 2014. "How Mexico's Cartels are Behind the Border Kid Crisis." *The Daily Beast.* June 23. https://www.thedailybeast.com/how-mexicos-cartels-are-behind-the-border-kid-crisis.

Dickerson, Caitlin. 2018. "Trump Administration in Chaotic Scramble to Reunify Migrant Families." *New York Times,* July 5. https://www.nytimes.com/2018/07/05/us/migrant-children-chaos-family-separation.html.

Dieng v. Holder, 698 F.3d 866 (6th Cir. 2012).

Dine Citizens Against Ruining Our Env't v. Jewell, 839 F.3d 1276 (10th Cir. 2016).

DL v. District of Columbia, 860 F.3d 713 (D.C. Cir. 2017).

Dobbs v. Jackson Women's Health Organization, 597 US __ (2022).

Doe 4 by and through Lopez v. Shenandoah Valley Juvenile Center Commission, 985 F.3d 327 (4th Cir. 2021)

Doe v. ORR, 884 F.3d 269 (5th Cir. 2018) (per curiam).

Doe v. Robertson, 751 F.3d 383 (5th Cir. 2014).

Doe v. Rumsfeld, 341 F. Supp. 2d 1 (D.D.C. 2004).

Doe v. Shenandoah Valley Juvenile Ctr. Comm'n, 355 F.Supp.3d 454 (W.D. Va. 2018).

Drake, Shaw and Bernardo Cruz. 2021. "Unaccompanied Children's Well-Being Must Come First at Fort Bliss and Across Texas." *American Civil Liberties Union.* June 24. https://www.aclu.org/news/immigrants-rights/unaccompanied-childrens-well-being-must-come-first-at-fort-bliss-and-across-texas/.

Dreierr, Hannah. 2023. "Alone and Exploited, Migrant Children Work Brutal Jobs Across the U.S." *New York Times*, February 25. https://www.nytimes.com/2023/02/25/us/unaccompanied-migrant-child-workers-exploitation.html.

Duchesne v. Sugarman, 566 F.2d 817 (2nd Cir. 1977).

E. A. C. A. v. Rosen, 985 F.3d 499 (6th Cir. 2021).

EAFF v. Gonzalez, 600 Fed.Appx. 205 (5th Cir. 2015).

Earnest, David. 2006. "Neither Citizen nor Stranger: Why States Enfranchise Resident Aliens." *World Politics* 58 (1): 242–275.

Eddings v. Oklahoma, 455 U.S. 104 (1982).

Edwards v. Arizona, 451 U.S. 477 (1981).

Epstein, Lee, and Jack Knight. 1998. *The Choices Justices Make*. Washington, D.C.: C.Q. Press.

E.O.H.C. v. Sec'y, U.S. Dep't Homeland Sec., 950 F.3d 177 (3d Cir. 2020).

Equal Access to Justice Act, 28 U.S.C. § 2412 ("EAJA").

Espenshade, Thomas, and Charles Calhoun. 1993. "An Analysis of Public Opinion Toward Undocumented Immigration." *Population Research and Policy Review* 12 (6): 189–224.

Escobar-Batres v. Holder, 385 F. App'x 445 (6th Cir. 2010).

Escobar v. Holder, 698 F.3d 36 (1st Cir. 2012).

Executive Office for Immigration Review. 2007. "Operating Policies and Procedures Memorandum 7-01, Guidelines for Immigration Court Cases Involving Unaccompanied Alien Children." May 22. http://myattorneyusa.com/storage/ upload/files/matters/guidelines-for-immigration-court.pdf.

Executive Office for Immigration Review. 2008. "Unaccompanied Alien Children in Immigration Proceedings." April 22,. https://www.justice.gov/sites/default/files/ eoir/legacy/2008/04/24/UnaccompaniedAlienChildrenApr08.pdf.

Executive Office for Immigration Review. 2009. "Asylum and Withholding of Removal Relief, Convention Against Torture Protections." *U.S. Department of Justice*. January 15. http://www.justice.gov/eoir/press/09/AsylumWithholdingCATProtections.pdf.

Executive Office for Immigration Review. 2013. "Department of Justice and the Department of Homeland Security Announce Safeguards for Unrepresented Immigration Detainees with Serious Mental Disorders or Conditions." April 22. http://www.justice.gov/eoir/press/2013/SafeguardsUnrepresentedImmigrationDet ainees.html.

Executive Office for Immigration Review. 2014. Justice Department and CNCS Announce New Partnership to Enhance Immigration Courts and Provide Critical Legal Assistance to Unaccompanied Minors. June 6. https://www.justice.gov/eoir/ pr/JusticeAmeriCorpsRelease06062014.

Executive Office for Immigration Review. 2017. "Executive Office for Immigration Review: An Agency Guide." December. https://www.justice.gov/eoir/page/file/eoir _an_agency_guide/download.

Executive Order 13841, 83 Fed. Reg. 29435 (June 20, 2018).

Executive Order 14011, 86 Fed. Reg. 8273 (February 2, 2021).

Extension of Order under Sections 362 and 365 of the Public Health Service Act; Order Suspending Introduction of Certain Persons From Countries Where a Communicable Disease Exists, 85 Fed. Reg. 22424-01, 2020 WL 1923282 (April 22, 2020) ("April Order").

Farmer v. Brennan, 511 U.S. 825, 114 S.Ct. 1970, 128 L.Ed.2d 811 (1994).

Federal Emergency Management Agency ("FEMA"). "FEMA Awards $110 Million to the Emergency Food and Shelter Program to Assist Migrants." March 18, 2021.

Fed. Trade Comm'n v. Enforma Nat. Prod., Inc., 362 F.3d 1204 (9th Cir. 2004).

Fernandes-Alcantara, Adrienne. 2018. "Youth and the Labor Force: Background and Trends." *Congressional Research Service Report R42519,* August 20. https://sgp .fas.org/crs/misc/R42519.pdf.

Fernandez Aguirre v. Barr, No. 19 Civ. 7048 (VEC), 2019 WL 3889800 (S.D.N.Y. Aug. 19, 2019).

Fetzer, Joel. 2000. *Public Attitudes Toward Immigration in the United States, France, and Germany.* Cambridge: Cambridge University Press.

Finklea, Kristin. 2018. "MS-13 in the United States and Federal Law Enforcement Efforts." *Congressional Research Service Report R45292,* August 20. https://sgp .fas.org/crs/homesec/R45292.pdf.

F.L. v. Thompson, 293 F.Supp.2d 86 (D.C. Cir. 2003).

Flores v. Barr, 934 F.3d 910 (9th Cir. 2019).

Flores v. Barr, case 2:85-cv-04544-DMG-AGR, Document 690, (C.D. Cal. September 27, 2019).

Flores v. Barr, 407 F.Supp.3d 909 (C.D. Cal. 2019), affirmed in part, reversed in part by *Flores v. Rosen,* 984 F.3d 720 (Ninth Cir. 2020).

Flores v. Barr, Not Reported in Fed. Supp., 2020 WL 2758792 (C.D.Cal., 2020a).

Flores v. Barr, Not Reported in Fed. Supp., 2020 WL 2128663 (C.D. Cal., 2020b).

Flores v. Barr, Slip Copy, 2020 WL 5666551 (C.D. California 2020c).

Flores v. Barr, Slip Copy, 2020 WL 5491445, (C.D. Cal, 2020d).

Flores v. Barr, Slip Copy, 2020 WL 5666550, (C.D. Cal, 2020e).

Flores v. Barr, 977 F.3d 742 (9th Cir. 2020f).

Flores v. Garland, 3 F.4th 1145 (9th Cir. 2021).

Flores v. Lynch, 828 F.3d 898 (9th Cir. 2016).

Flores v. Meese, 681 F. Supp. 665 (C.D. Cal. 1988).

Flores v. Meese, 934 F. 2d 991 (CA9 1990), vacated 942 F. 2d 1352 (CA9 1991) (en banc).

Flores Munoz v. Holder, No. 13-60601, 2014 U.S. App. LEXIS 8974 (5th Cir., May 14, 2014).

Flores v. Reno, No. CV 85-4544-RJK(Px) (C.D. Cal. Jan. 17, 1997).

Flores v. Reno, Case No. CV 85-4544-RJK(Px), Stipulation extending the settlement agreement and for other purposes, and order thereon (C.D. Cal., 2001).

Flores v. Rosen, 984 F.3d 720 (Ninth Cir. 2020).

Flores v. Sessions, 862 F.3d 863 (9th Cir. 2017).

Flores v. Sessions, 394 F. Supp. 3d 1041(C.D. Cal. 2017a).

Flores v. Sessions, 862 F.3d 863 (9th Cir. 2017b)

Flores v. Sessions, No. CV 85-4544-DMG(AGRx), 2018 WL 10162328 (C.D. Cal. July 30, 2018).

Flores-Chavez v. Ashcroft, 362 F.3d 1150 (9th Cir. 2004).

Flores-Lobo v. Holder, 562 Fed.Appx. 262 (5th Cir. 2014) (per curiam).

Flores, Rosa, Sara Weisfeldt, and Catherine E. Shoichet. 2021. "Kids Detained In Overcrowded Border Facilities Are Terrified, Crying and Worried, Lawyers Say."

CNN, March 13. https://www.cnn.com/2021/03/13/us/border-detention-conditions
/index.html.

Forbes v. Perryman, 222 F. Supp. 2d 1076 (N.D. Ill. 2002).

Foreign Affairs Reform and Restructuring Act of 1998 ("FARRA"), 8 U.S.C. § 1231.

Foster-Frau, Silvia. 2021. "First Migrant Facility for Children Opens Under
Biden." *Washington Post*, February 22. https://www.washingtonpost.com/national
/immigrant-children-camp-texas-biden/2021/02/22/05dfd58c-7533-11eb-8115
-9ad5e9c02117_story.html.

Foucha v. Louisiana 504 U.S. 71 (1992).

Fountain, Joselynn, and Abigail Overbay. 2019. "The Corporation for National
and Community Service: Overview of Programs and Funding." *Congressional
Research Service Report RL33931*, July 16. https://sgp.fas.org/crs/misc/RL33931
.pdf.

Franco-Gonzales v. Holder, 767 F. Supp. 2d 1034 (C.D. Cal. 2010).

Freeman, Gary, 1995. "Modes of Immigration Politics in Liberal Democratic States."
International Migration Review 29 (4) 881–902.

Friends of the Earth, Inc. v. Laidlaw Env't Servs. (TOC), Inc., 528 U.S. 167, 120 S.Ct.
693, 145 L.Ed.2d 610 (2000).

Fritze, John. 2014. "Immigration Court Speeds Review of Cases Involving Children."
The Baltimore Sun, August 20. https://www.baltimoresun.com/maryland/bs-xpm
-2014-08-20-bs-md-immigration-rocket-docket-20140820-story.html.

Fuentes-Chavarria, No. 13-9503, 2014 U.S. App. LEXIS 6956 (10th Cir., Apr. 15,
2014).

Garcia v. Barr, 960 F.3d 893 (6th Cir. 2020).

Garcia v. Decker, 448 F. Supp. 3d 297 (S.D.N.Y. 2020).

Garza v. Hargan, 874 F.3d 735 (D.C. Cir. 2017).

Gates v. Shinn, 98 F.3d 463 (9th Cir. 1996).

George, Tracey, and Lee Epstein. 1992. "On the Nature of Supreme Court Decision
Making." *American Political Science Review* 86 (2): 323–337.

German Santos v. Warden Pike Cty. Corr. Facility, 965 F.3d 203 (3d Cir. 2020).

Ghaly v. INS, 58 F.3d 1425 (9th Cir. 1995).

Gibney, Mark, and Michael Stohl. 1988. "Human Rights and US Refugee Policy." In
Open Borders? Closed Societies? The Ethical and Political Issues, edited by Mark
Gibney. New York: Greenwood Press.

Gibney, Mark, Vanessa Dalton, and Marc Vockell. 1992. "USA Refugee Policy: A
Human Rights Analysis Update." *Journal of Refugee Studies* 5 (1): 33–46.

Gibney, Mark, Linda Cornett, Reed Wood, Peter Haschke, Daniel Arnon, and
Attilio Pisanò. 2021. "The Political Terror Scale 1976–2020." http://www
.politicalterrorscale.org.

Gil, Rebeca Garcia. 2017. "Running into the Arms of Expatriation: America's
Failure Addressing the Rights of Unaccompanied Migrant Children From Central
America." *Maryland Journal of International Law* 32 (1): 346–373.

Gillman, Howard. 2001. "What's Law Got to Do With It? Judicial Behavioralists
Test the 'Legal Model' of Judicial Decision Making." *Law & Social Inquiry* 26
(2): 465–504.

Givens, Terri. 2005. *Voting Radical Right in Western Europe*. Cambridge: Cambridge University Press.

Godinez v. U.S. Immigration & Customs Enf't, No. 2:20-cv-466 KWR/SMV, 2020 WL 3402059 (D.N.M. Jun. 19, 2020).

Gomez-Rodas v. Barr, No. 16-72852 (9th Cir. 2019).

Gonzalez v. Reno 212 F.3d 1338 (11th Cir. 2000).

Gonzales, Alberto R., and Patrick Glen. 2015. "Advancing Executive Branch Immigration Policy Through the Attorney General's Review Authority." *Iowa Law Review* 101: 841–921.

Gonzalez-Posados v. Att'y Gen., 781 F.3d 677 (3d Cir. 2015).

Gould, Jon, Colleen Sheppard, and Johannes Wheeldon. 2010. "A Refugee from Justice? Disparate Treatment in the Federal Court of Canada." *Law & Policy* 32 (4): 454–486.

Government Accountability Office. 2018. "Unaccompanied Children: Agency Efforts to Reunify Children Separated From Parents at the Border." October. https://www .gao.gov/assets/gao-19-163.pdf ("GAO Report").

Government Accountability Project. 2021. "El Paso Times: Fort Bliss Migrant Children Shelter Contractor Receives Nearly $1b Contract Despite Mismanagement Allegations." September 10. https://whistleblower.org/in-the-news/el-paso-times -fort-bliss-migrant-children-shelter-contractor-receives-nearly-1b-contract-despite -mismanagement-allegations/.

Greenberg, Mark. 2021a. "U.S. Government Makes Significant Strides in Receiving Unaccompanied Children but Major Challenges Remain." *Migration Policy Institute,* May.

Greenberg, Mark. 2021b. "Hampered by the Pandemic: Unaccompanied Child Arrivals Increase as Earlier Preparedness Shortfalls Limit the Response." *Migration Policy Institute*, March. https://www.migrationpolicy.org/news/unaccompanied -child-arrivals-earlier-preparedness-shortfalls.

Greenberg, Mark. 2021c. "This Week in Immigration Episode 94." *Bipartisan Policy Institute*, May 17. https://open.spotify.com/episode/7lzXPApHY56N5HZ3jQ3JWz.

Greenberg, Mark. 2021d. "U.S. Government Makes Significant Strides in Receiving Unaccompanied Children but Major Challenges Remain." *Migration Policy Institute*, May 17.

Gryski, Gerard, Elanor Main, and William Dixon. 1986. "Models of State High Court Decisions Making in Sex Discrimination Cases." *Journal of Politics* 48 (1): 143–155.

Gutierrez v. Hott, 475 F.Supp.3d 492 (E.D. Virginia 2020).

Guzman-Garcia v. Attorney General United States, 860 Fed.Appx. 235 (Third Circuit, 2021).

Guzman-Vazquez v. Barr, 959 F.3d 253 (6th Cir. 2020).

G.Y.J.P. by and through M.R.P.S. v. Wolf, Slip Copy, 2020 WL 7318009 (District of Columbia 2020).

Haag, Matthew. 2019. "Thousands of Immigrant Children Said They Were Sexually Abused in U.S. Detention Centers Report Says." *New York Times*, February 27. https://www.nytimes.com/2019/02/27/us/immigrant-children-sexual-abuse.html.

Hairston v. Dir. Bureau of Prisons, 563 F. App'x 893 (3d Cir. 2014).

Hajnal, Zoltan and Marisa Abrajano. 2016. *The Forum* 14(1): 295–309.

Hall v. INS, 253 F. Supp. 2d 244 (D.R.I. 2003).

Harchenko v. INS, 379 F.3d 405 (6th Cir. 2004).

Hare v. City of Corinth Miss. 74 F.3d 633 (5th Cir.1996).

Harmon v. Holder, 758 F.3d 728 (6th Cir. 2014).

Harrington, Ben. 2021. "Asylum Processing at the Border: Legal Basics." *Congressional Research Service Legal Sidebar LSB10582*, March 19. https://sgp .fas.org/crs/homesec/LSB10582.pdf.

Harris v. McRae, 448 U.S. 297, 100 S.Ct. 2671, 65 L.Ed.2d 784 (1980).

Haughton v. Crawford, No. 1:16-cv-534, 2016 WL 5899285 (E.D. Va. Oct. 7, 2016).

Hausman, David. 2016. "The Failure of Immigration Appeals." *University of Pennsylvania Law Review* 164 (5): 1177–1238.

Healthy Teen Network v. Azar, 322 F. Supp. 3d 647 (D. Md. 2018).

Henriquez-Rivas v. Holder, 707 F.3d 1081 (9th Cir. 2013).

Hernández, Arelis. 2018. "Trump Administration is Holding Record Number of Migrant Youths." *Washington Post*, December 21. https://www.washingtonpost .com/local/immigration/trump-administration-is-holding-record-number-of -migrant-youths/2018/12/21/183470c0-03b7-11e9-b5df-5d3874f1ac36_story.html.

Hernandez v. Mesa, —— U.S. ——, 140 S. Ct. 735, 206 L.Ed.2d 29 (2020).

Hernandez ex rel. Hernandez v. Tex. Dep't of Protective & Regulatory Servs. 380 F.3d 872 (5th Cir. 2004).

Hernandez-Perez v. Whitaker, 911 F.3d 305 (6th Cir. 2018).

Herrera-Reyes v. Att'y Gen., 952 F.3d 101 (3d Cir. 2020).

Higher Taste v. City of Tacoma, 717 F.3d 712 (9th Cir. 2013).

Hlass, Laila. 2017. "Minor Protections: Best Practices for Representing Child Migrants." *New Mexico Law Review* 47: 247–290.

Homeland Security Act of 2002, Pub. L. No. 107-296, 116 Stat. 2202-2205, 2135 (Nov. 25, 2002) (codified, as amended, at 6 U.S.C. §279).

Honeywell Int'l, Inc. v. Nuclear Regul. Comm'n, 628 F.3d 568 (D.C. Cir. 2010).

Hoskin, Marilyn. 1991. *New Immigrants and Democratic Society: Minority Integration In Western Democracies*. New York: Praeger.

Hubbard v. Taylor, 538 F.3d 229 (3d Cir. 2008).

Hutto v. Finney, 437 U.S. 678, 98 S.Ct. 2565, 57 L.Ed.2d 522 (1978).

Hylton v. Decker, 20 cv 5994, 2020 U.S. Dist. LEXIS 220506, 2020 WL 6879067 (S.D.N.Y. Nov. 24, 2020).

Ibrahim v. U.S. Dep't of Homeland Sec., 835 F.3d 1048 (9th Cir. 2016).

Immigration Act of 1990, Pub.L. 101-649, §153, 104 Stat. 5005–5006 (Nov. 29, 1990) (codified, as amended at INA §101(a)(27)(J), 8 U.S.C. §1101(a)(27)(J)), 8 C.F.R. §204.11(c).

Immigration and Customs Enforcement Guidelines, Detention Standard 4.4, Medical Care (Women). December 2016. https://www.ice.gov/doclib/detention-standards /2011/4-4.pdf.

Immigration and Nationality Act, Pub. L. 82-414, § 101, 66 Stat. 163 (June 27, 1952) (codified as amended at 8 U.S.C. § 1101).

Immigration and Nationality Act ("INA"), 8 U.S.C. § 1101 et seq.

Immigration and Nationality Act (INA), H.R. 2580; Pub.L. 89-236, 79 Stat. 911 (1997).

Imon v. Keeton, Slip Copy, 2020 WL 4284378 (D. Arizona, 2020).

Inmates of Allegheny Cnty. Jail v. Pierce, 612 F.2d 754 (3d Cir. 1979).

Innovation Law Lab v. McAleenan, 924 F.3d 503 (9th Cir. 2019).

In re Gomez-Gomez, 23 I. & N. Dec. 522 (BIA 2002).

In re Hutto Family Detention Center, Case No. A-07-CA-164-SS (W.D. Texas 2007).

In re M-A-C-O-, 27 I. & N. Dec. 477 (BIA 2018).

In re Masters Mates & Pilots Pension Plan & IRAP Litig., 957 F.2d 1020 (2d Cir. 1992).

In re Meja-Andino, 23 I. & N. Dec. 533 (BIA 2002).

INS v. Cardoza-Fonseca, 480 U.S. 421 (No. 85–782, Mar. 9, 1987).

I.N.S. v. Elias-Zacarias, 502 U.S. 478, 112 S.Ct. 812, 117 L.Ed.2d 38 (1992).

INS v. Lopez–Mendoza 468 U.S. 103 (1984).

International Monetary Fund. 2020. "Direction of Trade Statistics." https://data.imf .org/?sk=9D6028D4-F14A-464C-A2F2-59B2CD424B85.

Japarkulova v. Holder, 615 F.3d 696 (6th Cir. 2010).

J. B. B. C. v. Wolf, et al., Docket No. 20-cv-1509 (D.D.C. filed June 9, 2020).

J.D. v. Azar, 925 F.3d 1291 (D.C. Cir. 2019).

JEFM v. Lynch 837 F.3d 1026 (9th Cir. 2016).

Jennings v. Rodriguez, ——— U.S. ———, 138 S. Ct. 830, 200 L.Ed.2d 122 (2018).

Jensen, Tine, Envor Skårdalsmo, and Krister Fjermestad. 2014. "Development of Mental Health Problems—A Follow-Up Study of Unaccompanied Refugee Minors." *Child and Adolescent Psychiatry and Mental Health* 8 (29): 29–39.

Jimenez-Castro v. Sessions, 750 F. App'x 406 (6th Cir. 2018).

J.L. v. Cissna, 341 F. Supp. 3d 1048 (N.D. Cal. 2018).

Johnson, Kevin. 2004. "Driver's Licenses and Undocumented Immigrants: The Future of Civil Rights Law?" *Nevada Law Journal* 5: 213–239.

Johnson v. Zerbs 304 U.S. 458 (1938).

Johnston v. Marsh, 227 F.2d 528 (3d Cir. 1955).

Jonathan White, Deputy Dir. for Children's Programs, email message to Scott Lloyd, Dir., Office of Refugee Resettlement, September 22, 2017.

J.O.P. v. U.S. Department of Homeland Security, 409 F.Supp.3d 367 (D. Maryland, Southern Division 2019).

J.O.P. v. U.S. Department of Homeland Security, 338 F.R.D. 33 (D. Maryland Southern Div., 2020a), Appeal Filed by J.O.P. v. DHS, 4th Cir., February 19, 2021).

J.O.P. v. U.S. Department of Homeland Security, Slip Copy, 2020 WL 2932922 (D. Maryland, Southern Division 2020b).

Jordan by Jordan v. Jackson, 15 F.3d 333 (4th Cir. 1994).

Jose L.P. v. Whitaker, 431 F.Supp.3d 540 (D.C. D. New Jersey, 2019).

José-Tomás v. Barr, 822 Fed.Appx. 354 (6th Cir. 2020).

Joseph v. Decker, No. 18 Civ. 2640 (RA), 2018 WL 6075067 (S.D.N.Y. Nov. 21, 2018).

J.S.G. ex rel. Hernandez v. Stirrup, 2020 WL 1985041, Not Reported in Fed. Supp. (D.C. D. Maryland, 2020).

Juan Antonio v. Barr, 959 F.3d 778 (6th Cir. 2020).

Juan-Mateo v. Sessions, 729 F. App'x 446 (6th Cir. 2018).

Jutus v. Holder, 723 F.3d 105 (1st Cir. 2013).

Kandel, William. 2019. "Unaccompanied Alien Children: An Overview." *Congressional Research Service Report 43599*. https://fas.org/sgp/crs/homesec/R43599.pdf.

Kandel, William. 2021a. "Unaccompanied Alien Children: An Overview." *Congressional Research Service Report 43599*, September 1. https://crsreports.congress.gov/product/pdf/R/R43599/29

Kandel, William. 2021b. "The Trump Administration's 'Zero Tolerance' Immigration Enforcement Policy." *Congressional Research Service Report R45266*, February 2. https://sgp.fas.org/crs/homesec/R45266.pdf;

Kandel, William, Andorra Bruno, Peter Meyer, Clare Seelke, Maureen Taft-Morales, and Ruth Wasem. 2014. "Unaccompanied Alien Children: Potential Factors Contributing to Recent Immigration." *Congressional Research Service R43628*, July 3. https://sgp.fas.org/crs/homesec/R43628.pdf.

Kanno-Youngs, Zolan, and Michael Shear. 2021. "Biden Faces Challenge From Surge of Migrants at the Border. *New York Times*, March 8. https://www.nytimes.com/2021/03/08/us/politics/immigration-mexico-border-biden.html.

Kante v. Holder, 634 F.3d 321 (6th Cir. 2011).

Karingithi v. Whitaker, 913 F.3d 1158 (9th Cir. 2019).

Karki v. Holder, 715 F.3d 792 (10th Cir. 2013).

Keith, Linda Camp, Jennifer Holmes, and Banks Miller. 2013. "Explaining the Divergence in Asylum Grant Rates among Immigration Judges: An Attitudinal and Cognitive Approach." *Law & Policy* 35 (4): 261–289.

Keles, Serap, Oddgeir Friborg, Thormod Idsøe, Selcuk Sirin, and Brit Oppedal. 2018. "Resilience and Acculturation Among Unaccompanied Refugee Minors." *International Journal of Behavioral Development* 42 (1): 52–63.

Keller, MaryBeth. 2017. "Operating Policies and Procedures Memorandum 17-03: Guidelines for Immigration Court Cases Involving Juveniles, Including Unaccompanied Alien Children." December 20. https://www.justice.gov/eoir/file/oppm17-03/download.

K.H. v. Barr, 920 F.3d 470 (6th Cir. 2019).

Kids Count Data Center. 2020. "Economic Well-Being Indicators." https://datacenter.kidscount.org/data#USA/2/16/17,18,19,20,22,21,2720/char/0,

Kiewiet, D. Roderick, and Matthew McCubbins. 1991. *The Logic of Delegation: Congressional Parties and the Appropriations Process*. Chicago: University of Chicago Press.

Kight, Stef. 2021. "CDC Lets Child Migrant Shelters Fill to 100% Despite Covid Concern." *Axios*, March 5. https://www.axios.com/cdc-child-migrant-shelter-full-capacity-coronavirus-41d1ae80-1ecf-4815-a755-7b01fac5850b.html.

Kight, Stef, and Hans Nichols. 2021. "Biden Opposes Reopening Controversial Child Migrant Shelter." *Axios,* March 16. https://www.axios.com/biden-homestead -shelter-migrant-children-crisis-256f5976-8642-4835-b051-0c7e81ad37b3.html.

Kim, Catherine Y. 2018. "The President's Immigration Courts." *Emory Law Journal* 68 (1): 1–48.

Kim, Ted. Acting Chief. 2013. "Updated Procedures for Determination of Initial Jurisdiction Over Asylum Applications Filed by Unaccompanied Alien Children." *USCIS Asylum Division,* May 28. https://www.uscis.gov/sites/default/files/ document/memos/determ-juris-asylum-app-file-unaccompanied-alien-children .pdf.

King, Shani. 2013. "Alone and Unrepresented: A Call to Congress to Provide Counsel for Unaccompanied Minors." *Harvard Journal on Legislation* 50 (2): 331–384.

Kitroeff, Natalie, and Daniele Volpe. 2021. "We Are Doomed: Devastation from Storms Fuels Migration in Honduras." *New York Times,* April 6. https://www .nytimes.com/2021/04/06/world/americas/migration-honduras-central-america .html.

K.O. v. U.S. Immigration and Customs Enforcement, 468 F.Supp.3d 350 (District of Columbia 2020).

Koh, Jennifer Lee. 2019. "Crimmigration Beyond the Headlines: The Board of Immigration Appeals' Quiet Expansion of the Meaning of Moral Turpitude." *Stanford Law Review Online* 71 (March): 267–280.

Koliada v. INS, 259 F.3d 482 (6th Cir. 2001).

Kopan, Tal. 2018. "ICE Arrested Undocumented Adults Who Sought to Take in Immigrant Children." *San Francisco Chronicle,* December 10. https://www .sfchronicle.com/politics/article/ICE-arrested-undocumented-adults-who-sought -to-13455142.php.

Lampkin v. District of Columbia, 886 F. Supp. 56 (D.D.C. 1995).

Lanard, Noah. 2019. "Judge Promoted by Trump Administration Threatened a 2-Year-Old with an Attack Dog." *Mother Jones,* September 10. https://www .motherjones.com/politics/2019/09/judge-promoted-by-trump-administration -threatened-a-2-year-old-with-an-attack-dog/.

Landon v. Plasencia, 459 U.S. 21, 103 S. Ct. 321 (1982).

Lands Council v. McNair, 537 F.3d 981 (9th Cir. 2008).

Langlois, Joseph. 2007. "Updated Procedures for Minor Principal Applicant Claims, Including Changes to Raps." August 14. https://www.uscis.gov/sites/default/files/ document/memos/procedures-minor-children-raps.pdf.

Langlois, Joseph. 2009. "Implementation of Statutory Change Providing USCIS with Initial Jurisdiction Over Asylum Applications Filed by Unaccompanied Alien Children." March 25. https://www.uscis.gov/sites/default/files/document/memos/ jurisdiction-provision-tvpra-alien-children2.pdf.

Lassiter v. Dep't of Soc. Servs., 452 U.S. 18, 101 S.Ct. 2153, 68 L.Ed.2d 640 (1981).

League of Women Voters of N.C. v. North Carolina, 769 F.3d 224 (4th Cir. 2014).

Lecky v. Holder, 723 F.3d 1 (1st Cir. 2013).

Leighton, Andres. 2018. "Nearly 15,000 Migrant Children in Federal Custody Jammed Into Crowded Shelters." *CNBC,* December 19. https://www.cnbc.com

/2018/12/19/nearly-15000-migrant-children-in-federal-custody-jammed-into
-crowded-shelters.html.

Leiva-Barrios v. Attorney General United States, Not Reported in Fed. Rptr., 2021 WL 3415087 (3rd Cir. 2021).

Leonard v. Whitaker, 746 Fed. Appx 269 (4th Cir. 2018).

Leslie v. Holder, 865 F. Supp. 2d 627 (M.D. Pa. 2012).

Levinson, Daniel. 2018. "Memorandum: The Tornillo Influx Care Facility: Concerns About Staff Background Checks and Number of Clinicians on Staff." *U.S. Office of Inspector General A-12-19-20000*, November 27. https://oig.hhs.gov/oas/reports /region12/121920000.pdf.

Linares Martinez v. Decker, No. 18 Civ. 6527 (JMF), 2018 WL 5023946 (S.D.N.Y. 2018).

Lincoln, Elizabeth. 2017. "The Fragile Victory for Unaccompanied Children's Due Process Rights After Flores v. Sessions." *Hastings Constitutional Law Quarterly* 45 (1): 157–186.

Lind, Dara. 2014. "The Process Congress Wants to Use for Child Migrants is a Disaster." *Vox,* July 15. https://www.vox.com/2014/7/15/5898349/border-children -mexican-central-american-deport-quickly-2008-law.

Lind, Dara. 2018a. "New Statistics: The Government is Separating 65 Children a Day from Parents at the Border." *Vox*, June 19. https://www.vox.com/2018/6/19 /17479138/how-many-families-separated-border-immigration.

Lind, Dara. 2018b. "It's Official: The Trump Administration has Replaced Family Separation With Indefinite Family Detention." *Vox*, June 30. https://www.vox.com /2018/6/30/17520820/families-together-detention-separate-camp-military.

Lind, Dara, 2018c. "Jeff Sessions Is Exerting Unprecedented Control Over Immigration Courts—by Ruling on Cases Himself." *Vox*, May 14. https://www.vox.com/policy -and-politics/2018/5/14/17311314/immigration-jeff-sessions-court-judge-ruling.

Lind, Dara. 2021. "No Good Choices: HHS Is Cutting Safety Corners to Move Migrant Kids Out of Overcrowded Facilities." *ProPublica*, April 1. https://www .propublica.org/article/no-good-choices-hhs-is-cutting-safety-corners-to-move -migrant-kids-out-of-overcrowded-facilities.

Loescher, Gil, and John Scanlan. 1986. *Calculated Kidness: Refugees and America's Half-Open Door, 1945 to the Present*. New York: Free Press.

Lopez, Rebeca. 2012. "Codifying the Flores Settlement Agreement: Seeking to Protect Immigrant Children in U.S. Custody." *Marquette Law Review* 95 (4): 1635–1677.

Lopez-Cruz v. Attorney General United States, 765 Fed.Appx. 707 (3rd Cir. 2019).

Lopez Santos v. Clesceri, Slip Copy, 2021 WL 663180 (N.D. Illinois, Western Division 2021).

Lovett, Ian, and Louise Radnofsky. 2018. "Amid Chaos at the Border, Some Immigrant Families Reunite." *Wall Street Journal*, June 24. https://www.wsj .com/articles/trump-administration-reunites-522-immigrant-children-with-adults -1529850825.

Lucas v. Hadden, 790 F.2d 365 (3d Cir. 1986).

Lujan v. Nat'l Wildlife Fed'n, 497 U.S. 871, 110 S.Ct. 3177, 111 L.Ed.2d 695 (1990).

Luke, Douglas A. 2004. *Multilevel Modeling*. Thousand Oaks, CA: Sage Publications.
Madan, Monique. 2020. "Sex Abuse Claims Revealed at Homestead Shelter, Where Staff Was Not Vetted for Child Abuse." *Miami Herald*, July 15. https://www .wlrn.org/local-news/2020-07-16/sex-abuse-claims-revealed-at-homestead-shelter -where-staff-was-not-vetted-for-child-abuse.
Maher v. Roe, 432 U.S. 464, 97 S.Ct. 2376, 53 L.Ed.2d 484 (1977).
Maldonado v. Houston, 157 F.3d 179 (3d Cir. 1998).
Maldonado-Perez v. INS, 865 F.2d 328 (D.D.C. 1989).
Manuel, Kate, and Michael Garcia. 2014. "Unaccompanied Alien Children—Legal Issues: Answers to Frequently Asked Questions." *Congressional Research Service Report R43623*, July 18. https://sgp.fas.org/crs/homesec/R43623.pdf.
Mapp v. Reno, 241 F.3d 221 (2d Cir. 2001).
Maraziegos-Morales v. Garland, Not Reported in Fed. Rptr., 2021 WL 3140322 (Sixth Circuit 2021).
Marikasi v. Lynch, 840 F.3d 281 (6th Cir. 2016).
Martin v. Gentile, 849 F.2d 863 (4th Cir. 1988).
Martin-Mendoza v. INS 499 F.2d 918 (9th Cir. 1974).
Martinez, Oscar. 2014. "How the Zetas Tamed Central America's Coyotes." *Insight Crime*, May 1. https://insightcrime.org/news/analysis/how-the-zetas-tamed-central -americas-coyotes/.
Marzouk, Julie. 2016. "Ethical and Effective Representation of Unaccompanied Immigrant Minors in Domestic Violence-Based Asylum Cases." *Clinical Law Review* 22: 395–443.
Masters, Jeff. 2019. "Fifth Straight Year of Central American Drought Helping Drive Migration." *Scientific American*, December 23. https://blogs.scientificamerican .com/eye-of-the-storm/fifth-straight-year-of-central-american-drought-helping -drive-migration/.
Matter of A-B, 27 I. & N. Dec. 316 (A.G. 2018)
Matter of A–E–M–, 21 I. & N. Dec. 1157 (BIA 1998).
Matter of A-R-C-G-, 26 I. & N. Dec. 338 (BIA 2014).
Matter of Bermudez-Cota, 27 I. & N. Dec. 441 (BIA 2018).
Matter of C-T-L-, 25 I. & N. Dec. 341 (BIA 2010).
Matter of Castro-Tum, 27 I&N Dec. 271 (A.G. 2018).
Matter of E-R-M- & L-R-M-, 25 I. & N. Dec. 520, 521–22 (B.I.A. 2011).
Matter of J-B-N-, 24 I. & N. Dec. 208 (BIA 2007).
Matter of Lozada, 19 I. & N. Dec. 637 (BIA 1988).
Matter of M-A-C-O-, 27 I. & N. Dec. 477 (BIA 2018).
Matter of M-A-M-, 25 I. & N. Dec. 474 (BIA 2011).
Matter of Rosas-Ramirez, 22 I. & N. Dec. 616 (1999).
Matter of S-E-G-, 24 I. & N. Dec. 579 (2008).
Matter of Urena, 25 I&N Dec. 140 (BIA 2009).
Mathews v. Eldridge, 424 U.S. 319, 96 S.Ct. 893, 47 L.Ed.2d 18 (1976).
Mauricio-Vasquez v. Crawford, No. 1:16-cv-1422, 2017 WL 1476349 (E.D. Va. Apr. 24, 2017).
Mazariegos-Diaz v. Lynch, 605 F. App'x 675 (9th Cir. 2015).

McHenry III, James. 2018. "Case Priorities and Immigration Court Performance Measures." January 17. https://www.justice.gov/eoir/page/file/1026721/download.

Meckler, Laura. 2018. "New Quotas for Immigration Judges as Trump Administration Seeks Faster Deportations." *The Wall Street Journal,* April 2. https://www.wsj .com/articles/immigration-judges-face-new-quotas-in-bid-to-speed-deportations -1522696158.

Menke, Julie. 2020. "Abuse of Power: Immigration Courts and the Attorney General's Referral Power." *Case Western Reserve Journal of International Law* 52(1): 599–626.

Medley v. Decker, No. 18 Civ. 7361 (AJN), 2019 WL 7374408 (S.D.N.Y. Dec. 11, 2019).

Mejia-Mejia v. U.S. Immigration and Customs Enforcement, Civil Action. No. 18-1445 (PLF), Not Reported in Fed. Supp., 2019 WL 4707150 (D.D.C. 2019).

Memorandum from David Siegel, Acting Dir., Office of Refugee Resettlement, on Medical Services Requiring Heightened ORR Involvement. March 21, 2008. https: //perma.cc/LDN8-JNL5.

Memorandum from Jonathan White, Deputy Dir. for Children's Programs, to Scott Lloyd, Dir., Office of Refugee Resettlement. December 6, 2017.

Memorandum from Kenneth Tota, Acting Dir., Office of Refugee Resettlement, to ORR Staff. March 4, 2017.

Memorandum of Agreement ("MOA") among the Office of Refugee Resettlement of the U.S. Department of Health and Human Services, and U.S. Immigration and Customs Enforcement and U.S. Customs and Border Protection of the U.S. Department of Homeland Security Regarding Consultation and Information Sharing in Unaccompanied Alien Children Matters. April 13, 2018. https://www .aila.org/File/Related/21031235a.pdf.

Mendez Ramirez v. Decker, ——— F.Supp.3d ----, 2020 WL 1674011 (S.D. N.Y., 2020).

Merchant, Nomaan. 2021. "Amid Surge, US Tries to Expedite Release of Migrant Children." *AP News,* February 24. https://apnews.com/article/health-us-news -coronavirus-pandemic-immigration-86f189f3c444d816ae0f8b704442203f.

Merck & Co. v. United States Dep't of Health & Human Servs., 385 F. Supp. 3d 81 (D.D.C. 2019), aff'd, 962 F.3d 531 (D.C. Cir. 2020).

Meyer, Peter. 2021. Central American Migration: Root Causes and U.S. Policy. *Congressional Research Service In Focus IF11151,* October 27. https://sgp.fas.org /crs/row/IF11151.pdf.

Michelson v. INS, 897 F.2d 465 (10th Cir. 1990).

Meyer, Peter, and Clare Seelke. 2015. "Central America Regional Security Initiative: Background and Policy Issues for Congress." *Congressional Research Service Report R41731,* December 17. https://sgp.fas.org/crs/row/R41731.pdf.

Mickinski, Nicholas. 2021. *UN Global Compacts: Governing Migrants and Refugees.* New York: Routledge.

Mikhailevitch v. INS, 146 F.3d 384 (6th Cir. 1998).

Miller, Banks, Linda Camp Keith, and Jennifer S. Holmes. 2015. *Immigration Judges and U.S. Asylum Policy.* Philadelphia: University of Pennsylvania Press.

Minneci v. Pollard, 565 U.S. 118 (2012).

Minto v. Decker, 108 F. Supp. 3d 189 (S.D.N.Y. 2015).

Miroff, Nick, Andrew Ba Tran, and Leslie Shapiro. 2011. "Hundreds of Minors Are Crossing the Border Each Day Without Their Parents. Who Are They?" *Washington Post*, March 11. https://www.bostonglobe.com/2021/03/11/nation/hundreds-minors -are-crossing-border-each-day-without-their-parents-who-are-they/.

Miroff, Nick and Maria Sacchetti. 2021. "Migrant Teens and Children Have Challenged Three Administrations, but Biden Faces Rush with No Precedent." *Washington Post*, March 22. https://www.washingtonpost.com/nation/2021/03/22 /unaccompanied-minors-immigration-obama-trump-biden/.

Misra, Tanvi. 2019. "DOJ Changed Hiring to Promote Restrictive Immigration Judges." *Roll Call*, October 29. https://rollcall.com/2019/10/29/doj-changed-hiring -to-promote-restrictive-immigration-judges/.

Moe, Terry. 1984. "The New Economics of Organization." *American Journal of Political Science* 28 (4): 739–777.

Moe, Terry, and Scott Wilson. 1994. "Presidents and the Politics of Structure." *Law and Contemporary Problems* 57 (2): 1–44.

Monsanto Co. v. Geertson Seed Farms, 561 U.S. 139, 130 S.Ct. 2743, 177 L.Ed.2d 461 (2010).

Montano, Elizabeth. 2020. "The Rise and Fall of Administrative Closure in Immigration Courts." *Yale Law Journal* 129: 567–589.

Monyak, Suzanne. 2020. "D.C. Judge Blocks Policy to Expel Migrant Kids from Border." *Law360*, November 18. https://www.law360.com/articles/1330144/dc -judge-blocks-policy-to-expel-migrant-kids-from-border.

Moore, Robert. 2018. "Tent City Operator's Request for Policy Shift Could Reduce the Mass Detention of Migrant Children." *Texas Monthly*, December 15. https: //www.texasmonthly.com/news-politics/private-operator-texas-tent-city-migrant -kids-may-not-renew-unless-new-policy-adopted/.

Moran-Taylor, Michelle. 2008. "When Mothers and Fathers Migrate North: Caretakers, Children, and Child Rearing in Guatemala." *Latin American Perspectives* 35 (4): 79–95.

Morton v. Ruiz, 415 U.S. 199, 94 S.Ct. 1055, 39 L.Ed.2d 270 (1974).

Mrs. Fields Franchising, LLC v. MFGPC, 941 F.3d 1221 (10th Cir. 2019).

Ms. L v. ICE, case 3:18-cv-00428-DMS-MDD, Document 83, (S.D. Cal. June 26, 2018).

Ms. L. v. U.S Immigration & Customs Enforcement, 310 F. Supp. 3d 1133 (S.D. Cal. 2018), modified, 330 F.R.D. 284 (S.D. Cal. 2019).

Nakamura, David. 2014. "Influx of Minors Across Texas Border Driven by Belief They Will Be Allowed to Stay in U.S." *Washington Post*, June 13. https://www .washingtonpost.com/politics/influx-of-minors-across-texas-border-driven-by -belief-that-they-will-be-allowed-to-stay-in-us/2014/06/13/5406355e-f276-11e3 -9ebc-2ee6f81ed217_story.html.

Natale v. Camden Cty. Corr. Facility, 318 F.3d 575 (3d Cir. 2003).

National Archives & Records Administration ("NARA"). 2016. Department of Homeland Security records management program: Records management inspection

report. Last modified January 11, 2016. https://www.archives.gov/files/records
-mgmt/resources/dhs-2016-inspection.pdf ("NARA DHS Inspection Report").

National Archives & Records Administration. 2018. U.S. Customs and Border
Protection Records Management Program: Records Management Inspection
Report. Last modified July 16, 2018. https://www.archives.gov/files/records-mgmt
/pdf/cbp-2018-inspection.pdf ("NARA CBP Inspection Report").

National Immigrant Justice Center. 2019. "Significant Asylum Policy Change for
Unaccompanied Children's Cases." Last modified June 6. https://immigrantjustice
.org/for-attorneys/legal-resources/copy/significant-asylum-policy-change
-unaccompaniedchildrens-cases.

Nat'l Mining Ass'n v. U.S. Army Corps of Eng'rs, 145 F.3d 1399 (D.C. Cir. 1998).

Navarro, Lisa. 1998. "An Analysis of Treatment of Unaccompanied Immigrant and
Refugee Children in INS Detention and Other Forms of Institutionalized Custody."
Chicano-Latino Law Review 19 (1): 589–612.

N.B. v. Barr, Not Reported in Fed. Supp., 2019 WL 4849175 (S.D. California 2019).

Ndayshimiye v. Att'y Gen., 557 F.3d 124 (3d Cir. 2009).

Neal, David. 2007. Operating Policies and Procedures Memorandum 07-01. Guidelines
for Immigration Court Cases Involving Unaccompanied Alien Children. Last
modified May 22, 2007. http://myattorneyusa.com/storage/upload/files/matters/
guidelines-for-immigration-court.pdf.

Nehimaya-Guerra v. Gonzales 177 Fed.Appx. 729 (9th Cir. 2006).

N.H. Hosp. Ass'n v. Azar, 887 F.3d 62 (1st Cir. 2018).

Nolasco, Claire. 2017. "Immigrant Access to Justice: Challenges and Reality."
Criminal Law Bulletin 53 (4): 866–878.

Nolasco, Claire. 2018. "Models of Legal Representation for Unaccompanied Minors."
Criminal Law Bulletin 54 (1): 274–282.

Nolasco, Claire Angelique, and Daniel Braaten. 2019. "The Role of Hospitable and
Inhospitable States in the Process of Refugee Resettlement in the United States."
Journal of Refugee Studies 34 (1): 634–662.

Nolasco, Claire, and Daniel Braaten. 2021. "Suffer the Little Children to Come:
Legal Rights of Unaccompanied Alien Children Under United States Federal Court
Jurisprudence." *International Journal of Refugee Law* 31 (1): 55–82.

Norton v. S. Utah Wilderness Alliance, 542 U.S. 55, 124 S.Ct. 2373, 159 L.Ed.2d 137
(2004).

Notice of Order Under Sections 362 and 365 of the Public Health Service
Act Suspending Introduction of Certain Persons From Countries Where a
Communicable Disease Exists, 85 Fed. Reg. 17060-02, 2020 WL 1445906 (March
26, 2020).

Novartis Consumer Health v. Johnson & Johnson—Merck Consumer Pharms. Co.,
290 F.3d 578 (3d Cir. 2002).

Obama, Barack. 2014. "Presidential Memorandum—Response to the Influx of
Unaccompanied Alien Children Across the Southwest Border." Last modified
June 2, 2014. https://obamawhitehouse.archives.gov/the-press-office/2014/06/02/
presidential-memorandum-response-influx-unaccompanied-alien-children-acr.

Ocepek, Melissa, and Joel Fetzer. 2010. "The Causes of Pro-Immigration Voting in the United States Supreme Court." *International Migration Review* 44 (3): 659–696.

Office of Refugee Resettlement. 2022. https://www.acf.hhs.gov/orr/resource/children -entering-the-united-states-unaccompanied ("ORR Policy Guide").

Office of Refugee Resettlement. 2015. "ORR Guide: Children Entering the United States Unaccompanied." January 30,. https://www.acf.hhs.gov/orr/resource /children-entering-the-united-states-unaccompanied.

Office of Refugee Resettlement. 2017. "Unaccompanied Alien Children Program Sexual Assaults by Date of Incident." https://s3.documentcloud.org/documents /5751021/NadUAC1213-Sexual-Assaults-by-Date-of-Incident.pdf.

Office of Refugee Resettlement. 2019. "Unaccompanied Alien Child Shelter at Homestead Job Corps Site, Homestead, Florida." August 6. https://www.hhs.gov/ sites/default/files/Unaccompanied-Alien-Children-Sheltered-at-Homestead.pdf.

Office of Refugee Resettlement. 2021a. "Unaccompanied Children Program." November 1. https://www.hhs.gov/sites/default/files/uac-program-fact-sheet.pdf.

Office of Refugee Resettlement. 2021b. Facts and Data: Length of Care. Last modified December 20. https://www.acf.hhs.gov/orr/about/ucs/facts-and-data.

Office of Refugee Resettlement. 2021a. "Unaccompanied Children Released to sponsors by State." December 30. https://www.hhs.gov/programs/social-services/ unaccompanied-children-released-to-sponsors-by-state-november-2021.html.

Office of Refugee Resettlement. 2021b. "Unaccompanied Children Released to Sponsors by County." December 30. https://www.hhs.gov/programs/social-services /unaccompanied-children-released-to-sponsors-by-county-november-2021.html.

Office of Refugee Resettlement. 2021c. "ORR Guide: Children Entering the United States Unaccompanied." June 7. https://www.acf.hhs.gov/orr/policy-guidance/ children-entering-united-states-unaccompanied.

Office of Refugee Resettlement. 2021d. "ORR Field Guidance #11, Temporary Waivers of Background Check Requirements for Category 2 Adult Household Members and Adult Caregivers." March 31. https://www.acf.hhs.gov/sites/default /files/documents/orr/FG-11%20Temporary%20Waiver%20of%20Background %20Check%20Requirements%202021%2003%2031.pdf.

Office of the Vice President. 2014 "Remarks to the Press With Q&A by Vice President Joe Biden in Guatemala." *The White House*. Last modified June 20. https://obamawhitehouse.archives.gov/the-press-office/2014/06/20/remarks-press -qa-vice-president-joe-biden-guatemala.

Ogayonne v. Mukasey, 530 F.3d 514 (7th Cir. 2008).

O'Leary, Brian. 2015. "Docketing Practices Relating to Unaccompanied Children Cases and Adult With Children Released on Alternatives in Detention Cases in Light of New Priorities." Last modified March 24. https://www.justice.gov/eoir /pages/attachments/2015/03/26/docketing-practices-related-to-uacs-and-awcatd -march2015.pdf.

Olmos Borja v. Holder, 550 Fed. App'x 517 (9th Cir. 2013).

Ordonez, Franco. 2021. "Biden Administration Rescinds Trump Policy Affecting Sponsors of Young Migrants." *NPR*, March 21. https://www.npr.org/2021/03

/12/976555366/biden-administration-rescinds-trump-policy-affecting-sponsors-of -young-migrants.

Osaghae v. INS, 942 F.2d 1160 (7th Cir. 1991).

Osuna, Juan. 2014. "Prepared Statement on the President's Emergency Supplemental Request for Unaccompanied Children and Related Matters." Last modified July 10, 2014. https://www.govinfo.gov/content/pkg/CHRG-113shrg24808/pdf/CHRG -113shrg24808.pdf.

Palma-Salazar v. Davis, 677 F.3d 1031 (10th Cir. 2012).

Parkell v. Morgan, 682 F. App'x 155 (3d Cir. 2017).

Parra v. Perryman, 172 F.3d 954 (7th Cir. 1999).

Parekh, Serena. 2020. *No Refuge: Ethics and the Global Refugee Crisis.* Oxford: Oxford University Press.

Pashby v. Delia, 709 F.3d 307 (4th Cir. 2013).

Passel, Jeffrey S., and D'Vera Cohn. 2019. "Mexicans Decline to Less Than Half the U.S. Unauthorized Immigrant Population for the First Time." *Pew Research Center,* June 12. https://www.pewresearch.org/fact-tank/2019/06/12/us -unauthorized-immigrant-population-2017/.

Patel v. Gonzales, 126 F. App'x 283 (6th Cir. 2005).

Patten v. Nichols, 274 F.3d 829 (4th Cir. 2001).

Pelley, Scott. 2018. "The Chaos Behind Donald Trump's Policy of Family Separation at the Border." *60 Minutes,* November 26. https://www.cbsnews.com/news/trump -family-separation-policy-mexican-border-60-minutes-investigation-greater-in -number-than-trump-administration-admits/.

Pereira v. Sessions, 138 S. Ct. 2105, 201 L.Ed.2d 433 (2018).

Perez v. Garland, Not Reported in Fed. Rptr., 2021 WL 4988351 (6th Cir. 2021).

Perez-Funez v. District Director INS, 619 F.Supp. 656 (C. D. California 1985).

Perez-Perez v. Holder, No. 13-1711, 2014 U.S. App. LEXIS 8786 (4th Cir. 2014).

Pirir-Boc v. Holder, No. 09-73671, 2014 U.S. App. LEXIS 8577 (9th Cir. 2014).

P.J.E.S. v. Chad F. Wolf, case 1:20-cv-02245-EGS-GMH, Document 80 (D.C., 2020).

P.J.E.S. v. Pekoske, No. 20-5357 (D.C. Cir. 2021).

P.J.E.S. by and through Escobar Francisco v. Wolf, 502 F.Supp.3d 492 (D.D.C. 2020).

Planned Parenthood v. Casey, 505 U.S. 833, 112 S.Ct. 2791, 120 L.Ed.2d 674 (1992).

Plyler v. Doe, 457 US 202 (1982).

Poelker v. Doe, 432 U.S. 519, 519–21, 97 S.Ct. 2391, 53 L.Ed.2d 528 (1977) (per curiam)

Portillo v. Hott, 322 F. Supp. 3d 698 (E.D. Va. 2018).

Prasad, Ritu. 2018. "Undocumented Migrant Families Embark on Chaotic Reunion Process." *BBC,* June 25. https://www.bbc.com/news/world-us-canada-44581240.

Preiser v. Rodriguez, 411 U.S. 475 (1973).

Preston, Julia. 2014. "Hoping for Asylum, Migrants Strain U.S. Border." *New York Times,* April 10. https://www.nytimes.com/2014/04/11/us/poverty-and-violence -push-new-wave-of-migrants-toward-us.html.

Primero Garcia v. Barr, 484 F.Supp.3d 750 (N.D. California 2020).

Public Law 113-4 Violence Against Women Reauthorization Act of 2013 (March 7, 2013).

Pursuing Am. Greatness v. Fed. Election Comm'n, 831 F.3d 500 (D.C. Cir. 2016).

Quintanilla v. Decker, Slip Copy, 2021 WL 707062 (S.D. N.Y. 2021).

Quineros-Mendoza v. Holder, 556 F.3d 159 (4th Cir. 2009).

Ram v. Mukasey 529 F.3d 1238 (9th Cir. 2008).

Ramirez v. Decker, No. 19-11012, 2020 WL 1674011 (S.D.N.Y. 2020).

Ramirez v. ICE, 338 F. Supp. 3d 1 (D.D.C. 2018).

Ramirez v. U.S. Immigration and Customs Enforcement, 471 F.Supp.3d 88 (D.C. Columbia, 2020).

Ramirez v. U.S. Immigration and Customs Enforcement, ——— F.Supp.3d ---- 2021 WL 4284530 (D.C. 2021), *appealed by Ramirez, et al v. Immigration and Customs Enforcement, et al.* (D.C. Cir. 2022).

Ramji-Nogales, Jaya, Andrew Schoenholtz, and Philip Schrag. 2007. "Refugee Roulette: Disparities in Asylum Adjudication." *Stanford Law Review* 60: 295–411.

Ramji-Nogales, Jaya, Andrew Schoenholtz, and Philip Schrag. 2009. *Refugee Roulette: Disparities in Asylum Adjudication and Proposals for Reform*. New York: New York University Press.

Ramos v. Holder, 589 F.3d 426 (7th Cir. 2009).

Rana, Shruti. 2009. "'Streamlining' The Rule of Law: How the Department of Justice Is Undermining Judicial Review of Agency Action." *University of Illinois Law Review* 2009 (3): 829–894.

Rangel-Zuazo v. Holder, 678 F.3d 967 (9th Cir. 2012).

REAL ID Act, Pub. L. No. 109-13, 199 Stat. 302 (2005).

Reno v. Flores, 507 U.S. 292, 113 S.Ct. 1439, 123 L.Ed.2d 1 (1993).

Report of the Attorney General's National Task Force on Children Exposed to Violence. December 12, 2012. https://perma.cc/G3F6-ACW2.

Reyes v. Lynch, 842 F.3d 1125 (9th Cir. 2016).

Ritonga v. Holder, 633 F.3d 971 (10th Cir. 2011).

Rivars-Garcia v. Garland, 856 Fed.Appx. 166 (10th Cir. 2021).

Rivera-Barrientos v. Holder, 666 F.3d 641 (10th Cir. 2012).

Rodas Godinez v. United States Immigration and Customs Enforcement, Slip Copy, 2020 WL 3402059 (D. New Mexico, 2020).

Rodas-Orellana v. Holder, 780 F.3d 982 (10th Cir. 2015).

Rodriguez Galicia v. Gonzales, 422 F.3d 529 (7th Cir. 2005).

Rodriguez, Sabrina. 2021. "It's Not a Border Crisis. It's a Climate Crisis." *Politico*, July 19. https://www.politico.com/news/magazine/2021/07/19/guatemala-immigration-climate-change-499281.

Roe v. Wade, 410 U.S. 113, 93 S.Ct. 705, 35 L.Ed.2d 147 (1973).

Romero v. Att'y Gen., 972 F.3d 334 (3d Cir. 2020).

Romero v Barr, 937 F.3d 282 (4th Cir. 2019).

Rosenblum, Marc. 2004. *The Transnational Politics of U.S. Immigration Policy* Boulder, CO: Lynne Rienner Publishing.

Rosenblum, Marc, and Idean Salehyan. 2004. "Norms and Interests in US Asylum Enforcement." *Journal of Peace Research* 41 (6): 677–697.

Rosenblum, Marc, and Kate Brick. 2011. "U.S. Immigration Policy and Mexican/ Central American Migration Flows: Then and Now." *Migration Policy Institute*, August. https://www.migrationpolicy.org/pubs/RMSG-regionalflows.pdf.

Rotkiske v. Klemm, 140 S. Ct. 355, 205 L.Ed.2d 291 (2019).

Rottman, Andy, Christopher Farris, and Steven Poe. 2009. "The Path to Asylum in the US and Determinants for Who Gets In and Why." *International Migration Review* 43 (1): 3–34.

R.R. v. Orozco, Slip Copy, 2020 WL 3542333 (D. New Mexico 2020).

Rreshpja v. Gonzales, 420 F.3d 551 (6th Cir. 2005).

Ruiz v. INS, 787 F.2d 1294 (9th Cir. 1996).

Rush, Nayla. 2021a. "CAM and PTA: Opening the Back Door: The Likely Revival and Expansion of the Programs for Central Americans." *Center for Immigration Studies*, January 21. https://cis.org/Report/CAM-and-PTA-Opening-Back-Door.

Rush, Nayla. 2021b. "The Biden Administration Expands Access to CAM: Eligibility to Petition for Children to Join Is No Longer Limited to Lawfully Present Parents. *Center for Immigration Studies*, June 15. https://cis.org/Rush/Biden-Administration -Expands-Access-CAM.

Rust v. Sullivan, 500 U.S. 173, 111 S.Ct. 1759, 114 L.Ed.2d 233 (1991).

Ryan, Kelly. 2011. *Trafficking Victims Protection Reauthorization Act: Renewing the Commitment to Victims of Human Trafficking*. Last modified September 13. https: //www.judiciary.senate.gov/imo/media/doc/11-9-14RyanTestimony.pdf.

Salazar by Salazar v. District of Columbia, 896 F.3d 489 (D.C. Cir. 2018).

Salehyan, Idean, and Marc R. Rosenblum. 2008. "International Relations, Domestic Politics, and Asylum Admissions in the United States." *Political Research Quarterly* 61 (1): 104–121.

Salmeron-Salmeron v. Spivey, 926 F.3d 1283 (11th Cir. 2019).

Santos v. Smith, 260 F.Supp.3d 598 (W.D. Va. 2017).

Santosky v. Kramer, 455 U.S. 745 (1982).

Saravia v. Sessions, 280 F. Supp. 3d 1168 (N.D. Cal. 2017).

Savchuck v. Mukasey, 518 F.3d 119 (2d Cir. 2008).

Savoy, Connor M. and T. Andrew Sady-Kennedy. 2021. "Economic Opportunity in the Northern Triangle." *Center for Strategic and International Studies (CSIS)*. September. https://www.csis.org/analysis/economic-opportunity-northern-triangle.

Sawyer, Cheryl, and Judith Márquez. 2017. "Senseless Violence Against Central American Unaccompanied Minors: Historical Background and Call for Help." *Journal of Psychology* 151 (1): 69–75.

Schallhorn, Kaitlyn. 2018. "What Trump's 'Zero-Tolerance' Immigration Policy Means for Children Separated from Families at Border." *Fox News*, June 19. https: //www.foxnews.com/politics/what-trumps-zero-tolerance-immigration-policy -means-for-children-separated-from-families-at-border.

Schoenholtz, Andrew. 2005. "Refugee Protection in the United States Post-September 11." *Columbia Human Rights Law Review* 36: 323–364.

Scott v. Vargo, 2014 WL 11514067 (E.D. Va. September 5, 2014).

Segal, Jeffrey, and Harold Spaeth. 2002. *The Supreme Court and the Attitudinal Model Revisited*. Cambridge: Cambridge University Press.

Segal, Jeffrey, Robert Howard, and Christopher Hutz. 1996. "Presidential Success in Supreme Court Nominations: Testing a Constrained Presidency Model." Paper presented at the annual meeting of the Midwest Political Science Association.

Seelke, Clare. 2016. "Gangs in Central America." *Congressional Research Service, CRS Report RL34112*, August 29. https://crsreports.congress.gov/product/pdf/RL/RL34112/25.

Seghetti, Lisa. 2014. "Unaccompanied Alien Children: A Processing Flow Chart." *Congressional Research Service Report IN10107*, July 16. https://sgp.fas.org/crs/homesec/IN10107.pdf.

Seghetti, Lisa, Alison, and Ruth Wasem. 2014. "Unaccompanied Alien Children: An Overview." *Congressional Research Report R43599*, September 8. https://trac.syr.edu/immigration/library/P8978.pdf.

Seide, David, and Dana Gold. 2021. "Protected Whistleblower Disclosures of Gross Mismanagement by the Department of Health and Human Services at Fort Bliss, Texas Causing Specific Dangers to Public Health and Safety." *Government Accountability Project*, July 7. https://whistleblower.org/wp-content/uploads/2021/07/070721-Fort-Bliss-Whistleblowers-Disclosure.pdf.

Sepulveda v. U.S. Att'y Gen., 401 F.3d 1226 (11th Cir. 2005) (per curiam).

Sesin, Carmen. 2019. "Difficult to Watch: House Democrats Tour Housing for Migrant Children." *NBC News*, February 19. https://www.nbcnews.com/news/latino/difficult-watch-house-democrats-tour-housing-migrant-kids-n973286.

Shah, Bijal. 2016. "The Attorney General's Disruptive Immigration Power." *Iowa Law Review* 102: 129–165.

Shahoulian, David. 2021. "Unaccompanied Children at the Border: Federal Response and the Way Forward." *U.S. Department of Homeland Security,* June 10. https://www.congress.gov/117/meeting/house/112743/witnesses/HHRG-117-HM11-Wstate-ShahoulianD-20210610.pdf.

Shanks, Cheryl. 2001. *Immigration and the Politics of American Sovereignty, 1890–1990.* Ann Arbor: University of Michigan Press.

Shavell, Steven. 1995. "The Appeals Process as a Means of Error Correction." *Journal of Legal Studies* 24 (2): 379–426.

Shea, Wendy. 2014. "Almost There: Unaccompanied Alien Children, Immigration Reform, and a Meaningful Opportunity to Participate in the Immigration Process." *UC Davis Journal of Juvenile Law & Policy* 18 (1): 148–171.

Shear, Michael D., Katie Benner, and Michael S. Schmidt. 2020. "'We Need to Take Away Children,' No Matter How Young, Justice Dept. Officials Said." *New York Times*, October 6. https://www.nytimes.com/2020/10/06/us/politics/family-separation-border-immigration-jeff-sessions-rod-rosenstein.html.

Shear, Michael, Zolan Kanno-Youngs, and Eileen Sullivan. 2021. "Young Migrants Crowd Shelters, Posing Test for Biden." *New York Times*, June 14. https://www.nytimes.com/2021/04/10/us/politics/biden-immigration.html.

Shehu v. Attorney General of U.S., 482 F.3d 652 (3d Cir. 2007).

Sherley v. Sebelius, 644 F.3d 388 (D.C. Cir. 2011).

Shuchart, Scott. 2018. "Careless Cruelty: Civil Servants Said Separating Families was Illegal. The Administration Ignored Us." *Washington Post*, October 25. https:

//www.washingtonpost.com/news/posteverything/wp/2018/10/25/feature/civil
-servants-said-separating-families-was-illegal-the-administration-ignored-us/.

Sieff, Kevin. 2021. "The Reason Many Guatemalans Are Coming to the Border? A Profound Hunger Crisis." *Washington Post*, April 1. https://www.washingtonpost
.com/world/2021/04/02/us-border-migrants-guatemala/.

Siegel, Rachel. 2017. "The Trump Official Who Tried to Stop a Detained Immigrant from Getting an Abortion." *The Washington Post*, October 26. https://www
.washingtonpost.com/news/post-nation/wp/2017/10/26/the-trump-official-who
-tried-to-stop-a-detained-immigrant-from-getting-an-abortion/.

Singer, Audrey, and William Kandel. 2019. "Immigration: Recent Apprehension Trends at the

U.S. Southwest Border. *Congressional Research Service Report R46012*, November 19. https://sgp.fas.org/crs/homesec/R46012.pdf.

Singh v. Gonzales, 244 F. App'x 99 (9th Cir. 2007).

Singh v. U.S. Att'y Gen., 561 F.3d 1275 (11th Cir. 2009).

Siskin, Alison. 2015. "Alien Removals and Returns: Overview and Trends." *Congressional*

Research Service Report R43892, February 3, 2015.https://sgp.fas.org/crs/homesec/
R43892.pdf

Siskin, Alison, and Liana Rosen. 2014. "Trafficking in Persons: U.S. Policy and Issues for

Congress." *Congressional Research Service Report RL34317.*
https://www.everycrsreport.com/files/20140501_RL34317_83a44c8f0694b5792ff7b
96ee07298ca1a24ee20.pdf.

Smith v. Barr, 444 F. Supp. 3d 1289 (N.D. Okla. 2020).

Smith, Hillel. 2020. "Immigration Laws Regulating the Admission and Exclusion of Aliens at

the Border." *Congressional Research Service Report LSB10150*, May 19.
https://sgp.fas.org/crs/homesec/LSB10150.pdf.

Smith, McKayla. 2017. "Scared, but No Longer Alone: Using Louisiana to Build a Nationwide System of Representation for Unaccompanied Children." *Loyola Law Review* 63: 111–155.

Smole, David. 2013. "Postsecondary Education Issues in the 113th Congress." *Congressional*

Research Service Report R43302. https://sgp.fas.org/crs/misc/R43302.pdf.

Soboroff, Jacob, and Julia Ainsley. 2019. "Trump Admin Ignored Its Own Evidence of Climate

Change's Impact on Migration from Central America." *NBC News,* September 21. https://www.nbcnews.com/politics/immigration/trump-admin-ignored-its-own
-evidence-climate-change-s-impact-n1056381.

Sola v. Holder 720 F.3d 1134 (9th Cir. 2013).

Songer, Donals, Martha Humphries Ginn, and Tammy Sarver. 2003. "Do Judges Follow the Law When There Is No Fear of Reversal." *Justice System Journal* 24 (2): 137–161.

Sotomayor-Peterson, Marcela, and Martha Montiel-Carbajal. 2014. "Psychological and Family Well-Being of Unaccompanied Mexican Child Migrants Sent Back from the U.S. Border Region of Sonora-Arizona." *Hispanic Journal of Behavioral Sciences* 36 (2): 111–123.

Spagat, Elliot, and Nomaan Merchant. 2021. "Over 4,000 Migrants, Many Kids, Crowded into

Texas Facility." *APNews*, March 31. tps://apnews.com/article/joe-biden-immigration-texas-59d0eafb23d135f901dfc50ff326cfcd.

Standifer v. Ledezma, 653 F.3d 1276 (10th Cir. 2011).

Stanley v. Illinois, 405 U.S. 645 (1972).

Stenberg v. Carhart, 530 U.S. 914, 120 S.Ct. 2597 (2000).

Stern, Mark. 2018. "Bad Liars." *Slate*, May 16. https://slate.com/news-and-politics/2018/05/federal-judge-accused-ice-of-making-up-evidence-to-prove-that-dreamer-was-gang-affiliated.html.

Stoffel, Elizabeth, Adrea Korthase, and Melissa Gueller. 2019. "Assessing Trauma for Juvenile and Family Courts." *National Council of Juvenile and Family Court Judges.* https://perma.cc/K3SZ-V62X.

Tabbaa v. Chertoff, 509 F.3d 89 (2nd Cir. 2007).

Tate, C. Neal, and Roger Handberg. 1991. "Time Building and Theory Building in Personal Attribute Models of Supreme Court Voting Behavior, 1916–88." *American Journal of Political Science* 35 (2): 460–480.

Teitelbaum, Michael, and Myron Weiner, eds. 1995. *Threatened Peoples, Threatened Borders: World Migration and U.S. Policy.* New York: Norton.

Thach v. Arlington Cty. Dep't of Human Servs, 754 S.E.2d 922 (2014).

Thap v. Mukasey, 544 F.3d 674, 681 (6th Cir. 2008).

Thapa v. Holder, 572 F. App'x 314, 320–21 (6th Cir. 2014).

Tichenor, Daniel. 2002. *Dividing Lines: The Politics of Immigration Control in America.* Princeton, NJ: Princeton University Press.

Touvell v. Ohio Dep't of Mental Retardation & Developmental Disabilities, 422 F.3d 392, 403 (6th Cir. 2005).

Toyo Tire Holdings of Ams. Inc. v. Cont'l Tire N. Am., Inc., 609 F.3d 975, 982 (9th Cir. 2010).

Trafficking Victims Protection Reauthorization Act ("TVPRA"). Pub. L. No. 110-457, 122 Stat.

5044 (principally codified in relevant part at 8 U.S.C. § 1232).

Transactional Records Access Clearinghouse ("TRAC"). 2006. "Immigration Judges." https://trac.syr.edu/immigration/reports/160/.

Transactional Records Access Clearinghouse ("TRAC"). 2014, November 25. "Representation for Unaccompanied Children in Immigration Court." https://trac.syr.edu/immigration/reports/371/

Transactional Records Access Clearinghouse ("TRAC"). 2021. "Immigration Court Backlog Tool." http://trac.syr.edu/phptools/immigration/court_backlog.

Transactional Records Access Clearinghouse ("TRAC"). 2008. "Judicial Oversight v. Judicial Independence." https://trac.syr.edu/immigration/reports/194/include/side_4.html.

Transactional Records Access Clearinghouse ("TRAC"). 2022. "A Sober Assessment of the
Growing U.S. Asylum Backlog." December 22. https://trac.syr.edu/reports/705/.
Trias-Hernandez v. INS 528 F.2d 366 (9th Cir.1975).
Troxel v. Granville, 530 U.S. 57 (2000).
Ulloa Santos v. Attorney General, 552 Fed. App'x 197 (3d Cir. 2014).
Umaña, Isabel, and Jeanne Rikkers. 2012. "Nine Strategies to Prevent Youth Violence in Central America, Interpeace." https://www.interpeace.org/wp-content/uploads /2012/09/2012_09_18_IfP_EW_Nine_Strategies.pdf.
Umana-Ramos v. Holder, 724 F.3d 667 (6th Cir. 2013).
United Nations Convention on the Rights of the Child. 1989. G.A. Res. 44/25, U.N. G.A.O.R., November 20. http://www.unhchr.ch/html/menu2/6/crc/treaties/crc.htm.
United Nations Convention relating to the Status of Refugees. 1951. G.A. Res. 429(V) of December 14. https://www.ohchr.org/en/instruments-mechanisms/instruments/ convention-relating-status-refugees.
United Nations High Commissioner for Refugees ("UNHCR"). 1987. Refugee Children No. 47. https://www.unhcr.org/en-us/excom/exconc/3ae68c432c/refugee -children.html.
United Nations High Commissioner for Refugees. 1997. "Guidelines on Policies and Procedures in Dealing with Unaccompanied Children Seeking Asylum."
United Nations High Commissioner for Refugees ("UNHCR"). 2014. "Children on the Run: Unaccompanied Children Leaving Central America and Mexico and the Need for International Protection." https://www.unhcr.org/56fc266f4.html.
U.N. Office on Drugs and Crime ("UNODC"). "Global Study on Homicide 2013: Trends, Contexts, Data." Last modified August 2014. http://www.unodc.org/ documents/gsh/pdfs/2014_GLOBAL_HOMICIDE_BOOK_web.pdf.
United States ex. rel. the minor child K.E.R.G., et al. *v. Burwell* 2014 WL 12638877 (E.D. Pennsylvania 2014).
United States Ass'n of Reptile Keepers, Inc. v. Zinke, 852 F.3d 1131 (D.C. Cir. 2017).
United States v. Asarco Inc., 430 F.3d 972 (9th Cir. 2005).
United States v. Camero-Castaneda, Slip Copy, 2021 WL 4979406 (E. D. North Carolina, 2021).
United States v. Cisneros-Rodriguez 813 F.3d 748 (9th Cir. 2015).
United States v. Dominguez-Portillo, Case 3:17-mj-04409-MAT (W.D. Tex 2018).
United States v. Gomez-Salinas, No. 2:19cr10, 2019 WL 1141063 (E.D. Va. Mar. 12, 2019).
United States v. Munsingwear, Inc., 340 U.S. 36, 71 S.Ct. 104, 95 L.Ed. 36 (1950).
United States v. Perez-Arellano, 756 Fed. Appx. 291 (4th Cir. 2018).
United States v. Salerno, 481 U.S. 739 (1987).
United States v. Silvestre-Gregorio, 983 F.3d 848 (6th Cir. 2020).
United States v. Torres Zuniga, 390 F.Supp.3d 653 (E.D. Virginia, 2019).
Unterhitzenberger, Johanna, Rima Eberle-Sejari, Miriam Rassenhofer, Thorsten Sukale, Rita Rosner, and Lutz Goldbeck. 2015. "Trauma-Focused Cognitive Behavioral Therapy With Unaccompanied Refugee Minors: A Case Series." *BMC Psychiatry* 15: 260–268. https://doi.org/10.1186/s12888-015-0645-0.

University of Kentucky Center for Poverty Research. 2020. "National Welfare Data." http://ukcpr.org/resources/national-welfare-data.

Urbina v. Barr, No. 1:20-cv-325, 2020 WL 3002344 (E.D. Va. June 4, 2020).

U.S. Agency for International Aid and Development. 2020. "U.S. Overseas Loans and Grants:

Obligations and Loan Authorizations, 1946–2020." https://explorer.usaid.gov/reports .html.

U.S. Census Bureau. 2020. "Race and Ethnicity in the United States: 2010 Census and 2020 Census.."https://www.census.gov/library/visualizations/interactive/race -and-ethnicity-in-the-united-state-2010-and-2020-census.html

U.S. Citizenship and Immigration Service Asylum Division. 2009. "Asylum Officer Basic Training Course Guidelines for Children's Asylum Claims." https://www .refworld.org/pdfid/4f3e30152.pdf.

U.S. Customs and Border Protection. 2021. "CBP Announces June 2021 Operational Update." Last modified July 16. https://www.cbp.gov/newsroom/national-media -release/cbp-announces-june-2021-operational-update.

U.S. Customs and Border Protection. 2021a. "Southwest Land Border Encounters." https://www.cbp.gov/newsroom/stats/southwest-land-border-encounters?_ga=2 .133045070.1190483372.1642710060-1794336000.1642710060.

U.S. Customs and Border Protection. 2021b. "Southwest Land Border Encounters by Component." https://www.cbp.gov/newsroom/stats/southwest-land-border -encounters.

U.S. Department of Agriculture Rural Atlas Data. 2020. "Atlas of Rural and Small-Town America."

https://www.ers.usda.gov/data-products/atlas-of-rural-and-small-town-america/.

U.S. Department of Health and Human Services ("HHS"). 2021. "Latest UC Data— FY2021." Accessed November 15, 2021. https://www.hhs.gov/programs/social -services/unaccompanied-children/latest-uc-data-fy2021/index.html#tender-age.

U.S. Department of Health & Human Servs., Office of Refugee Resettlement. 2019. "Facts and Data." Last modified February 13, 2019. https://www.acf.hhs.gov/orr/ about/ucs/facts-and-data,

U.S. Department of Health and Human Services ("HHS") & U.S. Department of Homeland Security ("DHS"). 2018. "Apprehension, Processing, Care, and Custody of Alien Minors and Unaccompanied Alien Children." 83 Federal Register 45486-45534. September 7. https://www.govinfo.gov/content/pkg/FR-2018-09-07 /pdf/2018-19052.pdf.

U.S. DHS. 2019. "Apprehension, Processing, Care, and Custody of Alien Minors and Unaccompanied Alien Children." 84 Federal Register 44392- 44535. August 23. https://www.govinfo.gov/content/pkg/FR-2019-08-23/pdf/2019-17927.pdf.

U.S. Department of Health and Human Services ("HHS") & U.S. Department of Homeland Security ("DHS"). 2021. "HHS and DHS Joint Statement on Termination of 2018 Agreement." Last modified March 12. https://www.dhs.gov/ news/2021/03/12/hhs-and-dhs-joint-statement-termination-2018-agreement.

U.S. Department of Homeland Security. 2014. "Statement by Secretary Johnson on Increased Influx of Unaccompanied Immigrant Children at the Border." June

2. https://www.dhs.gov/news/2014/06/02/statement-secretary-johnson-increased -influx-unaccompanied-immigrant-children-border.

U.S. Department of Homeland Security. 2018. "Unaccompanied Alien Children and Family Units are Flooding the Border Because of Catch and Release Loopholes." February 15. https://www.dhs.gov/news/2018/02/15/unaccompanied-alien-children -and-family-units-are-flooding-border-because-catch-and.

U.S. Department of Homeland Security. 2019. "Updated U.S. Mexico Local Repatriation Arrangements." Last modified May 28. https://www.dhs.gov/ publication/updated-us-mexico-local-repatriation-arrangements.

U.S. Dep't of Justice. 2012. "Report of the Attorney General's National Task Force on Children Exposed to Violence." https://perma.cc/G3F6-ACW2.

U.S. Department of the Treasury. 2012. "Treasury Sanctions Latin American Criminal Organization." October 11. https://www.treasury.gov/press-center/press-releases/ pages/tg1733.aspx.

U.S. Department of State. 2021. "Restarting the Central American Minors Program." March 10. https://www.state.gov/restarting-the-central-american-minors-program/.

U.S. Government Accountability Office. 2015. "Unaccompanied Alien Children. Actions Needed to Ensure Children Receive Required Care in DHS Custody." July. https://www.gao.gov/assets/680/671866.pdf.

U.S. Immigration and Customs Enforcement. 2017. *Field Office Juvenile Coordinator Handbook Enforcement and Removal Operations*. September. https: //www.documentcloud.org/documents/4446357-Juvenileand-Family-Residential -Management-Unit.html.

U.S. Office of Inspector General. 2018. "Special Review—Initial Observations Regarding Family Separation Issues Under the Zero Tolerance Policy. *OIG-18-84.* September 27. https://www.oig.dhs.gov/sites/default/files/assets/2018-10/OIG-18 -84-Sep18.pdf.

U.S. Office of Inspector General. 2019. "Separated Children Placed in Office of Refugee Resettlement Care." *HHS-OIG Issue Brief OEI-BL-18-00511.* January. https://oig.hhs.gov/oei/reports/oei-BL-18-00511.pdf.

U.S. Office of the Inspector General. 2020a. "The Office of Refugee Resettlement did not Award and Manage the Homestead Influx Care Facility Contracts in Accordance with Federal Requirements." *Office of Public Affairs A-12-20-20001.* December. https://oig.hhs.gov/oas/reports/region12/122020001.pdf.

U.S. Office of the Inspector General. 2020b. "Office of Refugee Resettlement Ensured That Selected Care Providers Were Prepared to Respond to the Covid-19 Pandemic. *Report No. A-04-20-02031.* November. https://oig.hhs.gov/oas/reports/ region4/42002031.pdf.

Vargas-Hernandez v. Gonzales, 497 F.3d 919 (9th Cir. 2007).

Vatulev v. Ashcroft, 354 F.3d 1207 (10th Cir. 2003).

Vaughan, Jessica. 2018. "MS-13 Resurgence: Immigration Enforcement Needed to Take Back Our Streets." *Center for Immigration Studies*. February 21. https://cis .org/Report/MS13-Resurgence-Immigration-Enforcement-Needed-Take-Back-Our -Streets.

Vieira Garcia v. I.N.S., 239 F.3d 409 (1st Cir. 2001).

Villarreal, Danuta. 2004. "To Protect the Defenseless: The Need for Child-Specific Substantive Standards for Unaccompanied Minor Asylum-Seekers." *Houston Journal of International Law* 26 (3): 743–778.

Virtue, Paul. 1997. "Unaccompanied Minors Subject to Expedited Removal." Last modified August 21, 1997. https://www.aila.org/infonet/ins-advises-on -unaccompanied-minors-removal.

V.V. v. Orozco, Slip Copy, 2020 WL 3542480 (D. New Mexico 2020).

Wade v. Mayo, 334 U.S. 672 (1948).

Walker, Kyle, and Helga Leitner. 2011. "The Variegated Landscapes of Local Immigration Policies in the United States." *Urban Geography* 32 (2): 156–178.

Wasem, Ruth. 2007. "U.S. Immigration Policy on Asylum Seekers." *Congressional Research Service Report RL32621.* January 25. https://www.everycrsreport.com /files/20070125_RL32621_a48249ba722391d59d1edbb77ca4c92222e6f3ac.pdf.

Wasem, Ruth. 2011. "Asylum and 'Credible Rear' Issues in U.S. Immigration Policy." *Congressional Research Service Report R41753.* June 29. https://sgp.fas .org/crs/homesec/R41753.pdf.

Wasem, Ruth. 2013. "Asylum Abuse: Is It Overwhelming Our Borders?" *U.S. Congress, House Committee on the Judiciary.* December 12. https://docs.house .gov/meetings/JU/JU00/20131212/101588/HHRG-113-JU00-Wstate-WasemR -20131212.pdf.

Wasem, Ruth. 2014. "Asylum Policies for Unaccompanied Children Compared with Expedited Removal Policies for Unauthorized Adults: In Brief." *Congressional Research Service Report 45539.* July 30. https://crsreports.congress.gov/product/ pdf/R/R43664/3.

Wash. Legal Found. v. Henney, 202 F.3d 331 (D.C. Cir. 2000).

Webster v. Reproductive Health Servs., 492 U.S. 490, 109 S.Ct. 3040, 106 L.Ed.2d 410 (1989).

Weingast, Barry, Kenneth Shepsie, and Christopher Johnsen. 1981. "The Political Economy of Benefits and Costs: A Neoclassical Approach to Distributive Politics." *Journal of Political Economy* 89 (4): 642–646.

Weiss, Jeff. 1998. "Guidelines for Children's Asylum Claims, Memorandum to Asylum Officers, Immigration Officers, and Headquarters Coordinators (Asylum and Refugees)." Last modified December 10, 1998. https://www.refworld.org/ docid/3f8ec0574.html.

Weller v. Dep't of Soc. Servs. for City of Baltimore, 901 F.2d 387 (4th Cir. 1990).

White v. Napolean, 897 F.2d 103 (3d Cir. 1990).

Wild Rockies v. Cottrell, 632 F.3d 1127 (9th Cir. 2011).

Wilkie v. Robbins, 551 U.S. 537 (2007).

William Wilberforce Trafficking Victims Protection Reauthorization Act of 2008, Pub. L. 110–457 (December 23, 2008) (codified as 22 USC 7101).

Winter v. Nat. Res. Def. Council, Inc., 555 U.S. 7, 129 S.Ct. 365, 172 L.Ed.2d 249 (2008).

Woodall v. Fed. Bureau of Prisons, 432 F.3d 235 (3d Cir. 2005).

World Bank Group. 2018. "Internal Climate Migration in Latin America." *Groundswell*. https://documents1.worldbank.org/curated/en/983921522304806221 /pdf/124724-BRI-PUBLIC-NEWSERIES-Groundswell-note-PN3.pdf.

World Health Organization. 2021. "Estimates of Rates of Homicides." *The Global Health Observatory*. February 9. https://www.who.int/data/gho/data/indicators /indicator-details/GHO/estimates-of-rates-of-homicides-per-100-000-population.

Xin Yu He v. Lynch 610 Fed.Appx. 655 (9th Cir. 2015).

Yeboah v. U.S. Department of Justice, 345 F.3d 216 (3d Cir. 2003).

Youngberg v. Romeo, 457 U.S. 307, 102 S.Ct. 2452, 73 L.Ed.2d 28 (1982).

Yweil v. INS, 50 F. App'x 325 (7th Cir. 2002).

Zadvydas v. Davis, 533 U.S. 678, 121 S.Ct. 2491, 150 L.Ed.2d 653 (2001).

Zak, Danilo. 2021. "Explainer: Emergency Shelters and Facilities Housing Unaccompanied Children." *National Immigration Forum*. Last modified May 4, 2021. https://immigrationforum.org/article/explainer-emergency-shelters-and -facilities-housing-unaccompanied-children/.

Zaldana Menijar v. Lynch, 812 F.3d 491 (6th Cir. 2015).

Zapata-Matute v. U.S. Attorney General, 783 Fed. Appx. 1008 (11th Cir. 2019).

Zepeda-Melendez v. INS 741 F.2d 285 (9th Cir. 1984).

Ziglar v. Abbasi, 137 S. Ct. 1843, 1863 (2017).

8 C.F.R. §208.13(b)(2).

8 C.F.R. §236.3(b).

8 C.F.R. §1208.4(a)(5)(ii).

6 U.S.C. §279.

6 U.S.C §279(b)(1)(A).

8 U.S. Code § 1158(b)(1).

8 U.S.C. §1225.

8 U.S.C. §1225(b).

8 U.S.C. §1229a.

8 U.S.C. §1232(a)(2)(A).

8 U.S.C. §1232(a)(3) & (b)(3).

8 U.S.C. §1232(a)(4).

8 U.S.C. §1232(a)(5)(D).

8 U.S.C. §1232(b)(3).

8 U.S.C. §1232 (c)(5).

85 Fed. Reg. 16559–01, 2020.

8 C.F.R. § 235.3(b)(2)(iii).

8 C.F.R. § 1003.13.

8 C.F.R. § 1003.15 (b).

8 C.F.R. § 1003.18(b).

8 C.F.R. § 1208.13(a).

8 C.F.R. § 1240.10(a)(1), (2).

8 CFR 1240.26(b).

5 U.S.C. § 551(13).

8 U.S.C. § 1101(a)(27)(J).

8 U.S.C. § 1101(a)(42)(A).

8 U.S.C. § 1101(a)(48)(A).
8 U.S.C. § 1158.
8 U.S.C. § 1158(a)(2)(B), (E).
8 U.S.C. § 1158(b).
8 U.S.C. § 1158(b)(1)(A).
8 U.S.C. § 1158(b)(1)(B)(i).
8 U.S.C. § 1182(a)(6)(A)(i).
8 U.S.C. § 1182(d)(5)(A).
8 U.S.C. § 1232(c)(2)(B).
8 U.S.C. § 1225(b)(1).
8 U.S.C. § 1225(b)(1)(B)(ii).
8 U.S.C. § 1226(a).
8 U.S.C. § 1229(a)(1)(G)(i).
8 U.S.C. § 1229a(b)(4)(A).
8 U.S.C. § 1229a(b)(5)(C)(i).
8 U.S.C. §1229a(e)(1)).
8 U.S.C. § 1232(b)(4).
8 U.S.C. § 1232(d)(8)).
8 U.S.C. § 1232(c)(2)(A).
8 U.S.C. § 1232(c)(2)(B).
8 U.S.C. § 1232(c)(3)(A).
8 U.S.C. § 1253(h)(1).
8 U.S.C. § 1254.
28 U.S.C. § 2241.
28 U.S.C. § 2412.
28 U.S.C. § 2412(d)(1)(A).
42 U.S.C. § 1983.
44 U.S.C. § 2902.

Index

About the Authors

Dr. Claire Nolasco Braaten is Associate Professor in the Department of Criminology and Political Science at Texas A&M University-San Antonio. She has a PhD in Criminal Justice, a JD in law, and is licensed to practice law in both California and the Philippines. Her research interests are immigration studies, corporate and financial crime, cybercrime, and empirical legal research. She has published in several peer-reviewed journals, including *Deviant Behavio*r, *American Journal of Criminal Justice*, *Journal of Criminal Justice*, *Crime Law and Social Change*, *Journal of Criminal Justice Education*, and *Security Journal*.

Dr. Daniel Braaten is Associate Professor of Political Science in the Department of Criminology and Political Science at Texas A&M University-San Antonio. His research areas are in human rights, refugees, international organizations, and environmental politics. His research has been published in *Human Rights Quarterly*, *International Studies Review, Law & Policy,* and the *Journal of Refugee Studies*, among others.